STAGING MUSICALS

STAGING MUSICALS

An Essential Guide

Second Edition

MATTHEW WHITE

methuen | drama

LONDON · NEW YORK · OXFORD · NEW DELHI · SYDNEY

METHUEN DRAMA
Bloomsbury Publishing Plc
50 Bedford Square, London, WC1B 3DP, UK
1385 Broadway, New York, NY 10018, USA

BLOOMSBURY, METHUEN DRAMA and the Methuen Drama logo are trademarks of
Bloomsbury Publishing Plc

First published in Great Britain as *Staging a Musical* by A&C Black 1999
This edition first published 2019

Copyright © Matthew White, 2019

Matthew White has asserted his right under the Copyright, Designs and Patents Act, 1988,
to be identified as author of this work.

For legal purposes the Acknowledgements on pp. xiii–xvi constitute an extension
of this copyright page.

Cover design: Louise Dugdale
Cover image: *Top Hat* (Charlotte Gooch, Alan Burkitt). Photo, Hugo
Glendinning; graphic design, Dewynters

A catalogue record for this book is available from the British Library.

Library of Congress Cataloging-in-Publication Data
Names: White, Matthew, 1963– author.
Title: Staging Musicals : an essential guide / Matthew White.
Description: 2nd edition. | London; New York, NY : Bloomsbury Publishing, 2019. |
Includes bibliographical references and index.
Identifiers: LCCN 2018035522| ISBN 9781474247719 (hb) | ISBN 9781474247726 (pb)
Subjects: LCSH: Musicals—Production and direction.
Classification: LCC MT955 .W35 2019 | DDC 792.602/3—dc23 LC record
available at https://lccn.loc.gov/2018035522

ISBN: HB: 978-1-4742-4771-9
         PB: 978-1-4742-4772-6
         ePDF: 978-1-4742-4774-0
         eBook: 978-1-4742-4773-3

Series: Backstage

Typeset by RefineCatch Limited, Bungay, Suffolk
Printed and bound in Great Britain

To find out more about our authors and books visit www.bloomsbury.com
and sign up for our newsletters.

For Lindsey, Lydia and Xanthe

CONTENTS

PHOTOGRAPHS

DIAGRAMS

CONTRIBUTORS' BIOGRAPHIES

David Charles Abell (conductor/musical director)

Best known for the internationally televised *Les Misérables* Tenth and Twenty-Fifth Anniversary concerts, conductor David Charles Abell maintains an active career in musical theatre, opera and symphonic music. His West End credits include Andrew Lloyd Webber's *Love Never Dies*, and he has appeared five times at the BBC Proms. At English National Opera, he conducted *Sweeney Todd* with Emma Thompson and Bryn Terfel and *Carousel* with Katherine Jenkins and Alfie Boe. Together with his husband Seann Alderking, he created the first authoritative critical edition of the score of a Golden Age hit musical, Cole Porter's *Kiss Me, Kate*.

Sharon D Clarke MBE (actor)

Sharon is a British theatre and television actor and singer with an extensive career. She is best known for playing Dr Lola Griffin in the BBC1 drama *Holby City*. She originated the role of Killer Queen in *We Will Rock You* and has appeared in many West End shows, including *Caroline, or Change*, *Ghost*, *Hairspray*, *Guys and Dolls*, *Fame*, *The Lion King*, *Chicago*, *Rent* and *Once On This Island*. She received an Olivier Award for *The Amen Corner* at the National Theatre. Sharon achieved chart success with Nomad's 'I Wanna Give You Devotion'.

Paule Constable (lighting designer)

Paule is an associate director of the National Theatre (NT) and has designed productions for all the major UK companies including *Warhorse* (NT and worldwide) and *The Curious Incident of the Dog in the Night-Time*. Recent productions include *Follies* and *Angels in America* for the National Theatre. She has received four Olivier awards, two Tony Awards, the Helpmann Award and numerous Critics' Circle and Drama Desk awards. Her opera designs have been seen all over the world and include *Giulio Cesare* and *Billy Budd* at Glyndebourne; *Medea* at English National Opera (ENO) and *Ariodante* for Vienna Stadtsoper plus *Satyagraha* at the Metropolitan Opera. She is an associate of Matthew

Bourne's company and designed *Sleeping Beauty*, *The Red Shoes*, *Dorian Gray* and *Play Without Words* for him.

Soutra Gilmore (set designer/costume designer)

Soutra's credits include *Into the Woods* (Regent's Park Open Air Theatre), *Strictly Ballroom* (Piccadilly Theatre), *Urine Town* (Apollo Theatre), *From Here to Eternity* (Shaftesbury Theatre), *Antigone* and *Moon on a Rainbow Shawl* (NT), *Duchess of Malfi* (Old Vic), *Reasons To Be Pretty* (Almeida), *Inadmissible Evidence* and *Polar Bears* (Donmar Warehouse), *Who's Afraid of Virginia Woolf?* (Sheffield Crucible/Northern Stage), *The Little Dog Laughed* (Garrick Theatre), *Three Days of Rain* (Apollo) and *The Pride* (Royal Court). Operas include: *Down By The Greenwood Side/Into The Little Hill* (Royal Opera House), *Hansel and Gretel* (Opera North), *A Better Place* (ENO) and *Don Giovanni*, *Anna Bolena* and *Mary Stuart* (English Touring Opera).

James Orange (casting director)

James established James Orange Casting in 2007 after working for four years as casting director for Sir Cameron Mackintosh. West End productions include: *The King and I* (London Palladium), *Strictly Ballroom* (Piccadilly), *An American in Paris* (Dominion), *Miss Saigon* (Prince Edward), *Les Misérables* (Queens), *The Phantom of the Opera* (Her Majesty's), *Betty Blue Eyes* (Novello) and *La Cage Aux Folles* (Playhouse). Other productions include *On the Town* and *Seven Brides for Seven Brothers* (Regent's Park), *A Damsel in Distress* (Chichester Festival) and *Sweeney Todd* (Welsh National Opera). UK tours include: *Dr. Dolittle*, *The Addams Family*, *Shirley Valentine*, *Chitty Chitty Bang Bang*, *The Producers*, *Oklahoma!* and *Barnum*.

Emma Rice (director)

Emma Rice is the proud and excited Artistic Director of Wise Children. Between 2016 and 2018 she was the artistic director of Shakespeare's Globe; productions included *Twelfth Night*, *The Little Matchgirl*, *A Midsummer Night's Dream* and *Romantics Anonymous*. Prior to this she was Artistic Director of Kneehigh where she directed *The Red Shoes*, *The Wooden Frock*, *The Bacchae*, *Tristan and Yseult*, *Cymbeline* (RSC), *A Matter of Life and Death* (NT), *Rapunzel* and *Brief Encounter*. West End productions include *The Umbrellas of Cherbourg*, *The Empress* (RSC) and *Oedipussy* (Spymonkey).

Susan Stroman (director/choreographer)

A five-time Tony Award winner, Susan's work has also been honoured with Olivier, Drama Desk, Outer Critics Circle, and Lucille Lortel awards, and a record five Astaire Awards. Most notably she directed and choreographed *The Producers*, winner of a record-making twelve Tony Awards including Best Director and Best Choreography. Broadway credits include: *Prince of Broadway*, *Bullets Over Broadway*, *Big Fish*, *The Scottsboro Boys*, *The Producers*, *Contact*, *Crazy for You*, *Show Boat*, *Oklahoma!*, *Young Frankenstein*, *The Frogs*, *The Music Man*, *Steel Pier* and *Big*. She is the recipient of the George Abbott Award for Lifetime Achievement in the American Theater and a member of the Theater Hall of Fame in New York City.

ACKNOWLEDGEMENTS

There are so many people who have contributed to this book, in large and small ways. In fact almost everyone I have ever worked with has in some way had an influence on the content of these pages.

First I would like to thank my contributors, starting with Sir Cameron Mackintosh, who not only gave me my first West End acting job, but subsequently hired me as an assistant director and therefore helped to send my career off in a new and exciting direction. I would also like to thank, for their insightful observations and great expertise: David Charles Abell, Sharon D Clarke, Paule Constable, Soutra Gilmore, James Orange, Emma Rice and Susan Stroman.

I would also like to thank the following:

Louise Davidson, Paul Farnsworth, Ciara Fanning, Joel Fram, Artie Gaffin, Caroline Humphris, Sally Irwin, Sam Spencer Lane, Kezia Lock, Lucy McNally, Gareth Owen, Jason Taylor, Sarah Travis and Amy Wildgoose – my marvellous team of specialist advisors.

Anna Brewer, John O'Donovan and Lucy Brown – my supportive team at Methuen Drama/Bloomsbury Publishing.

David Babani, Bob Bailey, Hildegard Bechtler, Simon Blakey, Alan Burkitt, Alison Chapman, Adam Cooper, Kylie Anne Cruikshanks, Alistair David, Bill Deamer, David Farley, Tony Fisher, Charlotte Gooch, David Grewcock, Hannah Halden, Karen Large, Alastair Lindsey-Renton, Katy Lipson, Martin Lloyd-Evans, Martin Lowe, Celia Mackay, Anne McCluskey, Stephen Mear, Charlotte Medcalf, Jon Morrell, Daniel Nicolai, Omar Okai, Diego Pitarch, Stuart Matthew Price, Ana Sanderson, Tim Shortall, Tom Siracusa, Helen Snell, John Stalker, Dan Trenchard, Kate Warnaby, Kenny Wax, Caroline de Wolfe, Matthew Wright and James Yeoburn – my inspirational group of friends and colleagues.

'Imagem' for allowing me to use some of the text and lyrics from Rodgers and Hammerstein's masterpiece, *Carousel*.

My parents, Gerald and Sheila White, for tirelessly encouraging me in all aspects of music and drama, and for slavishly following me to every performance throughout my childhood and beyond; to Louise Child, my first music teacher, who helped me to understand that music and drama can never be separated; and to John Caird for supporting and encouraging me early in my career, especially with regard to my first foray into producing and directing on the London Fringe.

FOREWORD

How do you produce a musical? This is a question I am often asked and though there is no definitive answer, Matthew White has certainly set out clearly and simply the key areas of organisation that need to be addressed in order to take a project from an idea to a First Night.

This is quite an achievement as staging a musical is a tremendously complex undertaking. The dream of putting on a show must be matched by the practicality of putting all the pieces together and Matthew has expertly tracked the entire process of staging a production so that by the end of the book anyone wishing to stage a musical, whether for the amateur stage or perhaps as an aspiring professional, will understand the complicated and wide-ranging areas involved. Musical theatre is the most collaborative of arts and with any such endeavour, hand in hand with talent must go a certain amount of ego. Having chosen the team to put on the show it is the producer's job to get the best out of everybody. Therefore, a good producer needs a combination of charm, common sense, instinct and flair and must be able to keep cool under fire. He or she must also be good with figures and not be frightened of taking the odd calculated risk. But, above all, to have a hit you must enjoy what Alfred P. Doolittle immortally declared in *My Fair Lady*, 'a little bit of luck'.

This second edition of *Staging Musicals* is even more informative than the first, not least because Matthew himself has considerably more theatrical experiences to call on but also because it contains some terrific observations from some of the most brilliant talents working in musical theatre today. So with Matthew's handy guide to help you on your way, find a piece of material you believe in, put it together as well as you can and then hopefully your dreams will come true!

Sir Cameron Mackintosh (April 2018)

PREFACE

Putting together a stage production isn't a job for the faint-hearted, and musical theatre brings with it a special set of challenges since there's a variety of different disciplines involved. My intention in this book is to de-mystify the process, and to bring some sort of clarity to the overall procedure. By drawing on my own experiences as an actor, director and writer I hope to illuminate the joyful, but often complex process of staging a musical from start to finish. In this second edition I have taken the opportunity to re-examine this process by interviewing a number of experienced theatre practitioners whose input appears sporadically throughout the book. Their contribution has been invaluable and I am indebted to them for helping to shed light on this ever-changing, always-absorbing business.

My earliest recollections of the theatre are dimly remembered excursions to the ballet with my mother. As the heavy red curtain rose to reveal one breath-taking, fantastical vista after another, it was the magic of this experience which really captured my youthful imagination. I soon discovered light opera and the quirky, colourful operettas of Gilbert and Sullivan and subsequently Jacques Offenbach. What I failed to realise at the time, of course, was that this was my first introduction to the musical; I was, and still am, drawn to theatrical experiences where music and drama are expertly woven together. It was only a matter of time before I would stumble upon two great musicals of the twentieth century: a joyful production of *Guys and Dolls* at the National Theatre in London, and the stunningly choreographed original Broadway production of *A Chorus Line* in New York.

My own theatrical career began a few years later with a national tour of *Evita*. Subsequent work as an actor introduced me to the West End and a string of diverse musicals, several of which are still running today. My interest in theatre wasn't, however, confined to my work as a performer, and having produced and directed several shows on the London Fringe, I began working as an assistant director on larger commercial shows, whilst continuing to direct my own productions at various drama schools. With hard work and a dose of good fortune I was lucky enough to start directing professional productions of my own, some of which I also wrote or adapted. Having mainly learned on the job rather than studying a particular college course, my process had something of the magpie about it, collecting information and insight from each individual project and every creative person that I came into contact with. This process, I am happy to say, continues today with every new theatrical opportunity that presents itself.

These eclectic experiences have led me to the conclusion that the process of putting on a musical is essentially the same whether producing large-scale or small-scale work, whether amateur or professional. In spite of the obvious differences, size of budget, length of rehearsal time and availability of actors, the same principles apply; collaboration, communication and creativity should be at the heart of any theatrical enterprise. None of these, though, will be entirely effective unless the process is underpinned by good organisation.

The great news for anyone wishing to mount a production from scratch is that there is a plethora of different works to choose from. Some are well-loved and endlessly revived; others are more obscure and just waiting to be re-discovered. And let us not forget the many new musicals, some of them works of dazzling originality, which are yet to be produced. Whatever shape they come in, whether tried and tested or new and unheard, musical theatre productions will always require vision, energy and commitment. The task of transporting these works from page to stage is the main focus of this book. By examining this process, and by giving detailed information about each department and each member of the production team, I hope to help facilitate the smooth-running of any musical theatre project, from the initial idea to the last triumphant curtain call.

1
SELECTING THE SHOW

Producer

At the heart of every theatrical enterprise there's an individual known as the **producer**[*] who oversees the entire project from start to finish, and who has overall responsibility for putting the show together. This job requires someone with real passion and huge amounts of energy and enthusiasm. Under normal circumstances it's the producer who takes responsibility for the financial and organisational aspects of the production and is therefore both the business head and the administrator. In my experience, though, the producer is much more than that and will have a fairly significant creative input too, often overseeing the overall design concept, the casting and the marketing. Other responsibilities of the producer include:

- Organising the production finances. In the professional sphere this will involve raising investment, allocating funds to the various different departments, managing any **income** generated by the sale of tickets, and working with the production accountants to generate the production accounts. With college or amateur productions the producer will often have to work with a pre-existing **budget**, and may also need to organise bank loans based on the projected box office income.

- Securing the **performing rights** and paying the appropriate fees to the **licensing company**. In the case of new work this will involve acquiring the rights or signing an exclusive contract with the writers.

- Selecting the other members of the **creative team** (see Chapter 2). These will usually include a **director, musical director, choreographer, set designer, costume designer, lighting designer** and **sound designer**. Most professional producers will also employ a **casting director**.

- Organising appropriate support for the creative team. This will include securing a **production manager**, a **stage manager**, the other

---

[*] Please note that when a new term is used for the first time it is **emboldened** and will be included in the index at the back of the book.

members of **stage management** and all other technical personnel. There may also be assistants for the various members of the creative team.

- Overseeing all aspects of **publicity**. This will often involve delegation. Many producers will outsource the advertising, marketing and PR to other companies, or employ individuals within their own company to deal with them. The producer will keep a close eye on all areas of publicity and will usually have a strong opinion concerning the way in which the show is marketed to the public.

- Paying wages. This usually applies to professional productions only. Amateur theatre companies will generally rely on people offering their services for free, although there is sometimes some payment where musicians are concerned.

- Securing and hiring a suitable performance space. This may not necessarily be a recognised theatre but it will usually incur some sort of cost.

- Scheduling an overall timetable for the production (see Chapter 3). This is often done in conjunction with the director and the production manager.

- Organising **auditions**. With professional productions this will often be done in association with a casting director. An audition **venue** will need to be hired and it is usually necessary to enlist the services of a pianist with good sight-reading skills.

- Selecting a **company manager** who will liaise with the producer and with all the different departments in the theatre including stage management, **front-of-house**, the **wardrobe department**, the **actors** and the **band**. In a professional theatre the company manager will usually liaise with the producer to organise the payment of company wages and will also offer pastoral care to the company. It's a job of many parts and requires someone with excellent communication skills and bags of diplomacy (see Chapter 6).

- Organising a guest list for the **opening night.** This will usually include invitations for the investors, the press, reviewers, the creative team and for anyone else connected with the production.

- Providing some sort of celebration after the official opening night performance. This can be as simple as a glass of wine in the bar or as extravagant as a champagne reception at the Savoy.

- Managing the production during the **run**. This will involve liaising with the other members of the **production team** on a regular basis and keeping a close eye on the production. It's also important to ensure that standards are maintained, box office receipts are checked regularly, wages and royalties are paid (if applicable) and that publicity is ongoing and effective.

In the theatre it's usually the producer who initiates a project, although it's not unknown for a director or writer to approach the producer with a specific piece in mind. There are, of course, thousands of existing musicals just waiting to be re-discovered, re-invented and re-staged. There's a rich pool of subjects to explore, from the sublime to the ridiculous, the bizarre to the mind-numbingly banal. There are musicals about cartoon dogs, man-eating plants and serial killers; there are epic accounts of revolution and revolt, nuclear wars and presidential assassinations. There's even one about a certain little whore-house in Texas! The range is bewildering. What's more, there's a huge and exciting array of new musicals just waiting to be selected, developed and produced.

Finding the right show

I need a personal connection in everything I do. I have a simple rule, say 'no' until the story is so compelling you have no choice but to say 'yes'.
EMMA RICE

Some producers or directors will have a very clear idea right from the start about the type of musical they are hoping to present. Others will need to do some searching; the internet is an obvious first port of call. There's a bewildering amount of audio and audio-visual material available, and within seconds it's easy to access cast recordings, film footage, synopses and other useful bits and pieces of information. Alternatively, some producers prefer to go straight to the publisher or licensing company to find out what's currently available for hire; this information is easily accessible online.

Licensing companies

The main licensing companies in the UK include the following: Samuel French Ltd, MusicScope, Music Theatre International Europe (MTI Europe), Rodgers and Hammerstein Europe (R&H Europe), Warner/Chappell Music Ltd and Josef Weinberger Ltd. A selection of US **licensors** include: Dramatists Play Service Inc. (DPS), Music Theatre International (USA), Rodgers and Hammerstein (USA) and Tams-Witmark (Music Library, Inc.).

These online catalogues generally contain author/writer credits, a brief description of the show, an indication of cast size and cast type, a list of available **rehearsal** material (scripts, **vocal books** and conductor's score), and details of the existing orchestrations. Some websites also include extra information in the form of sound recordings and film clips from previous productions. It's hard to find comprehensive catalogues of all available material, mainly because the shows, whether amateur or professional, are divided up between various different licensing companies. A quick search online, though, will usually provide the required information.

Once a potential show has been identified the next step will be to request a **perusal copy** from the licensing company. This will usually include a libretto and a vocal book (often just the vocal lines without the piano part). Since this material is sent out electronically there's usually no fee for this service. The script and score are 'read only' for obvious reasons and it's not, therefore, possible to print out any of this perusal material. With amateur shows the licensor is usually willing to send out hard copies of the script and score, but there's often a charge for this.

Affordability

Whilst it may be tempting to weed out those shows which appear to require multiple sets, expensive costumes and complex lighting, it's worth remembering that with a positive attitude and lots of imagination many design challenges can be met successfully without spending a fortune. In fact, I've seen (and been involved in) a number of productions which have worked extremely well despite having only a limited budget. Where a skilfully crafted show exists, and where there's talent and originality in the cast and production team, it's quite possible to produce an innovative and successful production without breaking the bank. However, with shows on a small budget it's important that adequate funds are available for the sound department and for the band (assuming that there is one). In my experience compromises made in these departments can often have a profoundly detrimental effect on the overall quality of the show (see Chapter 3).

Suitable casting

It's important to make sure that the actors auditioning for the prospective production have the necessary skills for the piece. Does the show require performers who can act, sing and dance? If so, what style of dancing is required? How big is the **ensemble** and what is the age range? Are there rôles in the show requiring specific performance skills? It's no good trying to produce a production of Candide* without a stunning, virtuosic soprano to play the taxing part of

---

* Please note that the writers of each musical mentioned in this book are listed at the back (see Appendix: Referenced musicals).

Cunégonde. Likewise, a production of *42nd Street* without a fabulous tap dancer to play the chorus girl-turned-star, Peggy Sawyer, is never really going to raise the roof.

I've already suggested that in most cases design challenges can usually be overcome with flair, ingenuity and a dash of optimism. This is not, unfortunately, the case with performers. There is absolutely no point in being unrealistic about the necessary talent required to play certain musical theatre rôles. 'I'm sure that her vocal range will develop in rehearsals', and 'We can easily teach her to tap', are expectations which will probably land everyone in the soup. Being realistic about your pool of potential performers is essential, and your choice of show should reflect the talent available. This is particularly important with school or community projects.

Age-appropriate shows

It also makes sense to consider whether the piece is going to be suitable for the age group of the actors hoping to audition. If, for example, it's a school production, and the majority of the performers are teenagers, then it's not a great idea to select shows such as *Follies* or *Cabaret*, which include substantial rôles for older character actors. On the other hand, *Grease* or *Legally Blonde* are perfect vehicles for young performers since they focus on the joys and agonies of school and college life. Given the difficulties of **staging** a musical in the first place, it really does make sense to utilise any natural advantages such as the youth or maturity of the available pool of performers.

Cast size

If the production is to be presented at a school or college, is the plan to include a whole class or a whole year in the show? Could the piece be expanded to incorporate extra characters on stage? A school production of Lionel Bart's *Oliver!*, for example, might work extremely well with an expanded ensemble, since there's no limit to the number of orphans and urchins that could appear in the show.

On the other hand, if you are intending to use professional performers, how many actors can you afford to employ? Could the actors double up on parts, thereby reducing numbers and subsequent costs? Some shows work extremely well with this sort of economical approach. If you do decide to make such a decision, though, the writers (in the case of a new show) and the licensors (in the case of an established published work) need to be consulted at an early stage.

Photo 1 Production photo: *Sweet Charity*, Theatre Royal Haymarket (Tamzin Outhwaite, Mark Umbers). (Photo, Nigel Norrington.)

A few years ago I directed a production of Cy Coleman's Sweet Charity *at the delightful Menier Chocolate Factory in London. My concept involved having Charity's three lovers all played by the same actor. Initially there was some concern about this and the estate only agreed to this casting idea on the understanding that the show was a 'try-out' and that if they didn't like the result of this triple casting they would veto any future life for this particular production. In the event the audiences and the estate were won over by a virtuosic performance from our leading man (who played Charlie, Vittorio and Oscar) and the show not only enjoyed a successful run at the Chocolate Factory, but subsequently transferred into the West End.*

Intended audience

Will the show be suitable for its intended audience? This is a question which will no doubt preoccupy the producer, and one which must be given some serious thought. If the audience is likely to be a younger crowd, it may be wise to opt for something upbeat and energised such as *Little Shop of Horrors*, or the slightly more risqué pleasures of *Avenue Q*. Smart urban adults may favour *Company* whilst an older demographic may prefer the comfortable familiarity of *The King And I* or *My Fair Lady*. Sometimes, of course, it's good to challenge an audience and give them something outside their comfort zone – but this will depend on your finances and whether or not you can afford to take the risk. Most producers will make their decision based on a combination of research and instinct. In my experience the best producers aren't just looking for a hit but are eager to be involved in a theatrical experience which they'll find challenging and fulfilling. There's little point in choosing a show, no matter how profitable it turns out to be, if there's no real love for the piece to start with.

Venue

Will the show suit the available theatre space? If the venue has already been fixed, this will certainly have a bearing on which show to choose. If it's a small **theatre-in-the-round**, for example, with no **orchestra pit** and little room for the musicians, the band will need to be small too, and this will inevitably affect your choice. A big belter of a show like Cole Porter's *Anything Goes* or George Gershwin's *Crazy for You* will clearly suffer in these circumstances, since the power of such pieces is partly the result of the fabulous razzmatazz of the orchestrations. This isn't to say that it's impossible to stage such shows in small venues, but there are probably other choices which are more suitable. Small venues need not necessarily be an obstacle however, and as I've already suggested, some shows work surprisingly well in a scaled-down form, especially those where character and story take precedence over spectacle.

There's a certain amount of common sense needed when it comes to matching the right show with the right venue, and as long as the producer is very clear as to the demands of the piece then it should be a fairly straightforward process. Some matches are particularly felicitous. A memorable production of *Into the Woods* worked perfectly at the beautiful open-air theatre in Regent's Park surrounded by a forest of tall trees; the subsequent transfer to Central Park's Delacorte Theater made perfect sense. A notable production of another Sondheim masterpiece, *Sweeney Todd*, felt suitably claustrophobic when performed in the oldest pie shop in London. In this miniature venue the cast really were 'up close and personal', which had the effect of heightening the comic moments, and making the darker, more sinister aspects of the piece really resonant and chilling. This production was subsequently re-created off-Broadway at the Barrow Street Theater, a choice of venue which proved similarly atmospheric.

Site-specific theatre really can add a new dimension to the whole experience and finding a suitable venue doesn't necessarily have to cost the earth. *The Pajama Game*, for example, would work perfectly staged in an old factory building, since the story centres around a group of discontented factory workers campaigning for better wages. It's not always easy to secure the perfect venue, of course, but it's quite a coup when you do. I'm still waiting for the opportunity to stage a production of Joseph Papp's *The Pirates of Penzance* aboard a real nineteenth-century tea clipper!

Performing rights

Once a suitable musical has been chosen the next step is to apply for the performing rights through the licensing company which represents the show. Applying for amateur rights is pretty straightforward and simply involves filling in an online form. With professional productions there's a more bespoke approach and the producer will usually deal directly with the licensor. With both types of application, the producer will be expected to provide specific information such as details concerning the intended venue, overall seating capacity, ticket prices, number of performances and prospective dates. The licensing company will also want to know how many actors will be in the company and how many musicians in the band. With a professional production the licensor will often require information about the creative personnel, especially details concerning the prospective director, musical director and designer. The licence can be withheld if these key members of the team are deemed unsuitable for the project. The rights for a show are unlikely to be available if there's a conflict of interest involving another production of the same piece at a nearby venue, or if there's a national tour or large commercial production that's recently opened or is in the pipe-line. As far as tours are concerned, the licensor will need to be given some idea of the budget to ensure that the production has adequate financial backing to make it viable.

Once the application is accepted, the licensing company and the producer will sign an agreement allowing the production to go ahead, and confirming all practical details including royalty payments and hire charges for scores and libretti. The producer will be required to accept certain conditions stipulated by the contract; these will usually include an agreement that no changes can be made to the script or score without prior consent from the writers, or the writers' estates. This is an important clause and needs to be taken seriously. The licensor is, of course, working on behalf of the writers and will be protecting their interests. As long as the potential production appears to be well thought-out and financially viable, however, the licensor will usually do everything possible to make the arrangement work for both parties.

In my experience, licensing companies are often surprisingly flexible when it comes to the orchestration of a proposed musical. Many producers, particularly with amateur and fringe shows, are simply unable to afford the full complement of musicians stipulated for the piece. It's often the case, however, that alternative arrangements already exist for smaller numbers of players and these can usually be obtained directly from the licensing company. If there's no reduced orchestration available the licensor will sometimes allow a new one to be commissioned, generally at the expense of the producer. The copyright, though, will remain with the licensor once the specific production has finished. When resources are really limited – fringe productions in pub theatres, for example – the licensor will often agree to a simple piano accompaniment in place of a band or orchestra.

Once the licence has been signed by both parties the licensor will need confirmation of rehearsal dates so that written material such as libretti and musical scores can be sent out to arrive at the right time. With amateur productions, especially those that rehearse over an extended period, the band parts may appear at a later stage.

The licence also makes certain stipulations regarding printed information on posters, **programmes** and adverts. In addition, any material that appears on the internet in the form of **e-flyers** or online promotions will be scrutinised to ensure that correct billing procedures have been observed. Once the production goes into performance, the producer will collect the box-office receipts, determine what royalty payments are due, and distribute them to the licensor or directly to the rights holders. There's a slightly different arrangement, though, for productions which take place in smaller spaces – pub and fringe venues, especially. The producer of these may be asked to pay a flat fee for each performance rather than a fluctuating amount based on box office receipts. The agreement will also specify that scripts and scores are returned at the end of the run unmarked and in reasonable condition, and that compensation is paid for any material which is damaged or lost.

Once the producer has clarified that the rights to the show are available and that suitable funding is in place, it's time to start assembling the team. As shown in Diagram 1, the producer is ultimately in charge of the entire production and has overall responsibility for every other department. For this reason I've placed the producer in the centre of the **production wheel**, with other job titles located on the various concentric circles which radiate out from the middle. It's impossible to create a perfect formula for calculating the relative importance (or hierarchical position) of each member of the team, and there are always going to be exceptions and variations since no two productions are alike. It's probably better to see this wheel as an indication of the point at which each member of the team joins the production, and who defers to who within the overall job framework. I've purposefully left several departments to one side for reasons of clarity, such as front-of-house staff, **video designers** and wigs personnel. Job titles also differ in the US; for clarification see 'Stage management in the US' (Chapter 6, p. 94).

Whilst all productions differ – and some will operate with far fewer members of the team – Diagram 1 gives some idea of the allocation of duties and helps to give an impression of the overall chain of command. In certain situations a head

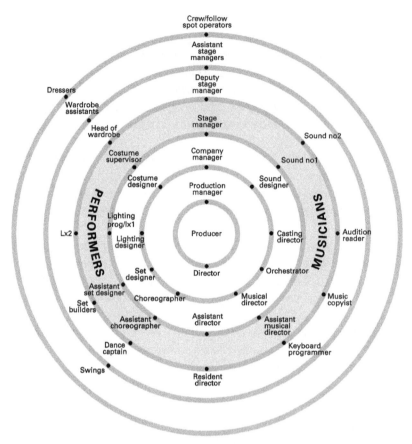

Diagram 1 Production wheel.

of department may take on more than one rôle; with musicals it's not unusual for a director to direct and choreograph the show or for a designer to design both set and costumes. Occasionally a musical director will appear on stage as part of the acting ensemble, especially in productions which involve **actor-musicians**. Nothing is set in stone and Diagram 1 should be used as a guide-line, not as a definitive model.

2
CREATIVE TEAM

It's important to define what I mean by the creative team. This is quite simply the group of people whose creative vision will determine the look, the sound and the overall feel of the show. For the sake of clarity I am not including the producer in this list, although as already discussed they will usually have a certain amount of creative input and will be in regular contact with the creative team at all times. This team will usually include the following:

Director
Musical director
Choreographer
Set designer
Costume designer
Lighting designer
Sound designer

With larger productions there may be additions to this list, including;

Musical supervisor
Casting director
Orchestrator
Costume supervisor
Wig designer
Prop supervisor
Make-up supervisor
Video designer
Puppet designer
Orchestral contractor

To avoid confusion, whenever the term creative team is used I'll be referring to the seven individuals listed above in the first category, and whenever the term production team is used it will signify the producer, the entire creative team, the stage management, the production manager and the company manager.

The **design team**, a sub-section of the creative team, will signify the set designer, the costume designer, the lighting designer and the sound designer. These are all involved in creating the look and the sound of the show.

Choosing a director

The relationship between the producer and the director is a crucial one – they will spend a large amount of time discussing and developing the show together, so it's vital that these two individuals have a strong working partnership. The producer will be looking for a director with creative vision, certainly, but one who can also handle the many varying personalities involved in the project, not only performers and creatives, but the many technicians whose work is so vital to the overall success of the production.

If a potential director isn't already known to the producer it's important to arrange a face-to-face meeting. An impressive CV isn't enough since a large part of the job involves communication; selecting a director sight unseen can potentially be a pretty risky business. An informal meeting to discuss the project and a chance for both people to find out a bit more about the other seems to be a sensible approach before any firm decisions are made. After all, the director is going to be the creative linchpin, and a mistake at this point can jeopardize the whole enterprise. The producer and the director really do have to see eye-to-eye; it's no use having a gifted director whose vision for the piece is entirely at odds with that of the producer.

SELECTING THE TEAM

Once the producer has secured a suitable director it's time to start selecting the other members of the team. Usually they'll discuss this together, and having drawn up a short-list of candidates, various meetings will take place. As a director, I'm much happier if I can have some input as far as the choice of musical director, choreographer and design team is concerned. Some directors like to work with the same team again and again. Others, like myself, prefer to mix the old and the new – to have one or two 'tried and tested' members of the team, and several new ones who've been highly recommended. This way there's always a new perspective and ideas remain fresh and challenging. With school, college or community productions, of course, there may not be a huge range of choices – sometimes it'll be a case of 'who's available and willing?' That's fine, of course, provided that the people chosen are enthused about the project and prepared to rise to the challenge.

The joy of long-term collaboration is something I have really enjoyed in my career. It has allowed me to become a better artist as it often creates an environment of truth and risk-taking that is vital to our development. That said, new relationships are also thrilling, as long as you really interrogate how you want to work together. They can make you question your process and see things afresh.

PAULE CONSTABLE

With the creative team in place someone must have overall artistic control of the production, and this should be the director. I'm certainly not advocating an artistic dictatorship, but simply suggesting that the director's job is to pull together the creative elements of the production and ensure that everyone is working towards the same artistic goals.

Once the production team has been selected the director will want to schedule regular meetings so that creative ideas can be exchanged and developed. These early discussions will usually take place between the director and one or more of the following: the musical director, the choreographer, the set and costume designers, and the lighting designer. In the early stages the director will probably spend most time with the set designer since the scenic design will provide the artistic framework for the whole production and other decisions can't really be made until some basic scenic ideas have been established.

Later meetings, called **production meetings**, will include members of other departments such as sound and stage management. Depending on the size and complexity of the show there's often at least one production meeting before rehearsals start and regular meetings during the rehearsal process. The producer will usually attend these meetings (see Chapter 11).

Director

A director must be able to command a room, delegate authority and make sure all the departments are on the same page. Plus, they must know how to get the best out of the actors, recognizing immediately the different work processes of each actor and respecting those differences.

SUSAN STROMAN

The director is sometimes misinterpreted as an omnipotent figure whose every command must be obeyed. In my experience good directors are nothing like this. They are almost always expert listeners, facilitators and collaborators. They don't pretend to have all the answers and are open to ideas and suggestions from other members of the team, and this includes the actors. The success of a musical theatre project is unlikely to rely on one person alone. The director will help to harness the creative abilities of the others, of course, but the end result will be achieved through an artistic collaboration.

It always amazes me when the director receives the credit for an entire production. What about the designs? What about the incredible lighting and flawless choreography? And those gorgeous orchestrations? Musicals, perhaps more than any other art form, require a group of people to work together with a unified vision to create a unique environment in which the performers can flourish and the story can unfold. This doesn't happen single-handedly. There's also a common misconception that the director's prime responsibility is to work with the actors in the rehearsal room **blocking** the scenes and staging the show. That, however, is just part of the job – the work begins the moment the director accepts the project, and there are lots of different aspects to it. These many directorial responsibilities include:

- Studying the piece, doing detailed research, and making overall decisions about style and interpretation based on discussions with other members of the creative team.

- Casting the show, usually with the assistance of the producer, the musical director and the choreographer. With professional productions a casting director may also be involved.

- Checking the suitability of the rehearsal venue before rehearsals begin.

- In conjunction with the producer and production manager devising a production timetable to include auditions, staging rehearsals, **technical rehearsals**, **dress rehearsals**, **previews**, and performances.

- Mapping out a **rehearsal schedule**. This schedule is usually sent out by the **deputy stage manager** at least a day before the specified calls.

- Depending upon the size and complexity of the production, appointing an **assistant director** to help in the rehearsal room and to work with **understudies**, if necessary.

- Rehearsing the actors, providing them with background information about the show, helping them to develop their characters, and staging the scenes.

- Overseeing all artistic aspects of the show, communicating regularly with the other members of the production team, and ensuring artistic unity throughout the project.

- Providing material for the programme, if required, and helping to publicise the show by giving interviews to the press (radio, television or online).

- In tandem with the stage manager, running the technical and dress rehearsals and ensuring that this process is well-paced, efficient and productive.

Photo 2 Artistic collaboration: *Candide*, Menier Chocolate Factory (Seann Alderking, Matthew White, David Charles Abell). (Photo, Nobby Clark.)

- In collaboration with the choreographer (and often the producer) deciding on the sequence of **bows** at the end of the performance. This tends to imply a cast hierarchy and will therefore need to be carefully considered, especially if there are celebrities involved.
- Maintaining the show after the opening night, attending performances, giving notes to the cast, and re-rehearsing problem areas, if necessary.
- Rehearsing understudies, if required, or delegating this task to stage management or to an assistant director.

Musical director

The skill-set for a musical theatre conductor must include clear conducting technique, an understanding of singers and singing, a theatrical frame of mind, flexibility, and diplomacy. It's not enough to simply be a good musician!

DAVID CHARLES ABELL

One of the many pleasures of working on a musical is the opportunity to work with excellent musicians. The musical director lies at the heart of the enterprise – after all, it's not called a musical for nothing. The best musical directors have an equal interest both in the music and the drama and will collaborate expertly with the director and choreographer to ensure that good story-telling is placed at the top of the agenda. Flexibility is a key attribute as musical directors are often faced with a wide range of challenges in the rehearsal room. Ideally, they will need to be excellent all-round musicians with knowledge of choral directing, vocal coaching and working with actors with little vocal training; other skills may involve devising **underscoring**, creating vocal arrangements and, in some cases, orchestrating some or all of the score. They are usually engaged either as a **conductor** or as a **keyboard MD** – the latter will conduct from the keyboard and will therefore need to have excellent keyboard skills. Most productions will require either an **assistant musical director** or a **rehearsal pianist** to assist in rehearsals.

The musical director is responsible for all the musical elements in the show. Not only will they attend auditions, help with casting, and subsequently work with the company in rehearsals, but they'll also be responsible for the band. **Band calls** will usually take place towards the end of rehearsals, and for this reason a rehearsal pianist will often be required in the rehearsal room whilst the musical director concentrates on the musicians. Chief responsibilities include:

- Attending meetings at an early stage with the production team to discuss scheduling, personnel, band placement, contracting of band musicians, budget and sound design.

- Meeting with the choreographer early on to work on dance arrangements and ensuring that there's a recording of the correct dance music prior to the start of rehearsals. It's best not to rely on existing cast recordings for dance arrangements as they can differ substantially from the printed music. With some professional jobs contracting a **dance arranger** to create bespoke dance music to the specifications of the choreographer.

- Assembling the music department personnel; this will sometimes include selecting a pianist for the auditions and an assistant musical director or second pianist for the rehearsal period. With student productions the musical director is very likely to double as the audition pianist and the rehearsal pianist.

- Booking a drummer for rehearsals; some musicals are very reliant on the rhythm section and it's not uncommon for a drummer to be engaged early to facilitate dance rehearsals. There's usually a cost implication here so this decision will need to be agreed with the producer beforehand.

- Attending auditions and assessing the vocal ability of each auditionee. This will usually involve checking vocal ranges, vocal quality, resilience and versatility, and ensuring that the candidate can sing in an appropriate vocal style. Ideally the director, the choreographer and the musical director will make up the panel for auditions, but on smaller productions the latter may need to double as the audition pianist, in which case sight-reading becomes a priority.

- In rehearsals, teaching the principals their vocal lines and, after assessing each of the ensemble members, allocating specific vocal parts according to their range, vocal ability and harmonic awareness. Musical theatre actors aren't always the strongest sight-singers, and the musical director will usually need to record individual lines so that the performers have something to refer to outside the rehearsal room.

- Helping the performers to overcome any musical difficulties. The musical director won't always be working with confident singers; there may be rôles in the show which require an actor to put across a song rather than to sing it perfectly. They will need to help these actors to develop and sustain a vocally robust technique for the duration of the run.

- In some situations creating the vocal arrangements from scratch or adapting them for a different number of singers. This can involve creating new harmonies or re-harmonising existing sections of the score.

- Adapting the underscore (music under dialogue) and **scene-change** music to suit the specific staging requirements of the production. Often it won't become apparent until the technical rehearsals exactly how long a piece of scene-change music needs to last. Potential alterations should be noted in rehearsals and fine-tuned on stage. If no suitable music exists for underscoring or scene changes the musical director's task will be to create something based on melodies and motifs from the existing score.

- On occasions, transposing songs and musical sections into different keys, depending on the vocal ranges of the chosen singers. This is more common with new shows where the specific range of a particular part will often be up for grabs. In the older, more established repertoire (Rodgers and Hammerstein, for example) a performer will usually be chosen specifically because of their ability to sing in the written keys. There are always exceptions to this rule, however, especially where **celebrity casting** is concerned.

- Booking the musicians for the band and rehearsing them. Professional musicians will usually have three band calls of three-hours each before the **sitzprobe** – this is a sing-through of all the music in the show involving the performers and the band. It's usually the first and only time they get to work together before the dress rehearsal. Most professional productions will use the services of an **orchestral contractor** to assist in the selection and booking of the musicians.

- Liaising with the sound department to ensure that there's a shared vision as far as amplification of the musicians and the singers is concerned and making sure that there's a suitable playing environment for the band. This is particularly important if the latter is placed at a distance from the performers (offstage or in a separate room).

- Helping to create a **click track**, if required. This is a pre-recorded vocal track which helps to supplement the live vocals on stage. It's often used during a particularly strenuous section of dance where the vocals are in danger of being compromised. In the US, a click track to reinforce the vocals is essentially frowned upon in most circumstances, will need to be authorised by Equity, and requires payment for the actors.

- Liaising with the lighting department so that, if necessary, television monitors can be positioned in convenient locations so that the cast can see the musical director, and also ensuring that lighting for the band is suitable.

- Conducting the band in performance, and in the case of a keyboard MD playing the keyboard part too.

- Approving and rehearsing band **deps** (**subs** in the US). Deps are alternative players who cover for the regular musicians if they are unavailable for a particular performance.

- Organising **vocal warm-ups** during rehearsals and throughout the run and ensuring that musical standards are maintained. This may involve giving notes and calling the cast for **clean-up calls**. In the US, vocal warm-ups are the responsibility of the performer and not the musical director. It's not uncommon, though, for the latter to lead a vocal warm-up if they choose to do so.

Choreographer

The person responsible for the **choreography** or movement in a musical is generally called the choreographer; however, there are some shows where the title **movement director** might be more appropriate, especially those where dance or musical staging is minimal. Input from a choreographer differs from show to show, some musicals requiring one to be present throughout the entire rehearsal process, and others needing only sporadic attendance. Some directors are fairly self-sufficient and may decide to choreograph the show themselves, whilst others will rely on their choreographer to do most, if not all, of the work in this area. There's no set way of approaching movement in a musical and each team will work slightly differently. From my own personal perspective as a director I particularly enjoy this relationship; early meetings with an instinctive and imaginative choreographer can be extremely inspiring and can help to establish a common language for the production and a specific style for the show. Key responsibilities for the choreographer include:

- Working closely with the director from the start of the process and coming to a common understanding about how movement in the show should be incorporated. It's a good idea to divide the work load and to make sure that between them the choreographer and the director are clear about their own particular staging responsibilities.

- Researching and developing dance and movement ideas after initial meetings with the director.

- Liaising with the musical director prior to rehearsals to determine which parts of the show are likely to be choreographed and which sections of dance music may require cutting, altering, extending or re-working.

- Liaising with the set designer and production manager to discuss the surface of the stage floor as they will need to know what type of dance is going to be used in the show, especially if this involves tap dancing, where the floor will need to adhere to certain criteria to make it suitable in terms of safety, durability and resonance. The costume designer will also need to be involved in these discussions as dance footwear will be a significant factor too.

- Attending auditions, devising a suitable dance routine for the auditionees, if required, and advising the director on casting, especially where the dancers are concerned.

- Choreographing all the danced sections in the show, and helping with the staging and blocking of scenes, if required.

- Selecting a **dance captain** from within the company. This job will involve keeping a close eye on all the dance sequences in the show and drilling the other dancers during rehearsals and beyond. The job may also involve slight modification of the dance routines in the case of injury or cast absence.

- Supervising **dance warm-ups** in rehearsal and helping to maintain the physical fitness of the cast. Choreographers will sometimes delegate this to the assistant choreographer or to the dance captain. In the US, dance warm-ups are the responsibility of the performer and not the choreographer. On occasions the dance captain may lead a group warm-up, but these aren't mandatory.

- Liaising with the costume designer to ensure that the designs are practical and that they won't inhibit the choreography. Making sure that show shoes and dance footwear are suitable and safe.

- Overseeing all aspects of dance during the technical and dress rehearsals and spacing the musical numbers on stage.

- In collaboration with the director, helping to organise the **curtain call** and bows. Depending on the type of show these can become fairly complicated and will often involve sections of dance.

- Maintaining the standard of dance during the run by liaising with the dance captain, visiting the show and taking notes, and calling extra rehearsals, if required.

Since it's a term which crops up repeatedly in this book it's worth taking a moment to define the meaning of the word staging, especially as it relates to the work of the choreographer. Whilst 'staging musicals', for the purposes of this book, refers to the whole process of putting on a musical, the use of the word 'staging' when referring to the movement of the actors in a scene is more specific. It generally implies sections of the show where there's a heightened physicality and it will often, though not always, involve non-naturalistic movement of some kind. Often staging occurs where there's musical accompaniment or when the actors are actually singing. It can, at its simplest, involve a single character crossing from one side of the stage to the other. Alternatively, it can indicate the intricate interaction of a number of different groups moving together to create specific stage pictures. The line between staging and choreography is sometimes fairly blurred, and it's often hard to tell where one finishes and the other begins.

DESIGN TEAM

As mentioned above, this is a sub-section of the creative team and it usually includes the set designer, the costume designer, the lighting designer and the sound designer. No man is an island when it comes to designing a show, and it's vital that the individual members of the design team communicate well with one another. If the set designer intends to have a gleaming white set, for example, the costume designer and lighting designer will need to know as soon as possible since this will inevitably inform their subsequent creative decisions. The set designer will always keep a close eye on the lighting design as this can significantly affect the look of the set. Often when it comes to selecting a lighting designer the set designer will be consulted, as these two individuals will be working in tandem during the whole process and a shared aesthetic approach is obviously desirable.

Set designer

Being a theatre designer is like being an architect; there is so much to learn. You have to have the ability to siphon everyone's thoughts through your own, the ability to stay personal and not become general, the ability to manipulate space, to contract and expand it, the ability to move the ideas through time and space, the ability to see the essential.

SOUTRA GILMORE

The set designer has a huge creative input and an enormous influence on the overall look of the show. In collaboration with the director, the set designer will create the visual world of the piece and this in turn will inspire the work of the costume and lighting designers. This key member of the team will also be responsible for making sure that scene changes are achieved swiftly and smoothly; there's nothing worse than a production grinding to a halt whilst stage management laboriously shift hefty bits of scenery into position. Equally importantly, the set designer will need to keep an eye on the budget. It's no use conjuring up the most ravishing of sets if there's no way that the production manager can actually afford to have it built. So there needs to be a careful balancing of creativity and practicality where set design is concerned.

The set designer is responsible for the overall look of the show, and whilst the main focus of the job is undoubtedly the scenic design they also have a major responsibility for **props** and **set dressing** (including **stage furniture** and soft furnishings). In a situation where the stage management are sourcing and buying the props, the set designer should always be involved in the final decision-making. Once the scenic design has been completed the designer will liaise with the production manager (see Chapter 6) and the set builders to ensure that the set is being built to the right specifications and to the highest possible standards. Main aspects of the set designer's job include:

- Liaising with the director and making clear decisions about the style and period of the show and deciding whether the set design will be naturalistic or stylised.

- Working out how to get from one scene to the next and deciding how the scene changes are to be achieved practically.

- If the piece is to be set in a specific period, doing detailed research and collecting useful design information. This may include areas such as architecture, furniture, furnishings and fashion.

- In consultation with the director and musical director, deciding on the position of the band. Will the players be in full view of the audience, in the bowels of the orchestra pit, or neatly tucked away in another room? It's also important for the set designer to be clear about the line-up of the band; finding space for drums, percussion and larger instruments can be quite a challenge in theatres with limited space.

- Creating a story-board showing the potential look of each scene. This can be a series of drawings, or a montage of computerised images. It won't be the finished version, but it will give the director some idea as to how the stage may look for each scene.

- Presenting a **white card model** to the producer after detailed discussion with the director. This will be a prototype of the final design, but will be less detailed than the finished product, usually lacking colour and texture. The director will generally be present at this meeting and sometimes other members of the creative team too.

- Making a **model box**. This is a scaled down model of the set which is used by the production manager and set builders as a template for the set design (see Chapter 4). The designer will usually photograph the model box in each scenic configuration so that the images can be used for reference by other members of the team and also by the actors.

- Having received the basic **ground plan** of the theatre, creating a second ground plan which includes details of the design including all permutations for each scene. In addition, creating a complete set of **technical drawings** (taken from the ground plan and the model). These are measured drawings of each piece of the set in front, back and side elevations. These measurements are all to scale and are vitally important when it comes to building and erecting the set.

- Showing the model box to the company on the first day of rehearsals. Alternatively, some designers prefer to use photographic images of the model box and project these onto a large screen.

- Discussing the set design and stage furniture with the stage management and deciding what substitutes will be sufficient for rehearsals (the actual stage furniture or specific set pieces aren't usually available for rehearsals).

- Supervising the buying of set dressing and props. In some professional productions there will be a **props supervisor** who will work closely with the set designer and design (and sometimes make) specific props or pieces of stage furniture.

- Liaising with the stage manager and production manager in case any aspects of the design need altering during rehearsals.

- Depending on the length of the run, visiting the show and checking that the set is being well maintained and that scene changes are running smoothly.

Costume designer

As mentioned previously, the rôles of set designer and costume designer are often combined. However, with larger productions, especially those involving a big cast, it sometimes makes sense to appoint two separate people. Although the main task facing the costume designer is to provide suitable costumes for all of the characters on stage, this job tends to spill over into other areas, especially on smaller productions where budgets are tight and resources are limited. Often the costume designer will help to coordinate wigs and hairpieces and will usually assist with jewellery and accessories such as hats, gloves and bags. In the absence of a **make-up supervisor** (these are pretty rare in my experience) the costume designer will also advise on make-up too.

The costume designer will work in close collaboration with the director and set designer so that the overall visual world of the piece is aesthetically consistent. Whoever designs the costumes will also need to be very conscious of the movement requirements for each character. With a dance-based show most of the cast will need costumes which allow for maximum movement and which will be able to withstand the rigours of leaping, jumping and spinning. A musical like *West Side Story*, for example, requires distinctive costumes for the two gangs, the Jets and the Sharks, which will allow the performers to navigate the most energetic of dance routines.

As with the set designer, the costume designer also needs to balance creativity with practicality by making bold, imaginative choices, but by keeping one eye on the budget. The main responsibilities of the costume designer are as follows:

- After discussion with the director and set designer, researching in detail the period of the show, and starting to gather together design ideas, often including swatches of material, photographs, computer images and rough sketches.

- Providing a design for each character in the show; with some characters this will involve multiple costumes. Where costumes are being made from scratch these designs will usually appear in the form of costume sketches, often with accompanying fabric samples.

On larger productions the following responsibilities will fall to the **costume supervisor** who is generally appointed by the costume designer.

- In association with the producer and the production manager, appointing a **head of wardrobe** who will look after the costumes during the run of the show, supervise the maintenance of the costumes (including cleaning and ironing) and return all hired costumes after the final performance.

- Drawing up a list of measurements for each actor, ideally before rehearsals begin.

- Where necessary, organising and supervising the making and hiring of costumes.

- Arranging fittings once the costumes have been made or hired and supervising any alterations that may be required.

- Where necessary, providing substitute costumes for rehearsals: these may include rehearsal skirts, assorted hats, coats, shawls and gloves, and anything else costume-related which may affect movement or blocking.

Lighting designer

The biggest challenge of lighting a musical is how quickly things move – stories, situations – they are in one place in one moment then somewhere entirely different.

PAULE CONSTABLE

A good lighting designer won't only influence the visual impression which the audience receives but will also affect its emotional response too. Lighting design can be an effective way of facilitating the story-telling – a good example of this is *City of Angels* in which the lighting design for the original Broadway and West End productions served a very clear purpose. Whilst the 'real' world of the movie studio was shown in colour, the story-within-a-story was presented like a film noir, with the emphasis on shades of black, white and grey. This visual effect helped to clarify which strand of the story the audience was watching – the 'real' one, or the fictional one. Of course, the costume design helped to make this distinction too.

The producer and the director will usually select the lighting designer together, but as previously mentioned the set designer often has an influence as well. After all, the lighting design will be crucial in helping to create the overall look of the piece, and the set designer's work will inevitably be affected by it, for better or for worse.

Before any lighting decisions can be made the lighting designer will need to have a detailed discussion with the director concerning style, interpretation and mood. Since the lighting will inevitably be affected by the colours and textures of the set, clear communication between these two departments is also vital throughout the whole process. The lighting designer will expect to be given a ground plan of the theatre (a technical plan showing the exact dimensions of the space), technical drawings of the set design, and any available images of the model box. These should all be provided as soon as possible so that early decisions can be made concerning the positioning of lights both on stage and in the auditorium. The chief duties of the lighting designer are as follows:

- After suitable discussion with the director and set designer, deciding on the style of lighting required for the production. This may, for example, be self-consciously 'theatrical' involving lots of colour and texture, or more naturalistic, using the lighting to create subtle nuance rather than eye-catching spectacle.

- Devising a preliminary **lighting plot** for the show. This will need to take into account the configuration of the particular performance space, whether that be **proscenium arch**, **thrust**, **traverse** (**alley** or **avenue** in the US), or in the round (see Chapter 4, Diagram 2).

- In consultation with the director, deciding which special effects, if any, will be needed for the show. These may include smoke effects, strobe lighting, pyrotechnic flashes or **gobos** (sharp-edged patterns placed in front of the light source to create textures and shapes).

- Deciding whether **follow spots** are being used, and if so, how many. This will inevitably have a financial implication since follow-spot operators will be required; the producer will therefore need to be involved in these decisions.

- Compiling a detailed list of lighting requirements and providing a plan showing the exact positioning of the lights in the theatre. This is called a **hanging plot**.

- Watching the show in rehearsal; this will enable the lighting designer to plot where the actors are likely to be standing at any one time, but also to appreciate the mood of each scene, and to see where the focus of the action needs to be. Some lighting designers appear for the last few runs in the rehearsal room, others like to get involved at an earlier stage.

- Ordering the necessary equipment from the suppliers (often with help from the production manager), supervising the rigging of the lights in the theatre, and once in position, **focussing** these lights. Depending on the size of production some of these duties may be taken by an assistant or in-house lighting technician.

- During the technical rehearsals, plotting in sequence all the lighting states for the show. These will need to be programmed into the lighting desk, usually by a **lighting programmer** (often the assistant lighting designer) and noted in the **prompt copy** or **prompt book** (**call/calling script** in the US) by the deputy stage manager. In performance the latter will cue a **board operator** to activate each lighting cue.

- Ensuring that the band members have adequate lighting so that in show conditions they can easily read their music (if the band are on stage this can be quite a challenge).

- Maintaining the quality of the lighting by attending performances, taking notes, and ensuring that **cueing** is accurate and consistent. Wear and tear can be a real problem with lighting, and on longer runs the individual lights will need to be checked on a regular basis to ensure that they're fit for purpose. Busy lighting designers will often delegate these responsibilities to an assistant or in-house technician.

Sound designer

Until the middle of the twentieth century performers were expected to project over the band or orchestra without vocal enhancement. It's only relatively recently that amplification of the actors' voices has become standard practice, and this is usually achieved with **radio mics**. This reliance on audio enhancement has created the need for the sound designer, a very skilled job which requires lots of technical know-how, an in-depth knowledge of acoustics and a sensitivity to the human voice, both sung and spoken.

But it's not just the actors who need amplification – once the voices are mic'd it's usually necessary to mic the band as well. This in turn often leads to the need for **vocal fold-back** so that the performers can actually hear themselves sing above the amplified band. If this sounds complicated, well it is! Hence the need for a skilful sound designer.

There's also a stylistic question to take into consideration – does the musical require amplification for aesthetic reasons and will it suffer from a lack of amplified voices? *Jesus Christ Superstar* is a good example of this, as are most rock musicals. Judas Iscariot's 'Heaven On Their Minds' will sound very under-powered, no matter how brilliant the singer, if the voice is heard acoustically. The distinctive, repetitive riff from the electric guitar is very much part of the fabric of this number, and there's no point using electronic instruments if the voices are acoustic – the latter will be drowned out completely. If you choose to present a musical which requires amplification, whether by radio or hand-held mic, you must ensure that you have a good sound designer with access to the right sort of equipment. And a decent budget too.

The sound designer will take overall responsibility for everything the audience hears and will supply the actors and the musicians with the necessary equipment to ensure that the overall sound quality is of the highest standards. The sound designer's responsibilities include:

- Discussing the style of the show and its musical content with the director and musical director and deciding upon a suitable approach to the sound design.

- Discussing with the musical director the positioning of the band and the number of players in it. The sound designer will also need to be clear about the orchestration and the specific line-up of instruments in the band.

- Assessing the natural acoustic of the theatre or performance space and deciding how best to amplify the sound and where to position the loudspeakers.

- Overseeing the hiring of all sound equipment and supervising its installation and maintenance. This is usually done in conjunction with the production manager. With larger productions these responsibilities may fall to an assistant.

- After consultation with the director, compiling a list of **sound effects** and sourcing a number of suitable samples so that the director has various different options to choose from.

- Providing amplification for the sitzprobe (first sing-through with cast and band) so that the actors can be heard above the instrumental accompaniment.
- Supervising the **sound check** in the theatre. This is the period allocated to the sound department to assess each voice and each instrument and to adjust levels accordingly.
- In collaboration with the musical director or choreographer, creating a click track for backing vocals or tap sequences, if required.
- With the producer and production manager, helping to appoint a **sound operator** to mix the sound during the show. There will often be sound assistants backstage maintaining the radio mics during performance and checking that the sound equipment is working properly at all times.
- Creating a suitable balance between the singers and the band; this will involve checking the sound from all parts of the auditorium.
- Subtly enhancing the dialogue so that sung and spoken material are evenly matched.
- Attending the show during the run to ensure that all aspects of the sound design are well maintained. With longer runs there will always be variables; the size of the audience, deps in the band, and understudies on stage will all have an effect on the consistency of the sound.

ADDITIONAL TEAM MEMBERS

Having discussed the responsibilities of the main creative team it's worth spreading the net a little wider and having a quick look at some of the other related jobs, those which tend to be associated with larger productions and bigger budgets.

Musical supervisor

The rôle of the **musical supervisor** can vary from job to job, but it mainly concerns the overseeing of the musical department. Sometimes the musical supervisor will help to teach the score to the cast, conduct preliminary rehearsals, and on occasions even conduct the show in previews and on the opening night. In my experience, though, the musical supervisor tends to work in a less hands-on, more advisory capacity. For this reason, they can be enormously helpful during the tech and the first few performances, as they are free to roam the auditorium and give incisive, detailed notes concerning the sound balance, cast projection and diction, and the overall aural effect of the show.

Casting director

I think it's essential that the audition room feels like a safe environment, so an artist should always feel supported and not exposed. Tension is useful, but it should only come from the natural anxiety of an artist presenting their work for consideration and not for any other reason.

JAMES ORANGE

The main job of the casting director is to work closely with the producer and the core members of the creative team to find out exactly what sort of cast they're looking for. As well as being familiar with the script and score they will also need to know the cast size, the ratio of men to women, and the age range and vocal range of each rôle. If the show has a strong dance element then it's important for the casting director to have a clear understanding about the style of the choreography, whether it's predominantly ballet, tap, jazz, contemporary, hip-hop or a mixture of different styles. As far as each individual rôle is concerned, only by quizzing the director, the musical director and the choreographer will the casting director begin to understand the dramatic, musical and physical requirements of each part.

The casting director will usually help the producer to organise auditions, ensuring that suitable venues are booked and that pianists are hired. On the day of the audition they'll often help to run the room, introducing the actors to the creative team, helping the latter to assess the suitability of each auditionee, and keeping detailed notes about each candidate. With professional productions they'll also liaise with the actors' agents concerning audition times and audition material, and will organise subsequent recalls where necessary.

The main reason for using a casting agent is to target the right sort of auditionee for the project. Casting directors need to be constantly on the look-out and will therefore spend a proportion of their time at the theatre watching new shows and scouting for talent. They need to maintain a good working relationship with agents, be familiar with their client lists and be aware of the type of performers that each agency represents.

Orchestrator

Orchestrators are, in my opinion, the great unsung heroes of musical theatre. They tend to be less self-promoting than composers, so their work is often under-appreciated. The best orchestrators know that their primary rôle is supporting, not leading.

DAVID CHARLES ABELL

There are often several options when choosing the orchestration for a show, especially one which has been produced many times before. On application to the licensing company the producer will be given specific information about the existing orchestration(s), including the size of the band and a list of instruments required. However, if the orchestration is unsuitable (it may, for example, require too many musicians to make the show financially viable) the producer can request permission to commission a new orchestration. If given the go-ahead the costs for this will fall to the producer, but once the new orchestration is completed it will legally belong to the estate or licensing company.

Once engaged in the project the **orchestrator** will work alongside the director, the composer (if the work is a new one), and the musical director to ensure that the style of the orchestration matches that of the production. If there are sections of dance or under-scoring which need adapting from the existing score this will often fall to the orchestrator too, though usually in collaboration with the musical director and the choreographer.

Costume supervisor

As mentioned earlier with reference to the costume designer, on larger professional productions there will usually be a costume supervisor who works alongside the costume designer making sure that the costumes are sourced, bought, hired, or made to the right specifications. The main job of the supervisor is to ensure that the costume designer's vision is realised as effectively as possible, whilst also keeping a close eye on the budget. The costume supervisor will usually draw up a **costume chart** which identifies exactly what each character wears in each scene.

Wig designer

Many productions, especially those which are set in the past (and occasionally the future), will require wigs or hairpieces. Wigs can make a huge difference to the overall look of the show, but it's important to remember that if they're to be used at all there needs to be someone experienced in charge. A bad wig is worse than no wig at all, and without proper instruction and supervision the results can be humorous, if not disastrous. Wigs will also need to be well maintained (often re-set and re-styled on a daily basis), and unless there's sufficient money in the budget to do the job properly it's probably best to steer clear of them altogether. However, if there's adequate money available a good **wig designer** will be a godsend. In collaboration with the director they'll decide on a 'look' for each of the characters and allocate wigs and hairpieces accordingly. In cases where the hair simply needs styling or cutting the wig designer will advise on that too.

Maintaining the wigs in performance is often a Herculean task, and usually falls to a dedicated team of **wiggies**. Usually appointed by the producer or company manager (with help from the wig designer), this team will re-set the wigs on a regular basis, often after each performance, especially if the show is a physical one and involves lots of movement. The wig designer will usually collaborate with the sound department since mic packs are often hidden in the wigs.

Props supervisor

As the title suggests, the props supervisor takes overall responsibility for the props, especially the more obscure ones or those which are likely to need specialist knowledge. They will keep in close contact with the designer, making sure that their aesthetic approach is similar, and will usually concentrate on the trickier, more complicated props, often those which require constructing from scratch. (For more information about specific show props see Chapter 11.)

Make-up supervisor

Sometimes the costume designer or wig designer will take charge of make-up too. If not, a make-up supervisor is occasionally brought in to help design a suitable 'look' for each of the characters. A memorable production of *The Addams Family* musical required us to create a group of Ancestors who ranged from bull-fighters and Roman emperors to Elizabethan noblewomen and geisha girls. To make things even more complicated we decided that they had all died in different, dramatic circumstances. Not only did our make-up supervisor have to advise the actors on their facial make-up, they also had to tell them how to create realistic gashes and stab wounds too! Once a make-up design has been decided upon the actor will be expected to replicate it for each performance.

Video designer

Since technology continues to improve by leaps and bounds it's now possible to create some extraordinary stage effects with the use of projection, LED panels and screens. This will usually be assigned to a video designer who'll work in close contact with the director, the lighting designer and the set designer, ideally from the very start of the project. One key aspect of projection is that it can be a very swift method of moving the action from one location to the next. This is particularly helpful when the stage design is fairly simple, but the story involves multiple locations. Obviously if video design is an integral part of the visual world of the piece then there will need to be suitable surfaces onto which the images, still or moving, can be projected. There will also need to be time allocated to this particular department when it comes to the tech since it's a specialism with its own technology and tools. Just as the lighting designer needs ample opportunity to assess the effect of the lighting on the surfaces of the set, the same goes for the video designer. Cueing the video effects with the music and stage action will also take time, and it's important to factor this in when devising a schedule for a show which features this type of visual enhancement.

There are those theatre practitioners who feel that complex video design pushes things too far in the direction of film and prefer to rely on more traditional theatrical techniques. My own feeling is that everything moves on, and if technology has created new opportunities it makes perfect sense for us to embrace them. Video design is yet another valuable tool which enables us to tell stories in a rich, imaginative way; for this reason, it is sensible to incorporate it and to explore its many possibilities.

At its best it can add a beautiful layer of textured light; it feels most successful when it adds to the emotional temperature of the scene rather than taking a narrative rôle.

SOUTRA GILMORE

Puppet designer

This is a specialist area and will only be required on certain shows. In my experience, if puppets are to feature in the production it's vital to get the **puppet designer** on board at an early stage so that the set, costume and puppet design feel cohesive. Often the puppet designer will take **workshops** in the rehearsal room to help the actors bring the puppets to life. This can be a particularly exciting time for the actors as they start to appreciate the skill involved in turning a lifeless prop into a fully-fledged character.

Orchestral contractor

The orchestral contractor will liaise with the musical director to determine what type of musicians are needed for the show. There may be specific requirements, especially if the musicians are expected to appear on stage. With *She Loves Me*, a delicate ensemble show set in a Hungarian perfumery, we needed a violinist who could not only play the fiendishly difficult solo violin part but would also be comfortable appearing in some of the scenes as an itinerant musician. In the event our orchestral contractor managed to find two such players who ended up sharing the job. Once a list of musicians has been drawn up, the contractor and the musical director will select those who are most suitable for the job. With professional productions the musicians will need to have deps and the contractor will be responsible for ensuring that suitable cover is available in the event that the regular musicians are absent from the show.

3

BUDGETS, SCHEDULES AND PUBLICITY

There's no getting around it, a musical is generally a more expensive undertaking than a play, not only because it often involves a larger production team and more performers, but because expectations tend to be higher in terms of its visual impact. Elaborate costumes and eye-catching sets, whilst not a necessity, are often associated with this particular theatrical genre. There are other expenses to consider too. Most musicals require some form of musical accompaniment, whether that's an orchestra, a band or simply a piano. Whilst actors, especially in the amateur or semi-professional sphere, usually give their services for free, musicians are less likely to do so, and the reasons for this are fairly obvious. Tucked away in an orchestra pit or an offstage room, they're often unseen by the audience and tend to remain somewhat anonymous. For the actors the production can be a showcase for their talents; for the musicians it can be a slightly less glamorous experience. Paying the musicians can take a large chunk out of the budget, especially when the show requires a sizeable band, and even when the musical accompaniment is limited to a single piano there are often hidden costs to consider, such as transport, maintenance and tuning.

It's also important to remember that if there are going to be more than two or three instruments in the band, or if the musical accompaniment is predominantly electronic, the actors will almost certainly need amplification. This will usually mean hiring radio mics, speakers and other pieces of sound equipment, not to mention specialists to install and operate them. Factoring sound into the equation at an early stage is advisable so that a realistic budget can be set in place.

Cast size is also worth taking into consideration. There's a danger of generalising here, but many musicals have a group of principals plus an ensemble (or **chorus**). The average play, if there is such a thing, tends to involve a designated number of principals but no chorus (Greek plays are, of course, an exception!). The greater the number of performers, the greater the number of costumes, footwear and radio mics. What's more, most of the musicals I've directed have required two rehearsal spaces, one for blocking, the other for dance work and staging. The hiring of rehearsal space, therefore, can be doubly expensive when it comes to the staging of a musical.

A word of caution. If money and resources are really tight, it's worth thinking twice before deciding to produce a musical. I'm not for a moment suggesting that musicals need to be inordinately lavish – some, as already suggested, work extremely well on a simple set with few costumes and minimal lighting – but there are areas which can't be compromised. By stinting on the music budget, for example, the result may be a second-rate band, and with a show that relies heavily on music, this can seriously affect the whole production. Likewise, if the actors need mics and the sound equipment is cheap and of low quality, the overall effect is likely to be disappointing. These are just two examples, particularly relevant with musicals, where under-funding can have a detrimental effect on the production as a whole.

Budget

Having assessed the situation and decided that a musical is financially viable the producer must draw up a realistic budget for the entire production taking into account the number of performances, ticket prices, running costs and production costs in each department. I emphasise the word *realistic* because it's all too easy to launch into a production with great gusto but to forget the practical details concerning the financing of the project. The producer, being the business head of the team, should try to ensure that the budget is drawn up as accurately and pragmatically as possible, and should avoid approaching the enterprise in an overly enthusiastic, rose-tinted fashion. The creative team can afford to go off on wild flights of fancy, but the producer can't. Encouraging the creativity of the team is one thing, being reckless with the finances is quite another; the producer must always have one eye firmly fixed on the practical details of the production.

When drawing up a budget, the producer will need to assess both the possible income from the project and the likely **expenditure**. Often outside financial assistance is required to mount a theatrical production. Sources of funding include subsidies from a local authority or grant-making organisation, donations from benefactors, use of Kickstarter or other crowd-funding websites, or sums of money invested in the production by a theatrical investor (or **angel**). These funding options mainly apply to professional or semi-professional productions; schools and colleges will usually be self-funding and tend to rely primarily on ticket sales.

The following list gives an idea of what constitutes income and expenditure as far as a theatrical enterprise is concerned. I've avoided referring to specific sums of money since this will obviously depend on the scale of the production, the overall budget, the size of the venue and many other variables.

Income

Ticket sales

Programme and merchandising sales

Investment (from theatrical investors or angels)

Sponsorship (from local businesses)

Grants (from local authorities)

Private donations (from patrons)

Advertising in the programme

Expenditure

Royalties (as stipulated by the licensing company)

Rental fees (for scripts and scores)

Rental of audition rooms and rehearsal rooms

Hire of venue

Set costs (materials, construction, transportation and maintenance)

Costumes, wigs and accessories (and ongoing maintenance)

Props (including replacement of running props and general maintenance)

Lighting hire (including ongoing replacement and maintenance)

Sound equipment hire (including maintenance)

Make-up (if not supplied by the actors)

Hiring and tuning of pianos for rehearsals and performances

Printing of tickets and programmes

Administration costs

Setting up a website (if required)

Insurance

Theatre costs, including get-in and get-out (load-in/load-out in the US)

Contingency

Professional productions may also include:

Salaries for the production team, the actors, musicians and theatre staff

Internet campaigns, e-flyers, adverts in newspapers and magazines, press events

Photo shoots with the actors

Hiring a PR company to handle the press

Hiring a marketing company to run the campaign and liaise with ticket agents

Securing a production photographer for programme and front-of-house photos

Opening night celebration and associated costs

Accommodation costs (if the show takes place outside the home town of the company).

Production costs and running costs

It's important to remember, especially with longer runs, that expenditure doesn't suddenly stop once the show has opened. The continuing costs may include salaries, on-going hires, cleaning and repairing costumes, regularly re-setting wigs, repairing and replacing lights, re-painting and maintaining the set, and repairing or replacing props. Certain props, such as food and drink, are referred to as **consumables** and will need to be replenished on a daily basis, whilst anything suffering wear-and-tear during the run, for example letters and magazines, fall into the category of **running props** and will need to be repaired or replaced regularly.

Keeping within the budget

The producer will decide on a budget once the scale of the production has been determined and will allocate specific amounts to each department. Once this allocation has been agreed upon it's the responsibility of the head of each department to keep within budget. It is also, however, the responsibility of the producer to set achievable goals and to allocate sufficient and appropriate funds to each department.

Reviewing the budget

The producer will continue to review the budget throughout the process so that it can be adjusted, if necessary. Since it's impossible to predict precisely how much each department will ultimately require the smart producer will ensure that there's some **contingency** money to draw on in extremis. None of this is an exact science and it's not unusual for funds to be re-allocated between departments. For example, if wigs were originally in the budget but are subsequently no longer required, the money may simply be re-directed elsewhere. In a creative environment such as the theatre no producer can predict every single potential expense so there does need to be some degree of flexibility surrounding the finances. As long as the producer keeps a watchful eye on each department and re-allocates money where necessary, it's often possible to solve budgetary issues without having to search for extra funding.

Contingency

Inevitably during rehearsals there will be unforeseen additions – an actor needs an extra jacket or hat, perhaps. Small things like this will usually be absorbed by the costume budget and shouldn't create too much of a problem. If it's something more significant, however – a wedding dress, ten pairs of tap shoes, or a tailored suit – then this may require extra money from the producer's contingency fund. And when it comes to additions to the stage furniture, props or set, these can be very costly indeed. Deciding to have the leading man make his first entrance on a motor bike may be an inspired idea, but if it's not already budgeted for the producer will have to dip into the contingency fund to make it happen. In my experience, if the producer likes the idea enough then the budget will miraculously expand to allow for this particular flight of fancy. If not, you can forget it! Directors and choreographers are creative people and not always realistic when it comes to production finances, so whilst it's to be hoped that large unforeseen costs won't suddenly arise, it's always a possibility. The contingency money is there to cover these unexpected costs and must be guarded carefully so that it's available when most needed.

And it's not just the directors and choreographers who struggle to understand the financial side of theatre-making. I've worked with several set and costume designers who find production budgets somewhat bewildering too. Since the process of producing a musical requires enormous energy and positive commitment from all departments, there's often a rose-tinted optimism about what can be achieved – a sense that by hook or by crook the show must and will go on. Much can be done on a wing and a prayer, of course, and it's extraordinary how often things can be begged and borrowed on a shoe-string budget. However, it's important to temper enthusiasm with some degree of reality, and the producer and production manager must be the ones to keep a firm grasp of the financial situation at all times and ensure that each department is spending its allocated money wisely. With professional productions a **reserve** will often be put in place. This is a sum of money to cover the first few weeks of performance before reviews, word-of-mouth, and advertising has had a chance to kick in.

Schedule

From the moment the actors pick up their scripts on the first day of rehearsals, the countdown begins and the pressure is on. A deadline in the theatre has to be met, and the biggest deadline of all is the first public performance. Cancellations do, of course, occur from time to time, but they should be avoided at all costs, since they can be financially disastrous for the producer, disappointing for the theatre audience, and unnerving for the actors too.

Once the rehearsal period has been set there's no going back on this decision. Everyone – the producer, the venue, the actors and the audience – will be expecting the performances to go ahead as scheduled. The responsibility for this inevitably falls on the shoulders of the director, even though a delayed first performance may be the consequence of illness in the cast, technical problems with the set, or a shortage of backstage personnel. Whilst it's impossible to foresee all eventualities, if the producer and production manager ensure that the **production schedule** is a realistic one and the director and production team follow it closely, the show will have the greatest chance of coming together in time for the first public performance.

In order to organise the production schedule the producer will start by working out when to have the opening night. This will, of course, depend on the date on which the production gains access to the venue, the length of time needed to do the **get-in**, the **fit-up**, the technical rehearsals and the dress rehearsal, and the number of previews required. Once the opening night has been fixed the producer will need to work backwards from here to work out the start date for rehearsals.

It's worth clarifying, at this stage, the meaning of the terms opening night and **press night** since there's sometimes some confusion. Essentially these terms both refer to the same thing – the performance when the press are invited to see the show, and when the production is considered to be in a fit state to be critically assessed. The performances will continue to develop and change throughout the run, of course, but this is the point when the rehearsal process officially comes to an end. A series of previews may precede the opening night, the number of these depending on the overall length of the run and the nature of the production (whether student, amateur or professional).

In order to maximise the impact of an opening night, producers will usually try to choose a date when there are no competing shows opening at the same time. This is especially true in the professional sphere since the opening night is a great PR opportunity and can generate lots of publicity. With professional productions in and around London (both West End and Fringe) the producer will need to contact the Society of London Theatre (SOLT) and ask to look at the press night calendar to check for potential clashes; producers in New York will need to contact The Broadway League.

As far as reviewers are concerned, gone are the days when they all pitched up to the opening night performance en masse. Nowadays they are permitted to attend previews on the understanding that their reviews won't be published until after opening night. The advantages of this are fairly obvious; an audience mainly made up of reviewers is never going to be an ideal one, partly because they'll be busy writing notes and therefore unlikely to be effusive and supportive, and largely because they don't necessarily represent the appropriate audience demographic. Having a good percentage of normal theatre-goers in the crowd is vital to ensure that the reaction is a realistic one and represents a typical audience response.

Planning the production schedule

There's no golden rule when it comes to allocating sufficient time to rehearse a musical. In my experience four weeks is fairly standard, but it does, of course, depend on the size and scale of the show. *Tick, Tick . . . Boom!* is a small-scale musical with a cast of three and could probably be rehearsed in less time. However, if the show is conceived on a larger scale and involves big casts and more ambitious story-lines, for example *Showboat* or *Ragtime*, it may well be worth adding an extra week to this basic four-week model. Most amateur, school and college productions won't rehearse in one single uninterrupted rehearsal block and are more likely to meet on a more sporadic basis, perhaps once or twice a week, in which case the rehearsals will take place over a period of months rather than weeks.

There's bound to be some degree of creative guesswork involved in scheduling rehearsals for a musical since there are so many variables to consider. No two actors will work at the same speed, no two dancers will assimilate the choreography at the same pace, and no two directors will collaborate with the cast in quite the same way. But a four-week rehearsal period will usually give the director, the choreographer, the musical director and the cast adequate time to explore the material in reasonable detail. Whilst the producer, for financial reasons, may be angling for a tighter schedule, it's important that everyone comes to an amicable agreement here. The producer will have the last word but may be influenced by the director if there are good reasons why the rehearsal period should be extended. On *Top Hat,* for example, we found that the sheer volume of dancing required by the leading couple was difficult to manage in four weeks and that it was worth bringing them in a week earlier to start on some of the more complex and challenging choreographic routines.

Preparatory rehearsals

On occasions it makes sense to think of having a pre-rehearsal period when some preparatory work can be achieved in advance of the official rehearsal block. This can be a useful time for the choreographer, for example, who may require some extra rehearsal days to prepare some of the more complicated dance sequences, usually with an assistant or with the dance captain. Where child actors are concerned, a period of rehearsal before the adult cast arrives can be very beneficial too – the young actors subsequently come to the main rehearsals well prepared and with some of the work already under their belts. As mentioned previously, with a show that heavily features one or two performers it's sometimes useful to bring these actors in early before the rest of the cast appears; this can be a very productive, focussed way of working, and it also avoids having other actors hanging around for hours feeling forgotten and ignored.

Production schedule

It's useful to think of the production schedule in three stages:

Stage 1: The period between the first creative meetings and the first day of rehearsals.

Stage 2: The period between the first day of rehearsals and the final run-through in the rehearsal room.

Stage 3: The period between the theatre get-in and the opening night.

The producer and production manager will generally decide how much time is needed for each stage, but this decision should be reached in consultation with the other members of the production team. If, for example, the performers are using radio mics, the sound designer will need time to balance the sound on stage. If the stage design is complex, with lots of scene changes involving cast or **crew** members, then the schedule will have to accommodate this too. Every show is different and scheduling decisions must be tailor-made to suit the specific requirements of each production.

Stage 1: Pre-production (see Chapters 3–5)

1 Holding initial meetings between the producer and the creative team.

2 Embarking on individual research; this will usually be undertaken by all members of the creative team.

3 Organising design meetings involving the director, the design team and often the producer.

4 Presenting the white card model. The set designer will take charge of this meeting, and the producer and director will usually attend.

5 Presenting the finalised model box to the producer, the production manager and other members of the creative team.

6 Publicising the show. This will, of course, continue throughout stages 2 and 3.

7 Holding auditions and recalls.

Stage 2: The rehearsal period (see Chapters 7–11)

8 Rehearsing in detail every aspect of the show, ensuring that the script, music, choreography and staging are thoroughly explored, blocked and memorised.

9   Constructing the set, buying, hiring or making the costumes, and sourcing the props. (Depending on the complexity of the show some of this may begin during stage 1).

10 Working towards a series of final run-throughs in the rehearsal room with piano accompaniment. Often the actors will use basic rehearsal props and wear some element of rehearsal costume, including their show shoes.

11 Rehearsing the band. These band calls will be supervised by the musical director and will need to take place in a room with reasonable acoustics ideally situated somewhere near the rehearsal venue.

Stage 3: At the theatre (see Chapters 12–13)

12 Holding a sitzprobe. This is where the cast and musicians meet for the first time and run through all the musical elements in the show. (This won't always take place at the theatre, but it does usually happen after the final rehearsal in the rehearsal room.)

13 Building the set on stage so that it's safety-checked and ready for the first technical rehearsal.

14 Rigging, focussing and plotting the lights.

15 Installing the sound equipment, rigging the speakers, carrying out a sound check with the cast and band members, and mixing the sound.

16 Working through the technical rehearsal (tech) ensuring that all aspects of staging are in place. Checking that all props are tested and approved, that lighting cues and sound cues are plotted, and that scene changes and costume changes are well rehearsed.

17 Holding at least one dress rehearsal under show conditions, with everything in place including props, costumes, lighting and sound. The band will be needed at this point. Full stage management, crew, and follow spot operators will also be required.

18 Performing the show in front of a preview audience; ticket prices are usually reduced for these early performances. During the preview period rehearsals will continue and improvements will be made, where necessary, in all departments. Previews will usually only apply to professional productions.

19 Performing the show for an opening night audience; this will generally include reviewers, investors and friends of the cast and production team.

Stage 3 is a time of frenetic activity when all the different pieces of the jigsaw finally slot together. Musicals will usually require a longer period of preparation in the theatre than plays because of the added complication of seating the band, balancing the sound and staging the dance routines.

Publicity

When I first started directing productions on the London Fringe the main focus for our publicity campaign was posters and flyers. We spent days putting up illegal posters on bill-boards and lamp-posts, and evenings trudging from pub to pub trying to off-load as many flyers as possible. Nowadays, I'm pleased to say, things are very different.

The internet has changed everything as far as publicity and marketing are concerned. We can now access a much wider audience by sending out e-flyers or promoting our shows on Facebook or Twitter. By setting up a website there's an immediate reference point for anyone who wants further information and at the touch of a keypad we can let everyone in our address book know about a forthcoming production. We can send out production photos, adverts and reviews to friends, business associates and local organisations such as schools and colleges. We can organise an **Electronic Press Kit** (EPK) (**B-roll** in the US); this usually includes film footage of the show, interviews with the cast and creative team, and **vox pops** (filmed audience reaction and comments). Often using a sound-track of music from the show, these can be skilfully edited to create a dynamic online advert for the production. Whilst EPKs can be quite an expensive investment – it's often necessary to pay the actors, the musicians and other personnel involved – there are cheaper alternatives for producers on a much tighter budget (see 'Free publicity'). Whilst these digital opportunities can be a great way of publicising the show, there's still a place for good old-fashioned posters and flyers, especially if the images used are striking and persuasive. Nowadays, though, this is just one method of advertising the show – thankfully there are many others to choose from.

Just as the budget and production schedule need to be drawn up long before the actors set foot in the rehearsal room, so too is it important to plan the show's marketing and publicity at an early stage; there's no point creating a great production if nobody comes to see it. With a professional production there will usually be a PR/marketing department which takes care of publicity, but in the case of a fringe production or a community/amateur/student project, the responsibility for selling the show will most probably land squarely on the shoulders of the producer.

Free publicity

Publicising a show can be an expensive business, and the degree of investment in this area will depend on the size of the overall production budget. At one end of the scale producers working on big, commercial productions can choose to invest in radio and television adverts, EPKs (see above), print ads (newspaper and magazine), digital advertising, and adverts on buses, taxis and large billboards. But for producers on a limited budget there are many ways to approach advertising and marketing which won't break the bank. These include sharing data bases with other venues, creating vox pops and putting them out on social media, running competitions with theatre tickets as prizes, sharing information on social media such as Twitter, Facebook, YouTube and Instagram, contacting local radio stations and newspapers, and organising publicity events involving cast members.

The main responsibilities for anyone organising the publicity and marketing are as follows:

1   To ensure that a suitable design image is created for the show. This, or a variation of it, will be crucial in helping to publicise the production. This artwork (sometimes created with the help of the show's designer) will be used on posters and flyers, on e-flyers and on the website, and will often become the main image for the theatre programme. If the show is being produced in the commercial sector then this image is likely to be the responsibility of the PR/marketing team and will probably end up being featured on a bewildering array of merchandise too.

2   To supervise all online marketing and publicity. This may include setting up a website, sending out e-flyers, organising an EPK (if funds are sufficient), managing social media accounts, and promoting the show on Facebook, Twitter and other suitable social media platforms.

3   To organise the printing of posters and flyers and to distribute them to shops, pubs, restaurants, schools, libraries, community centres and other local theatres.

4   To take out adverts in the local press, and to contact local television and radio stations.

5   To send out press releases and to ensure that all relevant information concerning the production is included, such as performance dates, performance times, the venue, the casting, the content of the show and the price of tickets. Also, to check that the show is included in local listings.

6   To contact local shops to organise promotional window displays; these may feature posters, handbills, production shots, cast photos and any number of suitable accessories which help to conjure up a sense of the show.

7   To organise the theatre programme.

8   To sell advertising space in the programme.

9 To invite reviewers and journalists to attend the opening night performance (or an earlier preview).

10 To deal with ticket agents, inviting them to see the show, and liaising with them about special ticket deals in exchange for marketing support.

11 If necessary, to liaise with the company manager about cast interviews and to organise **photo calls** for on-going publicity.

This list includes aspects of publicity and marketing which are relevant to amateur, semi-professional and professional productions. There are, of course, other ways of publicising a production, such as taking to the streets and performing excerpts from the show in front of the general public. This is a technique which is particularly effective when there are other shows vying for attention. During the Edinburgh Festival, for example, it is impossible to walk through the streets of this beautiful city without encountering actors from numerous shows, singing, dancing or acting, whilst handing out fistfuls of flyers to anyone who'll take them.

It's also possible to publicise a production by contacting local schools and colleges, especially if the show has some specific relevance to the course work. Discounts are often offered in these circumstances. Much needed publicity can also be obtained by contacting the local press and focussing on a specific aspect of the production. A quirky story, a local celebrity, or an unusual angle to the story-telling can be a good way to create some interest in the show. I directed a musical adaptation of David Walliams's wonderful children's novel, *Mr Stink*, which featured 'scratch and sniff' cards allowing the audience to experience the story not just visually and aurally but also via their sense of smell. This olfactory element proved to be a hit not only with our younger audiences, but also with the press and managed to generate some great publicity in the local papers.

Blogging can also be a useful way of publicising a show. In a recent production of *The Producers* one of our elderly female characters, 'Hold-Me-Touch-Me', was played by a male actor who decided to create a blog for his alter-ego and succeeded in securing quite a keen online following. This type of virtual journalism is a good way of generating a buzz about a specific production, without having to spend any money at all.

Poster

Finding an eye-catching image can be a very effective means of helping to publicise the show. For our production of *The Addams Family* the producer, designer and publicity department organised individual photo shoots with each of the principal actors and then created a composite image of the family which was subsequently used on posters, e-flyers, front-of-house displays, programmes and merchandise (see Photo 3).

Ideally the artwork for the poster should tie in stylistically with the production itself and should give some clear indication of the type of show that's being advertised. It's important to include key pieces of information on the poster, and details which are usually added to the basic design image are as follows:

- Name of the society or production company.
- Title of the show.
- Billing for the writer, lyricist and composer.
- Venue details including box office number and website address.
- Dates of performances.

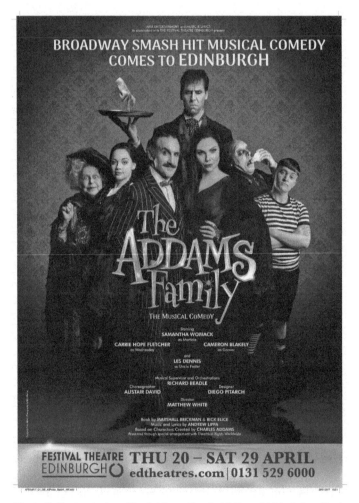

Photo 3 Poster design: *The Addams Family*, UK tour (Valda Aviks, Carrie Hope Fletcher, Cameron Blakely, Dickon Gough, Samantha Womack, Les Dennis, Grant McIntyre). (Photo, Matt Martin; graphic design, AKA.)

- Any information expressly specified by the licensing company. This sometimes includes details of the first production and the original creative team.
- Cast and creative team billing.
- If the production is an amateur one the licensing company will require this to be specified clearly on all publicity.

The producer may also want to include some additional information about the show informing the theatre-goer that it's a 'comedy classic' or 'Broadway sensation' or that it's based on a specific film, book or even pop group. Sometimes the use of a pithy quote taken from a review of a previous production may also help to catch the eye of the beholder.

As far as the printed matter on the poster is concerned, there will often be strict rules applied to the choice of font size for specific names attached to the production – for example, it may be a legal requirement that the name of the original writer is printed in a larger font than that of the current director, choreographer or designer. High profile performers are also likely to be in more prominent positions and often in larger print. Usually the flyer is a smaller version of the poster. Due to its size it probably won't have quite so much information on the front but will normally have a description of the show on the reverse side, including details about the cast and creative team. It may also have information concerning **access performances**; these can include audio described, captioned, sign interpreted, and relaxed performances (those which are aimed at theatre-goers with learning difficulties).

Programme

Revenue from the programme goes to the theatre, although proceeds from the sale of **souvenir programmes** are split between the venue and the producer. This tends to be a glossier, more glamorous version of the regular programme with plenty of photographs and extra information about the show. The content of the basic programme will usually include some or all of the following:

- Credits for the writers, and often for the original creative team too.
- Cast photos and biographies.
- Biographies for the creative team and the writers.
- A cast list and credits for the entire production team.
- A list of the band musicians.
- A list of understudies.
- A list of musical numbers in show order.

- An indication of the historical period of the piece.
- Additional information about the show, often supplied by the producer, the director or a theatre journalist, usually giving background information about the piece, some details concerning the writers, and sometimes an insight into the rehearsal process.
- A 'special thanks' section crediting various people who have contributed to the production by giving their time, money or expertise.
- Adverts for other shows, restaurants and businesses, concerts and other local events.
- Rehearsal photographs.

Programmes may also include a synopsis of the story, an interview with one or more members of the cast or creative team, and an approximate running time for the show.

4
RESEARCH AND DESIGN

There's no denying that rehearsing a show, particularly a musical, can be enormous fun and extremely rewarding. However, for me, part of the thrill of working on a new production is the preparation beforehand. I'm referring to that precious period of time between accepting the job and the start of rehearsals. This is the time when the creative team will begin to immerse themselves in the piece, researching many different aspects of it, and collaborating to find a common approach to its themes and nuances. A designer friend of mine refers to this period rather poetically as 'dream time'.

Some of this work will be done individually, and some of it will be shared. Good communication at this stage is, of course, very important. Whilst it's normal for the director and the designer to spend a fair amount of time together discussing the nature of the piece and how best to present it visually to the audience, other members of the team aren't always included in these early discussions. Where possible I will always try to disseminate relevant information so that no member of the creative team is left out of the loop. It's not always easy to get everyone together on a regular basis, but I find a well-crafted e-mail will usually do the trick.

Research

Having assimilated the script, the next port of call for most directors will be a decent recording of the show. Original cast recordings usually give a fair indication of how the writers intended the show to sound; later recordings can be confusing as they're inevitably influenced by subsequent directorial decisions, and also by the era in which they were recorded.

As a director I find that it's a good idea to listen to the music without referring to anything visual such as photographs or footage of the show. This helps to get a sense of the style and content of the music without being distracted by someone else's vision for the piece. There's a danger, though, that by listening to a recording over and over it's very easy to become attached to the phrasing, dynamics and tempi of that particular version. The director and musical director should try to avoid becoming over-familiar with any one recording – it's better to remain flexible so that the new company of actors are free to express themselves vocally without feeling as though they're being shoe-horned into someone else's performance.

Once I'm familiar with the script and the musical score I'll usually start gathering some background information about the show. This is where the detective work begins. In truth, what used to feel like intrepid sleuthing now feels remarkably straightforward. A quick trawl through the internet will usually come up with some very useful information. Wikipedia may have taken some of the thrill out of research, but it's also saved us an awful lot of time. It's good, however, to delve deeply into the subject, and it's worth taking the time to scour libraries and bookshops for suitable research material and where possible to access relevant recordings and film footage. These, of course, can often be accessed online.

Source texts

It's undeniably true that most pieces of musical theatre are based on something else. There are very few entirely original musicals which don't begin life as a novel, a play, a film, an opera or a collection of songs from a particular artist or band.

Adaptations of literary works include:

Lionel Bart's *Oliver!*	Dickens's *Oliver Twist*
Leonard Bernstein's *Candide*	Voltaire's *Candide*
Kander and Ebb's *Cabaret*	Isherwood's *Goodbye to Berlin*

Adaptations of plays include:

Lerner and Loewe's *My Fair Lady*	Shaw's *Pygmalion*
Rodgers and Hammerstein's *Carousel*	Molnár's *Liliom*
Bock and Harnick's *She Loves Me*	László's *Parfumerie*

Adaptations of films include:

Stephen Schwartz's *The Baker's Wife*	Pagnol's *La Femme du Boulanger*
Bacharach and Simon's *Promises, Promises*	Billy Wilder's *The Apartment*
Cy Coleman's *Sweet Charity*	Fellini's *Nights of Cabiria*

Adaptations of operas include:

Jonathan Larson's *Rent*	Puccini's *La Bohême*
Bell and Bowman's *Hot Mikado*	Gilbert and Sullivan's *The Mikado*
Boublil and Schönberg's *Miss Saigon*	Puccini's *Madama Butterfly*

Song catalogues adapted into stage shows include:

Beautiful (songs by Carole King)

Mamma Mia (songs by Abba)

Jersey Boys (songs by Frankie Valli and the Four Seasons)

Adaptations of autobiographies and biographies include:

Rodgers and Hammerstein's *The Sound of Music*	Maria von Trapp's *The Story of the Trapp Family Singers*
Lin-Manuel Miranda's *Hamilton*	Ron Chernow's *Alexander Hamilton*
Bock and Harnick's *Fiorello!*	Ernest Cuneo's *Life with Fiorello*

Whilst most musicals do seem to be based on some sort of urtext or previous artistic endeavour, there are some notable examples which are completely original. *A Chorus Line* takes as its subject a group of Broadway dancers auditioning for a new show. The idea was workshopped and improvised by its original cast under the expert guidance of its director/choreographer, Michael Bennett. *Dear Evan Hansen* is loosely based on the childhood memories of one of the show's writers (Benj Pasek) and charts the story of a young man whose life changes dramatically when a fellow student takes his own life. Similarly, *Caroline, or Change*, a musical which has at its heart an African-American woman struggling to make sense of her life working as a maid for a wealthy, middle-class family in 1960s Louisiana, was, to some extent, based on the childhood experiences of its writer, Tony Kushner. It's also appropriate to mention *Sunday in the Park with George*, a musical inspired by a painting by the post-impressionist painter Georges Seurat. The musical isn't based on any pre-existing narrative and the story revolves around the fictionalised characters in the painting; it is, therefore, largely original.

Where there's an obvious literary source, it makes perfect sense to try to get acquainted with this before exploring other areas of research. This approach can be very illuminating since it inevitably provides detail which is impossible to incorporate into the music, lyrics and script of a stage musical. *Les Misérables*, for example, is an effective, but massively condensed version of Victor Hugo's weighty and complex nineteenth-century novel. Reading the original text in translation is a useful way to help flesh out the characters, and to provide a clear historical angle on the events unfolding in the story. From a director's perspective, it's worth taking notes at this stage in the process; whilst you may find Hugo's *Les Misérables* a scintillating read, the cast may not, and it's helpful to be able to point them in the right direction when it comes to character descriptions and useful historical detail. Of course, if the actors are happy to read the whole book then they should be encouraged to do so – but in the case of *Les Misérables* they'll be lucky to finish it by end of the run, let alone the end of rehearsals!

I usually find that reading passages or scenes from the source text together can be a very useful way of helping the cast members to familiarise themselves with the themes and the overall tone of the original work (see Chapter 8). Later we may use these readings as the inspiration for an improvisation or some associated exercise. We may also look at another work from the pen of the same author – a poem, a short story or a play – comparing themes, characters and mood. In this way the source material can really help to kick-start the rehearsal process and encourage the cast to engage fully with the piece. Even if the director ultimately decides to move away from the tone of the original work, it's always useful to understand exactly what it is that you're leaving behind.

Films

Having got to grips with the source material some directors, designers and choreographers will want to take a look at a filmed version of the piece. Not all musicals have been adapted for the silver screen, of course, but it's usually possible to find some footage of a past production on the internet. Many well-known musicals, however, have been filmed, and some have made the transition from stage to film remarkably well – *The Sound of Music*, *Cabaret*, *My Fair Lady* and *Chicago* are good examples. Musicals on film can, however, be misleading and may differ from the stage show in quite significant ways. Apart from the fact that filmed musicals are often impossibly lavish and may be visually worlds away from anything that can be achieved on stage, they are usually heavily adapted for the screen. In Bob Fosse's 1972 film version of *Cabaret*, for example, two of the main characters, Fräulein Schneider and Herr Schultz, are replaced by a glamorous younger couple, Fritz Wendel and Natalia Landauer. There are also several pivotal songs which don't appear in the original stage show – 'Money' and the iconic 'Maybe This Time'. It's become common practice to insert these songs into subsequent stage productions of *Cabaret*, but permission from the licensing company must always be obtained in advance.

For obvious reasons, some directors much prefer to approach a new production with an open mind without images from past productions clouding their judgement. A filmed version of a show, however faithful to the original, will always be someone else's interpretation and may be an unwelcome influence at this early stage in the process.

The writers

It's always useful to know something about the writers. How did the collaboration come about? What else did they write together? How did the partnership work? What came first, the lyrics or the music? With long-term collaborators such as Rodgers and Hammerstein, there's a wealth of fascinating material to sift through. Finding out more about their working process and the types of subject matter that they were drawn to also helps to enrich the researcher's understanding of the specific show that's being examined. For example, when I first began work on a production of *Carousel* I was unaware of Rodgers and Hammerstein's fascination for the darker side of the human experience. As a child I was familiar with movie versions of their shows, but these were unsurprisingly sugar-coated and tended to gloss over the more sinister aspects of the stories. It's pretty clear, though, from an adult perspective, that at the heart of these works lie themes which are serious and challenging. With *The Sound of Music* it's Nazi Germany's annexation of Austria, in *South Pacific* racism is a key theme, and in *The King and I* imperialism, racism and capital punishment are brought into the spotlight. Even *Oklahoma!*, their first collaboration, presents the ambivalent character of Jud Fry, a man with a murky and possibly murderous past; the surface optimism of the show is very quickly undercut by the insidious threat of sexual violence. Discovering these darker elements in their other works made it clear to me that the writers weren't afraid to tackle important, serious subjects, and that their musicals were anything but 'light entertainment'. This gave me license to explore in much more detail Julie and Billy's disturbing and dysfunctional relationship in *Carousel*.

Biographical material can, of course, be accessed easily on the internet, and there are many fascinating books written about the more prominent writers of musical theatre – Kurt Weill, Leonard Bernstein and Stephen Sondheim to name but a few. There are even some films which focus on the lives of celebrated musical theatre practitioners, such as the 1946 film *Night and Day* starring Cary Grant as Cole Porter. Though interesting in some respects, the film is characteristically coy about Porter's sexuality and the devastating consequences of a riding accident which left him permanently disabled. Another example is Bob Fosse's 1979 film *All That Jazz*, a rich, somewhat hallucinogenic, semi-autobiographical film featuring Roy Scheider as a thinly-disguised Bob Fosse.

Personal research

How far can you go to research a musical? The answer is, in my case, a very long way. One particular journey involved travelling from London to the beautiful coast of Maine on the east coast of America to research a production of Carousel *which I was due to direct in Tokyo with an all-Japanese cast. My trip enabled me to take some fabulous photographs of the architecture and coast-line of New England which I was then able to show to my Japanese actors to help them visualise the exact locale in which the story unfolds. The intimate knowledge I gained of that particular place, and of its quirks and customs, helped me to give the cast a rare insight into a show which was as alien to them as an old Kabuki play would be to us.*

Everyone approaches research in their own, personal way, and what inspires and delights one person may irritate and bore another. Personally, I love having the time and opportunity to find out as much about a piece and its writers as I possibly can. Not only does this allow me a greater insight into the show, but it also provides me with lots of material to share with the company once rehearsals begin.

From the very start it's important that every member of the creative team has access to a decent recording of the show, a copy of the script, and ideally a copy of the score too. It's not enough to have 'a good idea what the piece is all about'; each member of the team must have a detailed understanding of the show, and be clear about its characters, themes, references and musical content.

Musical director

Whilst some musical directors will head off to find an existing cast recording so that they can get an overall sense of the show's musical content, others will prefer to immerse themselves in the score. It's generally useful for them to listen to other works by the same writers to get some sense of their musical style and a context for their work as a whole. The musical director may also want to make some early decisions about orchestration and instrumentation and will need to find out what arrangements already exist, and whether they're suitable for the particular production in hand. This information is easily accessed by contacting the licensing company.

Choreographer

The choreographer will almost certainly try to listen to an existing recording of the piece as soon as possible, in particular the dance sequences, and will want to get to know the music inside out so that options concerning staging and choreography can start to be explored. Depending on the period and location of the story the choreographer may also want to research specific dance styles, such as the waltz (*A Little Night Music*), the tango (*Kiss of the Spiderwoman*) or the Charleston (*Thoroughly Modern Millie*).

Designer

Once preliminary discussions have taken place between the director and the creative team, and decisions have been made about the period in which the show is set (and this may, of course, differ from the writer's original intentions), the designer can start to design the set. If it's intended to be naturalistic then this will involve some research into the period, making special reference to styles of architecture, types of furniture, and texture and colour of fabrics. Without doubt the internet can be a valuable resource when it comes to research, but there are many other illuminating ways of achieving this: consulting reference books, works of literature and life-style magazines, going to art galleries, visiting museums, and watching appropriate documentaries and feature films. It's quite possible that the finished design will make only a passing nod at authenticity, but even so, most designers will want to know something about the historical period before their creativity takes them off in a different direction. It's easy to generalise, of course, and no two designers will approach their work in quite the same way, but in my experience designers tend to be inveterate collectors and will usually have bookcases over-flowing with tantalising volumes referencing all sorts of different periods, countries, fashions and fabrics.

Costume designer

Costume designers will usually approach their work in a similar way. Detail is, of course, vitally important, and, assuming the production is set in a specific period, the costume designer will want to make absolutely certain that suitable reference material is available and that period detail is observed. If the show is likely to be dance heavy they will need to think about the best ways of creating costumes which are comfortable, durable and easy to move in. They will inevitably want to have some communication with the choreographer at this point so that they're aware of the type of choreography intended for the show; this will have some impact on the designs chosen for each individual character.

Design

Musical designs can feel less than perfect as they don't usually have the completeness and integrity of a design for a play; they are usually multi-locational so the challenge can often be to give them specificity.
SOUTRA GILMORE

Designing the set

The stage design will usually start to take shape after a number of meetings between the director and the designer. In my experience, other members of the creative team tend to join these discussions once the design is under way. An initial meeting between the designer and the director might include reading the script, listening to a cast recording and talking through the various scenes specified in the text. It will be the designer's job to find a neat, efficient way to get from one scene to the next, no matter how complicated this task may at first appear. *Top Hat,* a musical based on the famous Fred Astaire/Ginger Rogers movie, features a startling number of different scenic locations.

1   A Broadway stage, New York

2   Outside the stage door

3   A gentlemen's club, London

4   A London street

5   An elegant suite, the Excelsior Hotel, London

6   Dale's suite, directly below

7   The front of the hotel

8   The hotel foyer

9   A hansom cab

10 A bandstand, Hyde Park

11 Dale's suite, the Excelsior Hotel

12 The hotel foyer

13 A London street

14 The stage of the Prince's Theatre, London

15 Jerry's dressing room

16 The stage

And this is just Act 1! There are twelve different locations here, and fifteen changes of set (several scenes are visited more than once). Our inventive designer had to find a way of segueing from one location to the next, ensuring that the story continued to flow and that the narrative drive was maintained throughout. She rose to this challenge brilliantly by introducing a set of sliding screens which created different stage pictures whilst enabling us to change the scenery behind. It was very elegant, very smooth and very effective.

It's hard to generalise about what happens at this early stage in the design process because every designer/director team will approach the work in a slightly different way. However, in my experience it goes something like this. In consultation with the director, the designer will usually start by throwing lots of ideas about, trying not to get bogged down in too much practical detail. There is then a gradual honing of ideas until some sort of shape begins to emerge. At this stage some designers will begin by making rough sketches to illustrate certain aspects of the design. Others will use computerised images, often cut-and-pasted from various different sources, to create a sort of tapestry of ideas.

I look for flexibility, surprise, and someone who will provide me with a playground rather than a naturalistic world.

EMMA RICE

During the preliminary design discussions, it's important to ask some basic questions.

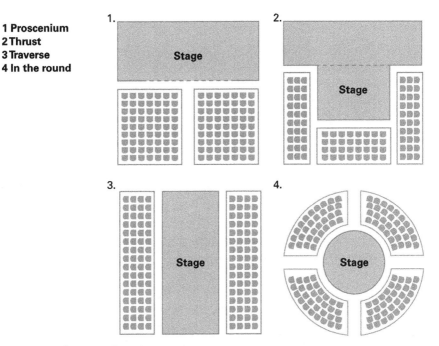

1 Proscenium
2 Thrust
3 Traverse
4 In the round

Diagram 2 Stage configurations.

How should the performance space be used?

If the theatre is a flexible space, the director and designer will need to decide how it should be utilised most effectively to tell their chosen story. Would it be best served in a conventional proscenium arch production with the actors contained within a rectangular frame, or should there be a thrust stage with the acting area extending out into the auditorium with the audience seated on three sides? What about a traverse configuration, with the audience divided into two banks of seating either side of the acting area, each facing the other? Or would the performance benefit from being **in the round**, with the actors in the centre of the space surrounded on all sides by the audience (see Diagram 2)?

There are other permutations too; would the show work as a **promenade performance** with the audience following the actors to various different locations? And what about placing a section of the audience on the stage itself, literally within spitting distance of the cast? The answer to these questions will depend upon the type of show that's being presented, the size and flexibility of the performance space, and the type of actor/audience relationship required by the director.

In which period is the piece set?

The director will usually decide if the show should be set in its correct historical period, or whether to shift the piece into a different era. Obviously, the designer will need to be informed about this as soon as possible, since it will affect most of the design decisions. It will also be of paramount importance to the costume designer. Some musicals, of course, are very difficult to uproot from their original historical context because of very specific events, references or themes. *Cabaret*, with its insidious Nazi threat, *Rent*, with its Aids-related story-line, and *Hair*, with its unabashed anti-Vietnam War stance, are shows which don't really make much sense unless placed within their correct historical framework. Other shows such as *Carousel* or *Guys and Dolls* might, perhaps, be set in a different era to that which was originally envisaged without affecting the overall integrity of the piece, but there has to be a good reason for this sort of historical tinkering.

Scene changes; how can they be achieved swiftly and smoothly without interrupting the flow of the piece?

This will be a major consideration both for the director and the designer since no one wants the story to come to a grinding halt whilst the scenery slowly and agonisingly shifts into position. Similarly, the audience will soon lose patience if they're sitting in a darkened auditorium with nothing to look at on stage. Scene changes, therefore, tend to become an important focus from early on in the process and can often take up a disproportionate amount of time in design meetings. It's also wise to decide who'll be doing the scene changes – the actors, or stage management? If the latter, will they be in **blacks** (all-black clothing required for work backstage) or costumed to help them blend in with the actors? This, of course, will need to be discussed with the costume department and will have financial implications. Rules are slightly different in the US where the crew generally move the set whilst stage management help to coordinate the scene changes.

How will the designer ensure that there's adequate space for the dance sequences?

The overall design will, of course, be influenced by the number of actors in the cast and by the physical nature of the piece. A musical often features more performers than a straight play, and many include dance sequences which require large areas of uncluttered onstage space. There is nothing worse than seeing a group of talented dancers squashed into a corner, hampered in every direction by pieces of intrusive scenery. Good collaboration at the start will mean that the designer is fully aware of the cast size and the choreographic requirements of the show. Conversely, if the cast is fairly small the designer may decide that a busy set actually makes the actors look less isolated and helps to create a more interesting stage picture.

Where will the band be situated?

Since musicals usually require some sort of instrumental accompaniment, this is an important question to ask and will inevitably have repercussions for other departments, especially the sound department. If, for example, the band is placed at the back of the stage, it will almost certainly be necessary to amplify it, both for the sake of the audience, and for the actors. If, on the other hand, the musicians are to be placed on stage in full view of the audience, this will affect the visual picture, and they risk becoming an unnecessary distraction. In addition, the light from their music stands may well interfere with the stage lighting and make it very difficult to achieve the right atmosphere for the story. With the band in view of the audience the musicians will usually require costumes to help them blend in with the actors, and this will have financial implications for the costume department. Once again, collaboration at an early stage is vital.

So, finding the ideal place for the band is an important decision, and needs to be very carefully thought through from the start of the process. Ultimately the director and designer, in consultation with the musical director, will make this decision, but it's likely to affect other departments too, so the sooner it's clarified the better for everyone.

Designing the costumes

Whether there's one designer for both set and costumes, or a separate person heading each department, it's useful to ask a few basic questions.

What type of movement will there be in the show, and how can the costumes facilitate this?

An early discussion with the choreographer will establish what style of dance or movement is likely to feature in the show. This will obviously have a bearing on the costumes and footwear. If it's a heavy dance piece such as *West Side Story* or *Chicago*, the costumes will need to be specially designed to accommodate this, and the fabrics will, by necessity, need to be flexible, durable and washable. Shoes will obviously be given top priority since they'll have to be practical, long-lasting and aesthetically appropriate.

Are there any quick changes in the show?

The costume designer must make sure that any **quick changes** are aided, not hampered by the costume design. There's no point in providing an actor with lace-up boots if they've only got twenty seconds to get into them. If these issues are addressed from the start, valuable time, not to mention money, can be saved and last-minute panic can be avoided.

What's the specific period of the show?

Since, as already discussed, the director may decide to deviate from the original intentions of the writers, it's important for the costume designer to receive this information as soon as possible. Some periods are easier to accomplish than others, not to mention cheaper. For obvious reasons it will be more economical to place a story in a contemporary setting than to locate it in the eighteenth century, for example, where clothes were elaborate, detailed and often required vast amounts of fabric.

Are the costumes likely to be hired, bought or made?

There are cost implications here, and the sooner the costume designer can answer this question the better. If there are large numbers of costumes to be designed and made the costs will soon start mounting up. Hiring costumes will, of course, be less time-consuming, though not always more economical. A word of warning, though; if most of the costumes are to be hired it's well worth factoring this into the rehearsal schedule. It often takes a considerable amount of time to get actors to and from the costume stores for fittings and alterations, time which is often vitally needed in the rehearsal room.

Clearly these early design meetings aren't just about throwing around creative ideas but are also concerned with facing practicalities. Musicals are complicated because they combine many different creative elements – music, drama, dance and design – and often a decision taken in one department can profoundly affect the work of other members of the team. With *Top Hat*, for example, we discovered that the dress designed for our leading lady for one specific number simply didn't give her maximum flexibility when it came to executing the dance moves. These included some gravity-defying leg kicks, and it was therefore imperative that the dress facilitated these moves rather than hampered them. Our designer worked tirelessly to come up with an alternative design which was elegant, which moved beautifully and, most importantly, gave the actress full choreographic freedom (see Photo 4).

Prioritising the story-telling

No matter how stimulating the design ideas may be in the initial stages, it's important for the director to remember that ultimately the show is about a group of actors telling a story. The set and costume designs must facilitate this story-telling, and not simply provide a beautiful, but lifeless piece of window-dressing. It seems fairly obvious, but in my experience designers, particularly inexperienced ones, can get so caught up with their creative ideas or 'concept' that they forget that the set has to function on a practical level, and that it's there to facilitate the

Photo 4 Costume in performance: *Top Hat*, Aldwych Theatre (Tom Chambers, Summer Strallen). Costume design by Jon Morrell. (Photo, Nigel Norrington.)

story-telling, not to **upstage** the actors. I've been involved in several shows, mercifully as an assistant rather than as the actual director, which have been spectacularly designed and gorgeous to look at, but which have been a complete disaster in terms of providing a suitable acting space for the performers. Bold designs can be a terrible distraction from the story, and it's vital to keep this in mind when the production is in its early stages.

Contemporary theatre design

Trends in theatre design are continually changing. Whilst it's hard to generalise about these things, and there are always going to be exceptions to the rule, it does seem to be the case that in musical theatre there's a current taste for economy. In the early seventeenth century, when the renowned architect Inigo Jones was designing for the court masque (a precursor of the modern musical, if ever there was one), the stage designs were opulent and ingenious, often using elaborate machinery to help conjure up sea battles, gilded chariots and exotic monsters. In America, during the early decades of the twentieth century,

Florenz Ziegfeld was equally intent on giving his audience lavish spectacle, with extravagant sets, hordes of beautiful show girls and hundreds of stylish costumes. Whilst the West End and Broadway are still able to deliver spectacle when it's needed, the emphasis seems to have shifted and the focus nowadays tends to be on finding the most effective means of telling the story – and this often involves opting for a simpler, less opulent style of presentation. Some of the recent Disney musicals would suggest otherwise, but I would argue that these are the exception rather than the rule.

Whilst in the past theatre-goers would expect a visual treat as each new scene unfolded, modern audiences are generally happy to accept something less flashy. Sets are often more unified, with each act taking place within the same basic framework. Variety can, of course, be achieved with scenic trucks, by the use of stage revolves and by flying in new pieces of scenery, but the basic set often remains the same. Lighting has also become much more sophisticated and can be used in all sorts of ways to help change the stage picture. And in recent years projection has become infinitely more advanced and is often used to alter the location without the need for complicated physical set changes. Modern audiences are simply not willing to sit in the dark for five minutes whilst an elaborate set change takes place, and nowadays scene changes will often occur in full view of the audience, instigated by the actors rather than stage management.

In design meetings I often find that we end up simplifying what started out as a complicated idea. This is sometimes financially motivated, but more often than not it's an attempt to avoid over-embellishing the stage picture and consequently allowing the audience's imagination to do some of the work. By 'suggesting' rather than 'presenting' it's possible to make the audience feel more engaged in the whole experience.

The model box

I start with my assistant trying out bad first ideas in the model box; things are never quite the same in your mind as they are in reality and you have to get them out and into the world to really see what you have, test it . . . and make it better.

SOUTRA GILMORE

'Dream time' is a valuable part of the process, but it can't go on indefinitely. Decisions concerning the set design have to be made so that the rest of the team can start their work.

Once these decisions have been made the designer will need to start work on the model box – this is a scaled down version of the set and will ultimately be the template used by the builders when constructing the real thing; accuracy is everything and it will need to be exact in all its dimensions. Creating the model box can be an intricate and time-consuming process, depending, of course, on the complexity of the design (see Photo 5). For this reason some designers have assistants to help them at this stage. The results are often breathtaking.

Most designers will start with a white card model which is a representation of the basic set, but without the colours and textures of the finished version. This will usually be shown to the director and the producer before a more robust version is constructed which will have the rest of the detail added. Once this is done a final model box presentation can be scheduled. At this meeting there will usually be the producer, the director, the lighting designer, the production manager, and often the costume designer and choreographer too. The designer will usually run through the scenes in chronological order explaining how each of the scene changes will be achieved. It's usual for photographs to be taken at this stage – very useful for reference once the model box has been commandeered by the production manager and the set builders. The showing of the model box is very important for each separate department; no matter how much discussion has taken place in advance there's nothing quite like seeing the finished model.

Once the set design is completed the other members of the creative team will have access to the visual language of the piece. Not only will the colours, patterns and textures be clear, but other aspects will also become apparent – whether the

Photo 5 The model box: *Sweet Charity*, Menier Chocolate Factory. Set design by Tim Shortall.

design is intimate or epic, whether it's a sparse or cluttered space, and whether the feel of the set is rough or refined. As far as the lighting designer is concerned it's now possible to see the lay-out of the stage and the colours and textures of the scenery and set dressings. Important decisions can now be made concerning the type of colour palette to use, where to hang the lights and how the lighting design can enhance certain aspects of the set. Viewing the model box will unleash all sorts of questions and creative ideas which can now be discussed and developed.

The thinking, the immersing yourself in the world of a piece, the model stage, the articulation of why light is in the space – these are all collaborative questions.

PAULE CONSTABLE

The sound designer will now be able to plan where to hang various pieces of equipment, such as loudspeakers and fold-back speakers. If the band is to be located on stage it will also be much clearer now how this will work and how it may affect the sound design. And the choreographer can now get a true sense of what the audience will see, how much space there'll be for the dance sequences, and whether there are problematic obstacles to avoid, such as tracks in the floor or trap doors.

Once the model box has been approved by the producer and director, it can be handed over to the set builders so that construction can begin. There should also be a ground plan and technical drawings to accompany it; these should be to scale and complete with all measurements.

Developing costume designs

Now that the set design has been clarified, the costume designs can start to develop from the many ideas which have been floating around since the early design meetings. Most designers will already have sketched out some costume ideas (see Diagram 3) and will now want to refine them choosing suitable colours, textures and fabrics.

One of the problems facing the costume designer at this point is that a crucial element is still missing – the actors. And until the show is cast nobody knows what they're going to look like. It's difficult to commit to a specific design without knowing details such as hair colour, weight, height and skin tone, but the costume designer will have to make a start, even if changes need to be made at a later date. Flexibility is key when it comes to costume design, and usually there's some opportunity to make adjustments once the casting has been finalised. Ideally the costumes will be designed with each specific actor in mind, and with shows with contemporary settings this is often possible as the costumes can be purchased swiftly via the internet or directly from high street shops at a

Diagram 3 Costume designs: *The Addams Family*. Designed by Diego Pitarch.

later stage in the process. In the majority of cases, though, especially when costumes are being made or hired, decisions will have to be taken earlier. This means that the actors often have very little say in the costumes that they'll be wearing and that can cause significant problems further down the line. 'But my character would never wear this!' is a complaint often heard from a disgruntled actor who feels compromised by a decision which was taken long before the actors ever set foot in the rehearsal room. Some designers will solve this particular problem by purchasing a variety of different costumes for each actor in the knowledge that they can, if necessary, be returned after the costume fitting.

As soon as the show has been cast the costume designer (and costume supervisor, if applicable) will need the actors' measurements. They are now working to a specific deadline (the first technical rehearsal) and will need to source the costumes as quickly as possible. Musicals can be complicated because the performers will often have a number of different outfits throughout the show and costume changes are frequently done at lightning speed. Most designers will organise a costume chart showing which actor wears which costume in each successive scene.

Radio mics: practicality and aesthetics

If radio mics are being used there will need to be a discussion at the planning stage between the sound designer and the director about the positioning of the mics on the actors as this will ultimately affect the look of the show. There are various options including attaching the mic to the cheek, to the forehead, underneath the curls of a wig (usually on female performers) or in some cases to a pair of glasses. In my experience, most sound designers will want the microphone to be reasonably close to the actor's mouth while most directors will prefer it hidden from sight. Obviously, it makes sense to use the smallest mics possible, but these are likely to be more expensive so this decision will often depend on the size of the budget. In some modern shows, particularly those with a predominantly electronic sound, the microphone may be placed on a visible rigid wire which contours the face and enables the mic to be as close as possible to the singer's mouth. The decision to use this type of **headset mic** is often visual as well as aural – it gives the performer a more contemporary look, whilst making life much easier for the sound department.

It's also important for the costume designer to flag up the use of hats at an early stage in the process so that the sound designer will have time to work round this particular challenge. The brim of a hat can, after all, often interfere with the sound quality, sometimes to disastrous effect. A show like My Fair Lady, for example, will always be problematic for the sound designer, especially a number like the 'Ascot Gavotte' in which almost every actor wears a different type of ostentatious hat – a costume designer's dream, and a sound designer's nightmare.

A flexible approach

Whilst it's evident that certain design decisions have to be taken before rehearsals begin, it is worth trying to retain some degree of flexibility. The best rehearsals are those which are full of exploration, inventiveness and fun. If we end up forcing the actors into pre-planned costumes, or rehearsing them into pre-blocked scenes, we're likely to end up with something solid but uninspiring. We need to be free to draw on the creativity of the company, and once everyone starts working together in the rehearsal room ideas will inevitably develop or change altogether; the director and the rest of the creative team should try to be responsive to this. Some decisions, of course, will have to be made before rehearsals begin – in most cases the set design will be finalised early in the process so that there's adequate time for construction and painting. Where possible, though, costume designs, lighting plots, choreography and staging shouldn't be set in stone from the outset. A production that's artistically frozen before the actors have set foot in the rehearsal room may be a competent piece of entertainment, but it's never going to be a thrilling piece of theatre.

5
CASTING

Casting is like dating; you have to feel a connection, a fizz and a warmth – you will be working together for a long time and you have to get along in a personal, professional, and creative way.
EMMA RICE

Casting the show

The musical is a unique combination of different disciplines and its success depends on how well these elements work together. But no matter how wonderful the set design, how gorgeous the costumes, how beautiful the music, and how dazzling the choreography, if the casting isn't up to scratch the whole thing will fall flat on its face. Good casting is paramount and should be a top priority from the start. From my perspective as a director, I'm well aware that if we don't get the casting right rehearsals will be an uphill struggle and the final results will be disappointing.

Auditions can be an exciting and sometimes nerve-wracking experience, not only for the auditionee, but also for the audition panel. Having already invested a large amount of time and energy in the production, the director, producer, musical director and choreographer will be quietly praying that the right people walk through the door. After all, there's no point in putting on a production of *Me and My Girl* without a charismatic charmer to play the loveable cockney, Bill Snibson, or mounting a production of *Gypsy* without an electrifying Mama Rose.

It's vitally important that the auditions are well publicised so that the panel has a wide range of options to choose from. If the production's a school or local community project, the producer and director will probably have a fair idea about the range of potential candidates and will hopefully have chosen a show which plays to their strengths. With school productions there are often many more female students auditioning than male ones. It's wise, then, to avoid shows such as *Jesus Christ Superstar* or even *Guys and Dolls* since the majority of the characters are disciples and priests in the former, and gamblers in the latter. It's not impossible to have girls playing boys, of course, but it makes things more complicated since vocal lines will probably need to be transposed and harmonies re-written. With school or community projects, auditions can be advertised in the follow ways:

1 Through word-of-mouth.

2 Via notice-boards, using posters or handbills.

3 Via local newspapers or school newsletters and bulletins.

4 Via online parent newsletters.

If the production is professional or semi-professional the audition panel will probably be familiar with some, but certainly not all, of the potential audition candidates. It's important, then, that the auditions are well publicised so that a wide-range of talented performers are attracted to the project. This can be achieved in a number of ways:

1 By contacting specific theatrical agents directly and supplying them with a casting breakdown.

2 By using the services of a casting director who will contact agents directly and then draw up a suitable list of audition candidates. The internet has many listings for casting directors.

3 By putting a casting breakdown in an online publication (*Spotlight* in the UK/Europe and *Backstage* in the US) and specifying the type of actor required for each role.

4 By pooling suggestions from the producer, director, musical director and choreographer and subsequently making a short-list.

Diversity

As a Londoner who went to a very diverse comprehensive school, I would love to see more of the London that I grew up in reflected on stage. And that needs to come from the casting directors and directors.
SHARON D CLARKE

It's important, when casting a show, to access a wide pool of talent. This involves casting the best people for the job, certainly, but it also means being inclusive and ensuring that there is a good mixture of diverse ethnicities and backgrounds represented at the audition stage. School or college productions are fairly straight-forward as there will be a self-contained pool of talent to choose from. With pro-fessional productions the casting department may have to work harder to ensure that **BAME** (black, Asian and minority ethnic) candidates are included on the audition lists. There's no doubt that some communities are under-represented in musical theatre – and until these communities begin to see themselves properly represented on the stage they will continue to assume that these options aren't open to them. Having a more focussed approach to drama training in schools would certainly help to overcome some of these issues, but more needs to be done to make vocational training available to aspiring actors from all sorts of different backgrounds.

It's only by greatly increasing the talent pool of BAME artists that the entire process becomes diverse without discussion.

JAMES ORANGE

Casting breakdown

This information is usually available online from the licensing company, but the cast details are often limited, listing the character's playing age and vocal range, but with little additional information. In order to make sure that you're targeting the right type of actors it's probably best to construct your own casting breakdown, ensuring that you provide detailed information about each individual character. This breakdown shouldn't only give a clear idea about the type of actor required for each rôle but should also specify any special skills required for the part. With a musical it's always important to indicate vocal type and vocal range.

The following example is a cast breakdown for two of the leading characters in *Carousel*. Since the information provided by the licensor is fairly limited I've constructed a more in-depth description of both characters.

Billy Bigelow:

    Voice: Baritone (bottom G to top G)
    Age: Mid 20s to late 30s

Billy works as a barker on a fairground carousel in New England, America. An outsider, he's tall, good-looking, tough and proud. His outward bravado masks an inner sensitivity and an innate lack of self-worth.

A charismatic actor with a strong baritone voice and excellent acting ability is required for this rôle. Must have a good American accent.

Julie Jordan:

    Voice: Soprano (middle C to top Gb)
    Age: Late teens to mid 20s

Julie is a young, attractive girl who works at a local mill on the coast of Maine. A loner and a dreamer, she is quiet, self-sufficient and serious. Like Billy she has a restless but sensitive nature.

A fine actress with an excellent singing voice is required for this rôle. Must have a good American accent.

When to hold auditions

For some commercial productions casting is often completed months before the start of rehearsals, but in most other circumstances the casting process occurs later, sometimes only a few weeks, or even days, before rehearsals begin. This is usually the result of a combination of factors including the availability of the production team for auditions and the unwillingness of actors to commit to a project too far in advance. Casting about six weeks prior to rehearsals seems to be a fairly good compromise – this gives the costume department time to measure the actors and to start work on their costumes, and also gives the choreographer some tangible idea of the dance ability of the chosen cast members. Choreographing sections of dance in advance is certainly easier if there are specific performers in mind.

Audition venue

The producer will usually be responsible for organising auditions, but if a casting director has been employed this job is most likely to be passed to them. A top priority will be to find a good audition venue. Ideally this will include:

1   A suitable room with good acoustics. Ideally it should be quiet, private, and large enough to contain a piano, a pianist, the audition candidate, and assorted members of the production team. For ensemble dance auditions the room will need to be larger.
2   A tuned piano or suitable keyboard.
3   A **green room**; a place for the actors to sit whilst waiting for their audition. Ideally there will be bathroom facilities too.

Audition venues come in all shapes and sizes. They can also vary in price enormously so it's best to shop about. Church halls and community centres can work very well and are often inexpensive. If in doubt, though, it's best to start by searching online. In my experience it's always sensible to check out these venues in person to make sure that they are suitable. On occasions I've turned up to find tiny rooms with non-existent sound-proofing, rooms with no heating, rooms with no chairs, and on one occasion a room with no piano!

Audition panel

For a musical the audition panel will generally include the producer, the director and the musical director. If the piece requires a lot of movement or dance there will also be a choreographer. With professional shows there's usually a casting director, and with larger productions and those in the commercial sector this group can expand to include a musical supervisor, an assistant director, an assistant choreographer and a **reader** (an actor brought in to read opposite the audition candidates). There will also be at least one person to help usher the actors in and out of the audition room; with professional productions this is likely to be the casting director, a casting assistant or a production assistant from the production office.

Last, and certainly not least, is the audition pianist. Sometimes the musical director will double as the accompanist, but this isn't an ideal scenario for obvious reasons – it's difficult to concentrate on a singer's performance whilst struggling to play a fiendish Sondheim accompaniment. A good audition pianist is a necessity and will be expected to sight-read a wide range of music whilst at the same time being sensitive to the needs of a potentially nervous candidate who may not necessarily sing the song at the given tempo, in the right style or even in the right key!

Auditions

I try and put people at their ease and give them every chance to show me, not only what they can do, but also a little of who they are.
EMMA RICE

What's an audition? From the point of view of the audition panel it's the opportunity to assess whether a performer is suitable for a particular show. From the point of view of the performer, it's the chance to sing, dance or act in front of a particular set of people in the hope of being cast in their production. Actually, I think it's more than that. Often an actor feels that an audition has gone badly just because they didn't get the rôle they were hoping for. The truth is, if the panel is impressed, the actor will usually go on a list and is likely to be considered for future shows. No good audition is a waste of time. It works both ways; the actors get the chance to be seen and assessed, and the various members of the audition panel get to meet new, talented performers.

There's no 'one size fits all' type of audition – they're all different, ranging from an informal chat around someone's kitchen table, to thirty seconds in a harsh spotlight on a huge West End or Broadway stage. Every director has a slightly different approach, and the potential candidate will need to adjust to each situation as it unfolds. If the tone is formal, it's best to go along with that. If it's casual and friendly, then it's fine to be relaxed and chatty.

Whilst the procedure may vary from show to show, every audition panel has the same basic objective – to find the best possible cast for their production. And it's not just a case of finding a group of excellent performers, they're looking to build a team. Talent is part of that, but it's not everything. They'll be looking for the right personalities to complement each other, actors who'll work together creatively in the rehearsal room with commitment, focus and good humour. And each member of the creative team will also be thinking: 'Will I enjoy working with this person?'

Private auditions

When I first started out as an actor I frequently attended **open auditions** in order to get seen for a particular production, usually a big musical. Hundreds of hopeful actors would turn up on a given day and wait patiently for the opportunity to sing sixteen bars to a punch-drunk audition panel. In the US these open calls remain a requirement of all Equity shows and are still, therefore, a common event. In the UK, however, they are, I'm pleased to say, a relatively rare occurrence.

With private auditions the actors are given a specific time slot and will usually have the opportunity to talk to the audition panel during the casting. It's a lot more personal, and much more actor-friendly. The advantages of this approach are fairly obvious; the actors feel more in control, have more of an opportunity to demonstrate their skills, and can ask questions if they need to. The audition panel, on the other hand, will generally witness a stronger overall performance and will also get a much better sense of the real personality of the actor.

First audition

I like a very focussed room. I want every actor to do well. In the end I want actors who are fearless. I can usually recognise that trait when an actor walks into the room.

SUSAN STROMAN

As I've already indicated, every team will have a slightly different approach to the casting process and no two musical theatre auditions are quite the same. However, in my experience it's usually the director who takes control in the room and leads the audition. My personal approach is to start by sitting the actor down, introducing the creative team, and having a quick chat. This can be about anything – their journey to the audition or their latest acting job. It's really just a device to get the actor talking and to enable us to get a sense of their personality, but it also helps to steady the actor's nerves and to ease them into the situation. This part of the audition is invaluable, I think, so that we can get a sense of the actor as a person and not just as a performer. This mustn't take too long, though – there's work to be done, and as soon as I feel that the actor has loosened up a bit I'll steer the conversation round to the audition material.

Two contrasting songs are often requested for an audition, usually one 'up tempo' and one ballad. The songs should ideally be in the style of the show – it makes sense to take along music from the same era or by the same composer. It shouldn't always be assumed, though, that any song by a given composer will be appropriate, as some writers employ many different styles. For example, it wouldn't be helpful to take a song from *The Phantom of the Opera* to an audition for *Jesus Christ Superstar*. Both shows are written by Andrew Lloyd Webber, but stylistically they're worlds apart.

The audition candidate will usually be asked to perform one of their two chosen songs; this will often be enough for the panel to assess their range and singing ability. Sometimes, though, a second song is requested in order to further explore vocal range and versatility. After this the actor may be required to read from the script. In some situations the director or assistant director will read opposite the candidate, and in extremis the casting director will occasionally lend a hand. It's better all round, though, if a reader can be introduced at this stage. Actors auditioning for principal rôles will sometimes be sent scenes and music from the show in advance of the audition. In most cases this won't need to be memorised, but it should be well-prepared so that the actor feels familiar and comfortable with the material.

Dance auditions

If the musical is essentially a dance show, such as *A Chorus Line* or *Chicago*, then the dance auditions will become a major priority, and will often take precedence over the other departments, at least initially. If, however, the dancing in the show is secondary, with the actors perhaps required to 'move' rather than dance, then the choreographer will often introduce movement sessions at the recall stage. In most cases it will be obvious, but it's worth ensuring that the actors are warned in advance if they're going to have to dance or do any specific movement work in an audition. This gives them the chance to bring appropriate clothes and shoes and to warm up before they arrive.

If dance ability is top of the agenda a large audition room will be required, and there will also need to be somewhere for the dancers to change. Often these dance auditions are divided into male and female categories, with the two groups only coming together for recalls. Auditions will usually start with the dancers learning a routine in a large group. This will be taught by the choreographer, or an assistant, and will often be quite challenging. With large numbers involved the dancers may be given a number to wear so that they can be easily identified. I'm not a huge fan of this impersonal approach, but from a practical perspective it does make some sense.

Having learned the routine the dancers will normally be divided into smaller groups; they'll then be asked to dance the routine a couple of times whilst being closely observed by the audition panel. At this stage a certain number of dancers will usually be 'let go', and the rest will be called back to sing and act, often later in the day. It's courtesy, though, to give the dancers a break so that they can cool down and change their outfits. It's important for the audition panel to be clear about who's who at this point because in my experience things can start to get rather confusing, especially if there are large numbers of dancers involved. Someone with scraped-back hair and a striking red leotard in the dance auditions may now return transformed with long, curly locks and a demure skirt and blouse. The audition panel will need to stay vigilant in order to make sure that the identity of each candidate is clear. It's the casting director's job to know who everyone is in the room, so if any confusion arises it's best to defer to them.

The performers will now sing a song of their choice, usually in a style requested in advance by the musical director. They may also be required to read from the script, especially if they're being considered for a featured rôle or an understudy part. Following these auditions the panel will decide who should be asked to return for further recalls, either for a principal rôle, a place in the ensemble, an understudy part or a **swing** track (see below).

Audition objectives

Auditions require research, good judgement, close attention and psychological finesse when trying to bring out the best in the singers.
DAVID CHARLES ABELL

Whilst I won't go into exhaustive detail about what actually goes on in the audition room since every director, choreographer and musical director will have a slightly different approach, it's important to make sure, from the point of view of the audition panel, that certain key areas are covered. The following list refers to a show such as *West Side Story* in which the majority of the performers will be expected to sing, dance and act.

1   Vocal ability. Does the singing voice of the candidate suit the musical style of the piece and is it strong and resilient? This is particularly important if the show is likely to run for any length of time.

2   Dance ability. What are the particular strengths of the candidate, and does their style suit the choreographic style of the show?

3   Acting ability. Is the candidate a convincing actor with clear diction and a good ear for accents? (*West Side Story* requires American and Puerto Rican accents.)

4   Rôle? If cast in the show, is the actor looking to play a principal rôle only, or would they consider an ensemble part, an understudy part or a swing track? With professional auditions this will usually be ascertained before the actor arrives to audition.

5   Company member. Is the performer likely to be an enthusiastic, hard-working, creative member of the company? Will they be fun to work with?

6   Availability. Whilst this should have been confirmed before the audition it's often worth checking that the actors are free to attend all rehearsals and performances.

One of the biggest problems when casting a musical, especially if there are large numbers involved, is comparing the actors with other candidates who may have auditioned on a different day, or even a different week or month. I tend to use a basic classification system for each of the different disciplines, ranging from A (excellent) to C (poor) with various pluses and minuses to help with differentiation. This is a fairly crude method, but it does at least provide some means of comparison. I also try to take detailed audition notes, not just with reference to performance ability, but also denoting physical characteristics too: a beard, long dark hair, piercing blue eyes, for example. Of course, we usually have **headshots** to help us, but actors change their look all the time and these photos can be very misleading. It's actually worth noting anything which may help to recall a particular actor, especially if auditions are spaced out over a period of weeks. These notes can also come in very handy for other productions, since an actor who's not suitable for your current show may be perfect for a future one. With large professional shows, especially where recalls are concerned, the producer will often arrange for auditions to be filmed so that there's some reference material should any confusion arise with casting. The audition candidates must always be warned in advance if filming is likely to take place.

Recalls

A good professional actor should only leave the audition room having not got the job for one of three reasons: they weren't right for it, they weren't what the team were looking for, one of their skills didn't match the requirements of the part.

JAMES ORANGE

For recalls we tend to allow each actor a longer time slot as there's usually more material to cover. It should be pretty clear now whether the actor is auditioning for a principal or an ensemble rôle, and they will usually have been given specific sections of music and script to look at in advance. A small word of warning here – it's best not to overload the actors with too much material at the recall stage. If they've been asked to prepare countless scenes and songs this can take up a huge amount of time and effort, especially if they don't read music. It also means that they'll be expecting to cover all that material in the recall, something which may not be possible in the allotted time.

Actors auditioning for principal rôles will usually be asked to look at more material than those auditioning for ensemble rôles and understudy parts. When looking for suitable audition material I always try to find a couple of contrasting scenes from the show which will demonstrate the range and versatility of the actor. I'll often edit these scenes so that the candidate doesn't have to learn too many lines. This isn't just benevolence on the part of the director – I find that if there's too much to learn the actor will end up with only a basic grasp of the material. Much better to give them several pithy scenes which they can really digest and perform with confidence and authority. It makes sense to give the actors a few days to learn this material – if they've only had twenty-four hours they may well be busking through it, especially if they've also had to learn some new music too.

In my experience, auditions at this stage tend to be between ten and fifteen minutes each, although this does, of course, depend on the size of the rôle and the complexity of the material. When organising the audition lists it's sensible to add the occasional empty catch-up slot, so that if one audition overruns it doesn't necessarily affect the rest of the day. If the audition team are constantly playing catch up it can make the auditions feel unnecessarily stressful. And even if they don't need the extra slot, it's always useful to have a few spare minutes to discuss the previous candidates. Or to have a sneaky coffee.

Recalls can actually be both enjoyable and exciting – they're a great chance to see the actors working with material from the show, and there's usually more time for discussion and experimentation. At this stage it's also possible to audition the actors in pairs or small groups to see how they work together. For example, for a production of *Rent* the director might wish to see how a prospective Roger and Mimi work together. If there's clearly no chemistry between these two actors one of the central relationships in the show will be seriously undermined.

Recalls are obviously an extremely valuable part of the audition process, but the creative team should try to limit the number of recalls they expect any actor to attend. If they're unable to come to a decision after two or three auditions, they're probably barking up the wrong tree. A certain laziness can creep in if the team feels free to recall actors repeatedly, and in my opinion, this isn't a particularly productive way of working. It's worth remembering that the actors may have to travel from a distance, spend money on transport and miss shifts at work in order to attend these auditions. Whilst it's important to get the casting decisions right, it's also important to respect the actors.

Finalising casting

If you get the cast right, the rehearsal process will unfold naturally and easily. No one will have to be shoehorned into a rôle that isn't appropriate.

DAVID CHARLES ABELL

Making the final casting decisions can be an agonising part of the process, and it's seldom that the creative team agrees on absolutely everything. The director needs to be very certain that everyone selected at this point absolutely earns their place in the company. Having a great voice, a great look and bags of personality may not be enough if that candidate doesn't have a strong enough dance technique. Similarly, a sensational dancer may be the choreographer's top choice, but if the singing doesn't match up, the musical director may feel that there are better all-round candidates for the job. Whilst it's the director who will need to supervise these final casting decisions, the producer will usually be heavily involved at this stage and may have some pretty strong opinions too. In commercial theatre there may be some pressure from the producer to cast some celebrity names, and this can generate a certain amount of controversy. In most cases, though, the team will work collaboratively at this stage, discussing each audition candidate individually and calmly assessing their suitability for the show. It usually helps to have headshots of each performer so that they can be laid out on the floor to give a visual impression of the potential cast. It's worth considering back-ups too; you may not end up getting your first choice for each rôle, and you'll need some viable alternatives.

Casting specific rôles

Often the casting of principal rôles is fairly clear-cut, and assuming that the candidates have all been through the recall stage, the creative team will usually have a fairly clear idea about which actors are most suitable. However, there are certain rôles requiring specific skills which make their casting more dependent on one member of the team than another. If a part is specifically intended for a dancer, for example, such as Louise in *Carousel* or the Frug Girl in *Sweet Charity*, the choreographer really should have a strong say in the casting. Likewise, the actress playing Cunégonde in *Candide* will need to be an exceptional soprano with a high coloratura range; if the musical director isn't happy with the choice there are likely to be all sorts of problems further down the line. As a director my motto is quite simple; 'Listen to the experts.'

Ensemble casting

There are lots of elements to take into consideration with ensemble casting, and this is often where disagreements can occur. Many musicals will require an ensemble who can sing, dance, play small cameo parts and often understudy the principal rôles too. Finding the right combination of performers really does feel like assembling a large and complicated jigsaw puzzle.

We usually start by laying out all the ensemble headshots and dividing them into groups of men and women. If appropriate we'll subdivide them into groups of singers, dancers and singer-dancers (those who'll be required to sing and dance to an equally high standard). Often, of course, there's an overlap in these categories. There'll usually be several actors who get a big thumbs up from every department, however no firm decisions should be made at this point; things can often change at the last moment, and in unexpected ways.

Next we discuss the pros and cons of each candidate. The director, the musical director and the choreographer may have very strong reasons for wanting a particular performer in the final cast, but they'll have to make a clear case and be prepared to defend them against other choices. An element of compromise is usually required at this stage, and each member of the team will need to remember that it's the overall good of the show that's important, not the supremacy of any one department. Sometimes we'll need to 'trade hostages' – if the choreographer wants a spectacular dancer in the cast, the musical director may have to accept a mediocre singing voice. In return, the musical director may get an amazing singer whose dance technique isn't as strong as the others. Only the separate members of the team, especially the director, will know whether these compromises are possible within the framework of the show. And there are often other things to take into consideration too; with professional shows the need to cast understudies, swings and dance captains can make ensemble casting particularly challenging.

Understudies

Although it's unusual for school, college or community productions to allocate understudies, with commercial, long-running shows it's a necessity. Whilst repertory theatres can often operate without covers since runs are usually pretty short, commercial theatres cannot and financial losses can be enormous if producers are forced to cancel performances.

Understudies will often, though not always, come from within the ensemble. Sometimes a smaller principal rôle will cover a larger one, and in some professional productions there may be **walking covers** (**off-stage covers** in the US). These are actors who are paid to understudy the main parts but who don't appear regularly in the show. Understudies generally don't get a huge amount of rehearsal time, so it's vital that they're diligent, focussed and self-sufficient. Ideally they'll be ready to go on from the first performance, if necessary, which means that they'll need to do a lot of the preparatory work themselves. In some cases they'll be blocked through the show by an assistant director or a member of stage management, but they'll also be expected to watch the principal rehearsals closely and take detailed notes for themselves. I have known situations where an understudy has been thrown on for a first preview with no rehearsal at all; it's clearly not ideal, but the understudy will need to be prepared for such an eventuality, just in case.

Swings

When an understudy moves up from the ensemble to take over a leading part there's usually a swing who will step into the vacated ensemble track. Swings have a complicated job; they will usually cover all the ensemble tracks in the show and will often be expected to go on with little or no rehearsal. The best swings are calm, well-organised and good-humoured, and enjoy rising to the many challenges of the job. They'll need to make copious notes in order to learn the physical moves of the ensemble tracks that they're covering and will also need to be very comfortable singing various different vocal lines. If they're **onstage swings** they will have their own performance track, which is easy to cut if they're covering for someone else, and which won't usually include featured solo moments. If they're **offstage swings**, they won't appear in the show at all unless they're covering someone else's track. Once the show is up and running it will usually be filmed and the swings will be able to refer to this in order to check the blocking and choreography for each of their tracks.

Dance captains

Dance captains are appointed from within the ensemble to look after all aspects of dance in the show, and they become the eyes and ears of the choreographer once the production has opened to the public. They'll usually take a physical warm-up before each performance (in the US dancers are responsible for their own warm-ups) and are expected to maintain choreographic standards by keeping a close eye on all dancing and staging. They will also re-rehearse sections whenever necessary and report back to the choreographer throughout the run.

If cast members are unable to perform for any reason it's usually the dance captain and the swings who will take responsibility for re-allocating lines and delegating stage business to the other actors (sometimes an assistant director or member of stage management will also be involved in these decisions). It can be a stressful and complicated job, so it's vitally important that they're up to scratch. Sometimes an actor will go off in the middle of a show, and it's usually the quick-thinking of the dance captain and swings that prevents the show from grinding to a halt. On occasions the dance captain will need to adapt the choreography as a result of injury or cast absence and will therefore need to understand the choreographic language of the show and be able to second-guess the wishes of the choreographer.

Offers

Once these complicated decisions have been made and the ideal cast has been selected, the actors will need to be notified as soon as possible. This is normally done by the producer or the casting director. With school, college or community productions it's most likely to be the producer or director who notifies the cast via e-mail or a communal notice board. At this stage it's always tempting to heave a huge sigh of relief; casting can take weeks or even months and it often feels as though a huge mountain has finally been scaled. Unfortunately the climb isn't necessarily over; just because you've offered the parts to your ideal cast doesn't mean that everyone's going to accept, and it's quite possible that an actor has had a better offer, or is suddenly unavailable for the job. It's important, therefore, to have other options up your sleeve. It's also prudent not to inform anyone that they haven't got a part unless you're absolutely certain that they won't subsequently be needed. It isn't unusual to have to move to a second or even third option after the initial choices have declined.

Once final offers have been accepted, though, it's important to let the unsuccessful actors know that they haven't been cast in the show. Far too many producers simply fail to notify candidates if they haven't got the job, even if they've attended numerous recalls and have had to learn huge sections of music and script. This, I think, is thoughtless and disrespectful; since everyone is easily contactable by e-mail, it's also inexcusable. Admittedly, with big professional shows there are often hundreds of audition candidates and in some cases it may not be practical to inform everyone individually once final decisions have been made. My own method is to ensure that everyone who's been recalled and has therefore spent considerable time and effort preparing extra material, should be notified, usually by the casting agent or the production office. In some cases I'll send a personal e-mail to the actor myself if I feel that feed-back would be beneficial. Often I'm able to tell them that they did a brilliant audition and that the panel were very impressed by their work; they just weren't right for this particular production.

Casting children

Watching talented children on stage can be a delightful experience; *Matilda*, *Billy Elliot* and *Charlie and the Chocolate Factory* have all recently introduced some phenomenally gifted young actors to theatre audiences. Other established musicals involving children – *Annie*, *Joseph and the Amazing Technicolor Dreamcoat* and *Oliver!* – have also provided fantastic opportunities for young performers in the UK, the US and further afield. Once you start casting children, though, there are all sorts of rules and regulations which have to be taken into consideration. There are strict guide-lines concerning the appearance of children on stage, and it's important to understand, before auditions begin, what rules apply, both in the locality in which the production is to take place, and in the child's own borough, county or state. If in doubt it's best to contact the local authority, or to get in touch with Equity (UK) or Actor's Equity (US).

With professional productions the producer will usually go through a children's casting director, and once a child has been offered the part the casting director, the child's agent (or a parent/carer) will then need to apply for a licence from the child's local authority. As far as amateur shows are concerned, if there's no payment involved and the child is rehearsing and performing outside school hours then no licence is required.

Professionally, children under a certain age (sixteen in the UK), unlike their adult counterparts, are permitted to appear in only a limited number of performances per year, and it's often necessary to double or triple cast these parts. There are other considerations too; children will need a **chaperone** (**child guardian/child wrangler** in the US) during rehearsals and performances, a dressing room with suitable bathroom facilities separate from the adult actors, and someone to ferry them to and from the theatre on a regular basis. Discipline can sometimes be a problem and it's important to choose children who are focussed and committed. The theatre can be a dangerous place and it's vital that the young actors are well behaved both on and off the stage. Since they will inevitably spend much of their time hanging around waiting to rehearse or perform, they'll also need to be able to entertain themselves whilst not disrupting the adult actors. Rehearsals and matinée performances will inevitably affect a child's daytime education from time to time, and there will therefore need to be good communication with the child's school.

Because of the laws surrounding child actors, another important aspect to consider is rehearsal time. If the show is double or triple cast then the scenes will obviously take longer to rehearse and when it comes to the tech everything will need to be done twice, if not thrice. So valuable rehearsal time can be eaten up if there are children in the cast, and it's important to factor this in from the start as it will inevitably affect the budget, not to mention the timetable for the adult actors. If time is tight, then, best not to choose *Oliver!* or *Bugsy Malone*.

Casting actor-musicians

Over the last couple of decades there's been a significant increase in shows featuring actor-musicians, and there's an obvious reason for this – it's cheaper than hiring a band. But this isn't, of course, the only reason. Stylistically it can work beautifully having a group of strolling musicians on stage, sometimes acting in the scenes, sometimes providing accompaniment, and often doing both at the same time. An inventive production of *Cabaret* which opened at the Donmar Warehouse in London and subsequently transferred to New York's Studio 54, featured a versatile ensemble who were mostly actor-musicians. This set-up not only worked perfectly in the club scenes, but in the rest of the show too where it seemed that the dissolute atmosphere of the Kit Kat Klub pervaded everything. 'Life is a cabaret, old chum' rang particularly true in this provocative production.

Casting shows involving actor-musicians isn't always straightforward, and inevitably more time will need to be allocated in auditions since the candidates will be acting, singing and playing their chosen instrument(s). Often the exact instrumentation for the show won't have been set, and the orchestrator will only start work once the cast has been chosen. Understudying inevitably becomes complicated with actor-musician shows because of the additional musical requirements. Finding people to cover the acting rôles is hard enough, but it's especially onerous trying to find performers who are able to cover the requisite instrumental tracks too.

Hiring actor-musicians may appear to be an economical way of putting on a musical, but there are hidden costs involved; the producer will need to make sure that the instruments are fully insured during rehearsals and performance, and in some cases may need to hire or buy extra instruments too. Producers are also likely to have to foot the bill for reeds, strings and other musical accessories since there will inevitably be some wear-and-tear during the run. With professional productions actor-musicians are also paid a higher basic minimum salary. (For further information about actor-musicians see Chapter 8.)

Respecting the auditionees

It's all too easy when casting a musical to start viewing the audition candidates as numbers rather than people. It's important to remember, though, that before setting foot in the room, each of them has spent time and energy preparing for that specific audition. They may have paid for extra singing lessons, spent more time at the gym, or hired an accompanist to help them prepare their audition song. At the recall stage they will almost certainly have been studying and learning a section of the script and quite possibly several songs too. In the event, they may not be quite what the creative team is looking for, but that's not the fault of the auditionee.

Everyone deserves to be treated with respect and that means giving the performers full attention when they're in the audition room. From an actor's perspective I've witnessed on many occasions an inattentive audition panel – some people who were palpably bored, and others who were glued to their mobile phones. No matter how experienced an actor may be, auditioning is still a challenging and often nerve-wracking event. It's important that the creative team recognises this, and that each candidate is treated with courtesy and consideration. Putting an actor in an uncomfortable position isn't only disrespectful but is also hardly likely to result in a good audition, which is, after all, the whole point of the exercise.

6
STAGE MANAGEMENT AND THE SUPPORT TEAM

Great stage management is what keeps the cogs of any show turning.

SHARON D CLARKE

Before explaining the function of each member of the supporting technical team, it's worth mentioning that job descriptions differ from country to country, and the US system of stage management is slightly different to that of the UK. Further information is provided at the end of this chapter.

Production manager

On most productions the producer will appoint a production manager to coordinate the technical elements of the show. It's a highly responsible and often stressful job since it involves a large degree of supervision and coordination. Throughout the process the production manager will communicate closely with the designer, the lighting and sound designers, and the stage management. Much of the job involves ensuring that the set design is successfully realised (this usually absorbs a large percentage of the budget), and the production manager will liaise regularly with the set builders and set painters to check on its progress. For obvious reasons it's vital that all the technical departments keep within budget and meet their deadlines, and it's the responsibility of the production manager to make sure that they do. Other responsibilities include:

- Pre-production: being involved in design meetings to ensure that the set is realistically achievable within the allocated budget.
- Helping the producer to allocate appropriate budgets to each individual department.

- Helping with staffing, especially where technical personnel are concerned. This will include the following departments: lighting, sound, video, set-building and prop making.

- Organising regular production meetings during the rehearsal period so that the creative and technical departments can get together to discuss general progress and flag up any potential problems (see Chapter 11). Representatives from all departments will try to attend these meetings, and for those who are unable to attend minutes will be taken and subsequently distributed by stage management.

- Helping to devise a **technical schedule** which will make best use of the time available in the theatre. This will include scheduling the arrival and installation of the set, the lighting equipment and the sound equipment, and also allocating adequate time for the band to be seated in the orchestra pit (or designated band area) and for a thorough sound check to take place.

- Negotiating the sound and lighting hire contracts, organising haulage, and booking freelance crew for the get-in, fit-up and **get-out (load-in/ load-out** in the US). This will, of course, involve liaising with the theatre or venue.

- Consulting with wardrobe to assess how many local dressing staff will be required during the performances.

- In consultation with the director, allocating suitable time for the technical rehearsals on stage. This is an opportunity for everyone to work through the show chronologically with all the technical elements in place: set, costumes, lighting and sound.

- Helping the producer and director to schedule the dress rehearsal(s) and previews.

- Doing a **risk assessment**. This involves monitoring the health and safety of the entire company and with the help of the stage manager ensuring that safety checks are carried out. Areas of particular concern include theatrical firearms, pyrotechnics, candles and naked flame, onstage smoking, ladders or steep staircases, trap-doors, revolves and anything which may potentially cause injury to the actors, musicians, stage management or crew.

- At the end of the run making sure that all hired equipment (set, sound and lighting) is returned to the correct hire company, and that the get-out is as swift and efficient as possible.

- Providing the theatre with a production rider; this will include crew numbers, power requirements and a suitable time frame for the get-in and get-out.

Company manager

Company managers are usually employed in the commercial sphere or in larger repertory theatres. Their job is multifarious and demanding, and they act as a conduit between the producer and the company. The job also involves preparing the payroll, organising petty cash, sorting out tickets for the company, booking physio sessions and medical appointments for the cast and stage management, entertaining guests, coordinating publicity events (especially those involving the cast), disciplining the actors when necessary, and organising photo calls and press events as required by the producer. In addition to these and other responsibilities, the company manager must be something of a therapist as their office is the first port of call when company members find themselves in need of tea and sympathy.

The company manager will also liaise with various organisations if performances are planned which require particular support for audience members with access needs, or which include **captioning** (using subtitles or surtitles). There may also be **audio described performances,** and **touch tours** where blind or partially-sighted audience members are invited onto the stage before the performance to handle props and costumes.

Company stage manager

With smaller professional productions the rôle of company manager and stage manager will sometimes be rolled into one resulting in the **company stage manager**. The job requires the juggling of office and pastoral duties with the technical duties on stage. (This job title doesn't exist in the US.)

Stage management

Every successful production depends not only on the quality of the cast and the inventiveness of the creatives, but on the expertise of the stage management team. This department is usually selected by the producer and production manager and will mainly deal with the practical elements of the production. The term stage management is something of a misnomer since the work that's carried out on stage is only one of a whole range of jobs which this team will undertake. Whilst the tasks involved vary greatly from one production to the next, the stage management team will provide a vital support mechanism for both the creative team and for the actors. They will organise the day-to-day running of the rehearsal room, keep all members of the creative team up-to-speed with progress in rehearsals, and will ultimately supervise the running of the show once it reaches the theatre or performance space. I cannot stress enough the importance of stage management since this department will provide the practical foundation upon which the entire production is built.

The size of the stage management team will, of course, depend upon the complexity of the show. In the UK it's usual to have a minimum of two, a stage manager and a deputy stage manager, and any number of **assistant stage managers** can be added to this core. Stage management job titles vary in the US (see 'Stage management in the US', p. 94).

Stage manager

I look for a stage manager that has the 'anticipatory' gene. Someone who knows what I want before I even say it.

SUSAN STROMAN

The best stage managers are invariably good communicators. They're also observant, calm, quick-thinking and efficient, and, perhaps most importantly, always reliable in a crisis. A good sense of humour is a valuable asset too, since the job has more than its fair share of challenges.

The stage manager will work in close contact with the director throughout the whole process, and together they will try to ensure that rehearsal time is used as productively as possible. At best a good stage manager is an unflappable problem-solver who deals with all sorts of difficulties calmly and efficiently as and when they arise. By shouldering most of the practical responsibilities, the stage manager allows the director and the other members of the creative team to concentrate on making the artistic decisions, and ensures that the rehearsals are as stress-free as possible. In short, the stage manager will take responsibility for running the rehearsal room and will ultimately be in charge of the show in performance, aided, of course, by other members of the stage management team.

With professional productions the stage management aren't usually engaged until the first day of rehearsals. The following job descriptions, though, include some responsibilities which relate to the pre-rehearsal period. In an amateur or student context stage management will usually undertake these various responsibilities, but with professional productions they'll be carried out by the casting agent (the auditions), the production manager (all things technical) and the production office (admin, booking of rehearsal venues and disseminating of rehearsal information). The main responsibilities of the stage manager, shown here at each stage of the process, are as follows.

Before rehearsals

- Helping to organise auditions, checking that there's a well-tuned piano in the audition room, and making sure that the necessary scripts and scores are available for the creative team and audition candidates.

- Contacting the cast and production team before the first day of rehearsals and giving them information about the rehearsal venue, including timings of the **meet-and-greet**, and a skeleton schedule for the first few days of rehearsal. The actors will also need to be reminded to bring in suitable rehearsal clothing or dance gear for staging and dance calls, and recording equipment for music calls.

- Ensuring that the rehearsal rooms are adequately proportioned, well-heated and generally fit for purpose. Also checking that there's a well-tuned piano or suitable keyboard in all the relevant rehearsal rooms.

- If there's a dance element to the show, making sure that the floor of the rehearsal room is suitable. Floors which are uneven, slippery or too rigid can sometimes lead to injury amongst the cast. In such cases the stage manager will sometimes hire a dance floor to go over the top of the existing surface. There will be a cost implication here, and the hire charges will need to be discussed with the producer in advance.

- Checking with the choreographer to see if mirrors are required in the dance space. These are often requested by the dancers so that they can watch themselves whilst learning the routines. Often there's also a curtain which can be pulled across to hide the mirrors when they're not in use since most actors prefer not to be able to see themselves whilst acting a scene.

- Where child actors are concerned, checking that licences have been obtained (see Chapter 11).

- Making themselves familiar with the terms of the children's performing licence so they can plan the children's attendance at rehearsals with the lead chaperone.

- Checking that performing licences have been obtained for any animals involved in the production (see Chapter 11).

- In the case of a show using fire, naked flame, pyrotechnical devices or fake guns, checking that the production manager has applied to the relevant authorities for the appropriate licences (see Chapter 11).

- In conjunction with the production manager, ensuring that the local fire officer has been contacted to organise a safety check on stage before the start of the technical rehearsals. This will involve checking that the scenery and scenic furniture are all adequately flame-proofed.

- Checking with the producer that scripts and scores have been hired so that they can be given to the cast on the first day of rehearsals. Sometimes the director will ask for these to be distributed before rehearsals begin so that the actors can start to learn their lines in advance.

During rehearsals

- Ensuring that the rehearsal room floor is marked out with tape to show the exact dimensions of the set. This is usually done in the first couple of days of rehearsal once the director is familiar with the room. The **mark-up** (**taping** in the US) is often a time-consuming activity so it's important to check which way round the director wants to use the space before starting it.

- In the absence of a company manager, ensuring that the **contact sheet** is kept up to date and distributed to everyone involved. This is usually supplied by the production office and contains contact details for the entire company, including phone numbers, e-mail addresses and agents' details. It's important that this personal information is handled sensitively and not shared indiscriminately.

- Supervising the assistant stage managers to provide suitable rehearsal furniture as requested by the creative team; this will often include items such as chairs, tables and sofas.

- Supervising the assistant stage managers to provide **rehearsal props** for the actors. Since the actual **show props** often aren't available until the technical rehearsals on stage, it's important that the actors have something similar to use as substitutes.

- In the case of illness or injury in rehearsal, organising medical appointments and physio sessions. Making sure there's a suitable first aid kit in the rehearsal room and, if necessary, finding out if there's a first aider in the building. On larger productions this job will usually be covered by the company manager.

- Ensuring that the rehearsal room remains a productive place of work, that it is clean, adequately heated and available for use whenever the actors are called. Where the rehearsal rooms are being shared with others it is a good idea to have access to a lockable cupboard or container to store props and other assorted pieces of equipment.

- Checking that the performers arrive punctually, know the times of their calls, and have regular breaks.

- Making sure that the actors get to and from photo calls, publicity events and interviews, and in consultation with the costume designer or wardrobe supervisor helping to schedule costume fittings during rehearsals.

- Liaising with the deputy stage manager (or an assistant stage manager) to ensure that rehearsal notes are sent out to the production team at the end of each rehearsal day.

- Checking that technical notes from rehearsals are relayed to the production manager who will then convey them to other technical departments including the workshop (where the set is constructed).

At the theatre

- Organising the cast once the production moves from the rehearsal room to the theatre, and, in the absence of a company manager, taking charge of dressing-room allocation. Also setting up a signing-in sheet at the stage door to monitor the whereabouts of everyone involved in the production.

- Giving the actors a tour of the stage and backstage areas prior to the start of the technical rehearsals and highlighting any potential dangers such as trap doors, steps or low-hanging lights. Also helping the cast to locate toilets and accessible drinking water near the stage.

- Coordinating and running the technical and dress rehearsals in the theatre and ensuring that the production schedule is followed as closely as possible.

- Liaising with the director during the technical and dress rehearsals and ensuring that all departments are kept up to speed concerning progress on stage.

- Coordinating scene changes and organising the backstage areas. Some of these responsibilities may be delegated to the assistant stage managers (or in the US to the crew).

- Addressing the audience if, for any reason, the show is delayed, interrupted or cancelled.

- Overseeing the general maintenance of the set and liaising with relevant departments should problems arise. Also supervising the assistant stage managers to ensure that damaged props are mended and supplies of consumables (food and drink) are regularly replaced.

- Supervising the deputy stage manager, who will keep a written account of all technical problems which occur during the run and will disseminate them in a daily **show report** (see Diagram 6, Chapter 13). Also, providing an **accident book** to record any physical injuries sustained by the cast, stage management or crew. In the US, Equity insists that members of the union are given contact details for the Office of Workers' Compensation Programs (OWCP) in case of injury during rehearsals or performance. These details will be provided by the stage manager on the first day of rehearsals.

After the run

- Supervising the striking of the set and liaising with the production manager to ensure that all hired items such as lighting and sound equipment are returned to the suppliers, checking that scripts and scores are sent back to the licensor, and making sure that the theatre is left in a reasonable condition. In the US the International Alliance of Theatrical Stage Employees (IATSE) has very strict rules concerning the responsibilities of the crew and won't allow stage management to touch the set during the get-out (or load-out).

Deputy stage manager

The deputy stage manager is another key member of the team and will usually be present throughout the entire rehearsal period, taking detailed blocking notes, observing where sound and lighting cues should happen, noting the position of stage furniture, identifying potential scene changes, and prompting the actors, if required. In performance the deputy stage manager will 'call' the show – this means letting the relevant departments know the precise moment when each lighting and sound cue should be activated, and when scene changes should occur. At this point in the process the deputy stage manager is often referred to as the **show caller**. In the US the title deputy stage manager doesn't exist and the head stage manager will call the show; after opening night other members of the stage management team will learn and rotate these responsibilities.

The best deputy stage managers are calm, efficient and quietly authoritative. If things go wrong in performance the job usually falls to them to make quick decisions to rectify the situation. This key member of the team is a vital ally and will work alongside the director in the rehearsal room making sure that everything's operating smoothly and that the creative team have everything that they need.

Deputy stage managers working in musical theatre will inevitably need to navigate their way around a musical score. Whilst I have worked with those who cannot actually read music, cueing a musical can be a complicated process and it certainly makes things significantly easier if the deputy stage manager does have some musical knowledge. I once worked as an assistant director on a lavish production of *Carousel* where the overture was an extraordinary visual treat taking the audience from the mill, to the boat yard, to the fairground, and then via various fairground rides to an extraordinarily beautiful carousel, which opened like a flower and started to revolve as the music reached its inevitable climax. It was one of the finest pieces of staging I've ever seen but was incredibly complex and required a deputy stage manager with great musicality to cue the many complex set and lighting changes throughout the sequence. Whilst the ability to sight-read a musical score isn't a necessity, it certainly can be a distinct advantage when working on a piece of musical theatre. The deputy stage manager's main areas of responsibility are as follows.

Before rehearsals

- Liaising with the stage manager in preparation for the first day of rehearsals (see above) and making sure that the scripts and scores have arrived from the licensing company.

During rehearsals

- Helping to organise a props table in the rehearsal room.
- Assisting the stage manager with the mark-up.
- Compiling a daily **rehearsal report** (see Diagram 5, Chapter 11). This involves taking detailed rehearsal notes concerning sound, lighting, props, set, wigs and costume and sending them out to the various departments at the end of each rehearsal day. If additional props, costumes or stage furniture are required by the director or choreographer it's important that this information is recorded in the daily rehearsal report and communicated swiftly to the appropriate department.
- After detailed discussion with the director, compiling a comprehensive list of sound effects and liaising with the sound designer.
- Ensuring that the rehearsal schedule (usually compiled by the director) is sent out to the company in advance of the next day's rehearsal. With larger productions this will often be handled by the company manager.
- Prompting, if required by the actors.
- Creating a prompt copy – a marked-up copy of the script and score (call/calling script in the US) which records the blocking (the actors' moves) and indicates cue points for each scene change, lighting change and sound effect. Cue lists for lighting and sound will usually come from the individual designers towards the end of the rehearsal process. Scene changes will be organised by the stage manager (often in conjunction with the choreographer) and the deputy stage manager will translate this into a cueing sequence.
- In consultation with the stage manager, checking that regular breaks are taken and that the actors return to rehearsals promptly after the break.
- In consultation with the director, recording script changes as they occur during rehearsals and including these changes in the daily rehearsal report. With professional productions these changes will need to be agreed with the licensing company.
- Making sure that rehearsal furniture is correctly positioned for each scene and **marking** these positions (the assistant stage managers will usually help with this). Towards the end of the rehearsal process these marks will need to be measured so that they can be transferred onto the set prior to the start of the tech.

- During **run-throughs** taking accurate timings for each act. These should be recorded in the daily rehearsal report.

- Writing the performance **cue sheets** for all members of stage personnel, including the rest of the stage management team, the crew and sometimes the wardrobe department. The cue sheets will need to be prepared before the production reaches the performance venue.

- Creating a **props setting list** (which will ultimately be handed over to the assistant stage managers) containing information about which prop is needed by which actor and where it needs to be set during the show.

- Creating a **running list** (or assistant stage manager plot) which the assistant stage managers will take over in tech and keep up-to-date. This will provide information concerning their personal tracks throughout the show.

At the theatre

- Issuing **show calls** via the theatre's paging system. This essentially means letting the cast members know how long they have before **curtain-up**. These will usually include the **half-hour call**, the **fifteen-minute call**, the **five-minute call**, and the **beginners call** (**places** in the US).

- Cueing the show from the **prompt desk** (this is usually backstage in the **wings**). This will include cueing scene changes, lighting changes, follow-spot cues and sound cues. During technical rehearsals (when the prompt desk is often placed in the auditorium) the deputy stage manager is the main thoroughfare for information. Whilst the stage manager will run the tech, usually from the stage, the deputy stage manager will liaise both with the latter and with the team out front (director, lighting designer and sound designer), keeping them fully informed about everything that's happening on stage and in the wings (the offstage areas surrounding the stage).

- In collaboration with the stage manager, sending out a show report to the production team at the end of each performance day. This will include: running times, audience numbers, cast absences, audience reaction, technical issues, accidents and any other useful pieces of information (see Diagram 6, Chapter 13).

- In lieu of a company manager, announcing cast changes to the audience, if necessary. Also alerting all departments backstage if any problems occur on stage, especially if there's a **show stop** (usually for health and safety reasons).

- In performance, calling the performers to the stage, if necessary. Most theatres, though, have a **show relay** which allows the actors in the dressing rooms to hear what's happening on stage and to time their entrances accordingly. This means that individual calls for specific actors are less common than they used to be. The deputy stage manager will, however, call the appropriate actors at 'beginners' as a matter of courtesy.

- Checking that the show starts on time, keeping an accurate account of the playing time of each act, and monitoring the length of the interval.

Assistant stage manager

Assistant stage managers are the ones who, in my experience, do most of the leg work, fetching and carrying, heaving bits of furniture around, making sure that rehearsal rooms are tidy and clean, running all sorts of errands, sourcing props, and often nipping around the corner to buy tea, coffee and biscuits. At their best they are resourceful, energetic, communicative and are able to turn their hand to pretty much anything. In performance they will often supervise the backstage activities, helping with scene changes, handing props to the actors and making sure that quick changes are speedily and efficiently managed. They will often supervise the crew members (who tend to do much of the heavy lifting) and will generally make sure that health and safety rules are observed backstage. As previously mentioned, job allocation for stage management differs in the US and responsibilities for the assistant stage managers and for the crew are somewhat different (see 'Stage management in the US', p. 94). Other duties for the assistant stage managers include the following.

During rehearsals

- Having liaised with the director and the designer, compiling a comprehensive **props list**. The earlier this can be done the better since the designer and props buyers (often the assistant stage managers themselves) will need time to source and purchase these items – or beg, borrow or steal them, depending on the state of the show's finances. When working to a budget, the assistant stage managers will generally include potential costs in their initial list, and also details as to which character uses which prop, and where they appear in the show.
- Helping the stage manager and deputy stage manager with the mark-up.
- Taking the actors to costume fittings, physio sessions and accent classes when not located in the rehearsal building.
- Buying tea/coffee and other provisions for consumption during breaks. Also encouraging the actors to wash their own cups!
- Moving and storing rehearsal furniture.
- Organising skeleton scene changes with rehearsal furniture.

- Printing rehearsal schedules, music and scripts.
- Re-setting the rehearsal room with the deputy stage manager before each run-through.

At the theatre

- Supervising the backstage areas.
- As far as costumes are concerned, helping with speedy quick changes, if required.
- Setting props and handing them to the actors as they enter and exit the stage. Having taken over the props setting list from the deputy stage manager, keeping this document up-to-date with props setting notes. Also **shout checking** the props with the stage manager before each performance to ensure they are all set correctly.
- Supervising and helping with scene changes.
- Taking over the running list from the deputy stage manager and keeping it up-to-date.
- Helping to maintain the set and the props. The latter will need checking regularly and mending when necessary. Consumables will need to be replaced on a day-to-day basis.

After the run

- Helping with the get-out, and ensuring that props are returned to the suppliers, or packed away in storage.

Crew

As mentioned above most musical theatre productions will require the services of a stage crew in addition to the stage management team. Unlike the latter, the crew won't usually get involved until the show reaches the theatre. Under instruction from the production manager and the heads of departments they will help to install the set, lights and sound equipment, and will generally assist the stage management in setting up the show. In performance they will usually handle any heavy lifting backstage, help with scene changes, and man the **fly towers** if scenery is to be flown in and out. After the final show they will always be on hand to assist with the get-out.

Stage management in the US

In the US there tends to be more flexibility as far as stage management is concerned. Individual members of the team change 'tracks' on a regular basis which means that they are required to know everyone else's job as well as their own. In the UK each job tends to be more strictly delineated and once defined doesn't alter much from one performance to the next.

Production stage manager

This title is generally used to denote the person in charge of stage management (often in the commercial sector). The other members of the team will be called stage managers or assistant stage managers. The production stage manager will generally run the tech in conjunction with the director (and sometimes the designer) and will usually stay out front in the auditorium and note cues in the prompt copy or call script. Often the production stage manager will also be responsible for rehearsing understudies (in the UK this is usually the responsibility of an assistant/resident director). This may even extend to rehearsing an entire replacement cast if the show runs for any length of time.

Stage management in rehearsals

In rehearsals the stage management team will do everything; assist with costume changes, move stage furniture, help with props and even run sound effects, if required. Once in the theatre, though, the crew will take over the bulk of these responsibilities.

Deputy stage manager

This job title doesn't exist in the US. The responsibilities of this member of the team will be divided up amongst the other members of stage management. As far as cueing is concerned, during performances the stage management will rotate and take turns to call the show.

Crew

The crew will handle all the manual work once the production reaches the theatre. Backstage they will move scenery, maintain the equipment and even handle the props (see below). Stage management aren't allowed to get involved with this manual work and the unions are very strict about this. Another key difference between the crew and the stage management team is that the former are members of the International Alliance of Theatrical Stage Employees (IATSE) and the latter are members of Equity.

Props crew

Whilst in the UK props are almost exclusively the responsibility of stage management, in the US a member of the props crew will take charge once the show reaches the theatre. This means that technically the stage management are no longer allowed to handle the props at this point. They may have to check that props are **pre-set** before a performance, but if anything needs moving or maintaining then a dedicated member of the props crew must take over. If a prop needs to be handed to an actor before going on stage this will also be done by one of the props personnel, and not by a member of stage management.

In the UK firearms are handled by stage management, but in the US they are the responsibility of the props crew. Stage management will, however, check that they are set correctly and will ensure that they are locked away after each performance.

7
FIRST DAY OF REHEARSALS

We do a lot of talking on the first day. Depending on the story, we talk about the history of the show – how it came to be – and the research and background that is pertinent to the narrative.
SUSAN STROMAN

The first day of rehearsals means different things to different people. For the actors it feels like a starting point; having successfully auditioned several weeks or even months beforehand they're usually raring to begin the exciting process of putting on the show. Some of the principal performers may have had their scripts sent out in advance, of course, but for the most part the actors are starting to engage properly with the material for the first time. For the production team, on the other hand, a huge amount of work will already have been accomplished. The set will have been designed, there will be costume charts and lists of provisional sound effects, the publicity department will be busy promoting the show, and the director will have done lots of research and been in frequent contact with all the other departments.

The producer should try to ensure that the whole company is present on the first day, including the actors, stage management, director, choreographer, musical director, set and costume designers, lighting and sound designers and the rehearsal pianist. With larger productions there may also be a production manager, company manager, casting director, representatives from PR and publicity, and various production assistants.

The first day of rehearsals is the first (and sometimes the last) opportunity for everyone to get together, and for that reason it's very important that the entire company should be present. Emotions are inevitably heightened – there's usually a potent mixture of nerves and excitement – and there's often a palpable sense of optimism too, with lots of creative challenges ahead and a general sense that there's everything to play for. From a directorial perspective the first day can be a mixture of excitement and trepidation; it's wonderful to see the company beginning to work creatively together, but it can be daunting too. They'll all be looking for clear guidance and will want to be assured that they're in safe hands, so it's important to ensure that the first day is well structured and that there's firm leadership from the outset. This doesn't, of course, have to be loud and bombastic; many excellent directors are quietly authoritative and inspire their companies with the minimum amount of 'sound and fury'.

Whilst the director may be champing at the bit to get rehearsals started, especially if there's limited rehearsal time, it's important that certain key goals are achieved on this first day. These will usually include:

1   General introductions (involving the entire company).

2   Introductory speeches (usually the producer and director).

3   The model box presentation and design discussion (set and costume designers).

4   Parish notices and house rules (stage manager or company manager).

5   Script **read-through** (full cast).

6   Cast measurements (wardrobe and wigs departments).

7   Equity meeting (all Equity members). This, of course, will only apply to professional productions. During this meeting an **Equity Deputy** will be elected to represent the company.

Meet-and-greet

Coffee and tea are always good ice-breakers, and it isn't a bad idea to start proceedings with an informal meet-and-greet so that everyone can say hello, gossip with old friends, and work off some excess nervous energy. If possible, the director and the other members of the production team should try to make sure that they know everyone's name at this early stage in rehearsals, so that introductions can easily be made without referring to lists. Not only does this preparatory name-learning save time in rehearsals, it also makes the company members feel much more welcome and helps to establish each person as an important part of the team. There's nothing worse than directors who spend all their time chatting up the principal actors, but who clearly don't have a clue who the assistant stage managers are. It's a fairly obvious point to make but feeling noticed and valued will inevitably make everyone feel more committed to the project. Once this informal meeting has taken place (a quarter of an hour should be sufficient) the stage manager will liaise with the director and assemble the company.

General introductions

For this part of the process I find that it's best to set out the chairs in a circle so that everyone can clearly see and be seen (Photo 6). A circle is, after all, the perfect democratic shape, and it's advisable to steer away from any sense of hierarchy at this early stage. Once everyone is seated it's a good idea to get the company members to introduce themselves again, even if most people have already done so informally. Not only does this help to ensure that everyone is properly introduced, but as far as the actors are concerned, it gives them a chance to speak in public for the first time. Not all actors are confident public speakers, and some, given half a chance, will fade into the background at the earliest opportunity. It's important that everyone feels that they have a contribution to make, and the sooner the actors realise this the better. Allowing them to take centre stage and introduce themselves, even if only for a few seconds, is a good way of kick-starting this process.

Introductory speeches

The producer will usually want to address the assembled company, welcome everyone to the project and say a few words about the forthcoming production. It's important for the company to feel that they are well supported, and that the production team is enthusiastic and excited about the show. The producer may also want to talk about ticket availability, publicity and the most effective way for

Photo 6 Company circle: *The Producers*, UK tour. (Photo, Russell Wilcox.)

the company to engage positively with social media to help market the production. The director will usually want to give some sort of introductory speech too; I usually try to give the company some background information about the piece itself, including details of the show's history, and information concerning the writers and the original production team. If the show is being presented for the first time this is an ideal opportunity to introduce the writers to the assembled company; they may be keen to say a few words to the cast too. I like to give the show some sort of context, and if the musical is derived from a well-known source (as with *Oliver* or *Candide*, for example) I may also read some excerpts from the original work. Photographs or short film clips can also be useful during these introductory talks.

Model box presentation and design discussion

For me it's where all the work is made, if it works in the model it will work on stage; they are very time-consuming and often frustrating – but invaluable.

SOUTRA GILMORE

The model box is the clearest and most accurate means of indicating how the final stage designs will look in the theatre (see Chapter 4). Scaled down and painted in the finest detail these exquisite replicas are often extraordinary to behold. The set designer will usually aim to present the model box to the cast on this first day of rehearsals; it's a unique theatrical moment for the actors, who will probably, up to this point, have very little idea about the visual elements of the show. Since this is the first time that the set design is revealed to the cast, it's best not to pre-empt this moment by leaving the model box uncovered in the rehearsal room. A discreet cloth thrown over the whole thing will obscure it until the dramatic moment of its unveiling.

Once the 'oohs' and 'ahs' have died down the designer, often with the assistance of the director, will talk through each scene, showing how set changes will be achieved throughout the course of the show. Once this has been done, the cast should be given an opportunity to question the designer about any aspect of the set which is unclear. The model box will usually be left in the rehearsal room for the rest of the day so that cast members can familiarise themselves with it at their leisure.

Since model boxes can be very cumbersome and aren't always easily transportable, the designer may prefer to photograph the model box in its various scenic variations and show these images to the assembled company instead. Whilst the advantages of this approach are fairly obvious – by enlarging the images it's easier to see details more clearly – the lack of three dimensions makes it harder for the actors to envisage how this design will translate to the stage. Whether or not the initial presentation involves a model box or a set of images, it's helpful if the designer can provide scene-by-scene photos of the model box which can be placed in their correct order along one wall of the rehearsal room. This is extremely useful for both cast members and stage management and helps to remind everyone what the set looks like in each scenic permutation. With school or college productions there may not always be a model box, and in such cases, especially if the design is simple, the designer may provide instead a series of drawings or computerised images so that company members have some idea about the overall design.

Once the set presentation has taken place costume designs will usually be shown to the cast (see Diagram 3, Chapter 4). Depending on the budget and the type of costumes required, these designs may be an approximation or an exact template intended to be scrupulously copied. In either case it's a good idea to put them up on the wall alongside pictures of the set as a point of reference for the cast and creative team.

Parish notices and house rules

If there's a company manager involved in the project this is a great opportunity for them to address the entire company and discuss various 'house rules' such as rehearsal room etiquette and first night tickets. In the absence of a company manager the stage manager will usually take the reins here. There are a wide variety of topics which may need to be discussed.

- The contact sheet. This is a comprehensive list which provides addresses, contact numbers and, where appropriate, agents' details for everyone in the production. All members of the company will need to check that their details are correct.

- Illness and late arrival. The actors will need to know who to contact in case they're unable to attend a rehearsal or are likely to be late for their call. This is usually the company manager or stage manager.

- Rehearsal calls. The actors will need to know how to find out about daily rehearsals. This is usually done via e-mail and will be sent out to everyone in advance. There will often be a duplicate schedule posted up somewhere in the vicinity of the rehearsal room too.

- Rehearsal clothing. The actors will need to be reminded that rehearsal gear should be worn to all rehearsals, unless otherwise stated. Clothes should be informal, comfortable, and shabby enough so that the actors won't worry about damaging them. If dancing is involved, they'll need to check with the choreographer about rehearsal footwear. Show shoes will often be provided during rehearsals so that the dancers can get used to them before the run of performances.

- House rules. The stage manager may also wish to mention one or two basic house rules before rehearsals begin. Smoking as a character choice won't be allowed in the rehearsal room – even herbal cigarettes aren't encouraged and are most likely to be introduced at the tech stage. The stage manager will usually mention local amenities and point out areas in the rehearsal building where the company members can make their own coffee and tea. There may also be specific rules about eating and drinking in the actual rehearsal space.

The stage manager may also ban bags and coats from the rehearsal room since they can often interfere with the rehearsal process, providing a constant source of distraction in the shape of chewing gum, newspapers, and crucially mobile phones. As far as the latter are concerned, my policy is to request actors to leave them turned off during rehearsals since they can easily disrupt a creative atmosphere and distract the actors from their work. If bags are to be forbidden in the rehearsal room then stage management will need to provide a safe place for them to be stored. A good stage manager will let the company know what they can and can't do in the rehearsal room, but will try to avoid sounding like a bossy school teacher. Actors are, on the whole, a fairly compliant lot, and if approached in the right manner, are usually pretty obliging.

Script read-through

Personally, I love a read-through. It's about hearing the piece lifted off the page, with voices other than your own.

SHARON D CLARKE

Some directors, myself included, find it very useful to have an informal read-through of the script on the first day of rehearsals. Not only does this ensure that everyone gets a chance to hear the dialogue spoken out loud (reading a script to oneself is a very different experience), but it also provides a clear starting point for everyone involved in the project. However, musicals which are more-or-less 'sung-through', such as *Hamilton*, *Les Misérables* or *Jesus Christ Superstar*, simply don't have enough spoken material to make a read-through worthwhile. *My Fair Lady* or *Fiddler on the Roof*, on the other hand, are shows with substantial book scenes and really do warrant a proper read-through at an early stage in rehearsals.

The read-through can often be a nerve-wracking occasion for the actors and it's important to keep it as relaxed and informal as possible so that no one feels that they're being judged. It needs to be stressed that it is just a starting point, an opportunity for everyone to begin to get to grips with the material, to understand the story, and to get a better sense of the characters. No matter what the director says, there'll always be some actors who feel that they have to throw everything at this reading, and some, conversely, who'll underplay everything and give an entirely colourless rendition. Ultimately it doesn't really matter; the most important thing is that the actors face the challenge together and that everyone starts the creative journey at the same point. Actually, it's amazing how liberating this read-through can be; whilst it can feel a bit like an endurance test at the time, there's a palpable sense of relief at the end and this experience will usually start to bind the company together in a very constructive way. There are directors who like to mix things up by re-allocating the parts for the read-through so that no one actually plays their own character. This, perhaps, makes for a slightly more entertaining reading, but doesn't necessarily help the group to get a better sense of the piece as a whole.

Following the read-through some directors will want to get straight down to the task of blocking the show, others will prefer to use improvisation as a means of experimenting with some basic ideas. And there are those who'll spend days discussing the project, focussing on its historical context, its social and political relevance, or its place in the history of musical theatre. Length of rehearsal time will, of course, influence the director's approach and sometimes there'll be no alternative but to knuckle down and start piecing the show together immediately. There are no hard-and-fast rules here; all these approaches are viable at the start of the rehearsal process, and some will be more suited to certain shows than others.

Personally, I like to follow the read-through with a discussion with the actors about the piece. I usually try to include the choreographer, the musical director and the set designer in these discussions, since each of them can help to illuminate the subject in subtly different ways. Most importantly, the actors are encouraged to start having opinions about the piece themselves. I'm always fascinated to find out what they think of the dialogue, the characters, the themes and the plot; after all, it's the actors who will ultimately be telling this story and it's vital that they feel thoroughly connected to it from the start.

Cast measurements

The wardrobe staff will probably want to check the actors' measurements and note down any that haven't already been submitted prior to rehearsals. It's often sensible to do this on the first day when the entire acting company is together under one roof. It may be days or even weeks before this opportunity presents itself again. If wigs are to be used in the show this is also an ideal time for head measurements to be taken and hairstyles to be discussed.

Prioritising the music

The rest of the first day is up for grabs although it's usual to give priority to the musical director so that vocal work can begin with the ensemble, individual voices can be assessed, and vocal lines can be allocated. Stage management should always warn the actors in advance of the first day that they'll need to bring in some type of audio equipment so that vocal lines can be recorded at this early stage; most actors will use their phones, of course. It's obviously vital for the cast to learn the music as quickly as possible since it's hard to undertake any choreography or staging until the music has been assimilated.

Rough rehearsal schedule

The following rehearsal schedule relates to a production with a standard four-week rehearsal block. It's an approximate guide and can be adapted to suit the specific requirements of the show being rehearsed. I've included references to understudies, but these won't, of course, always be applicable. We've already looked at a production schedule split into three stages: planning, rehearsals and 'at the theatre' (see Chapter 3). The following relates to the second stage of this ('rehearsals') but includes more detail.

Week 1

Main cast	Script read-through
Main cast	Teach music (whole show)
Main cast	Start work on blocking/choreography/staging for Act 1
Understudies	Script read-through

Week 2

Main cast	Continue blocking/choreography/staging for Act 1 (start work on Act 2, if time)
Main cast	Recap music (whole show)
Main cast	Stagger Act 1
Understudies	Start learning music (whole show)

Week 3

Main cast	Concentrate on blocking/choreography/staging for Act 2
Main cast	Stagger Acts 1 and 2
Understudies	Start blocking/choreography/staging (with assistant director)

Week 4

Main cast	Work through notes from previous staggered run.
Main cast	Run the show (ideally twice)
Main cast	Final run for producers and other members of the production team
Understudies	Continue blocking/choreography/staging

It usually makes sense to rehearse shows chronologically, but there are reasons why this may not be practical; the availability of some cast members or even the choreographer may make it more beneficial to work out of sequence. There may also be complicated sections of dance from the second half of the show which the choreographer really wants to tackle early in the process so that the cast have time to assimilate and learn them. If the show is being rehearsed over a longer period than four weeks, as will often be the case with school or community projects, this same schedule can be applied to each quarter of the rehearsal period, so that Week 1 refers to the first quarter, Week 2 to the second quarter, and so on.

Once the rehearsal process has begun, the director will, of course, need to specify which scenes are to be rehearsed in advance. It's simply not acceptable to call everyone to rehearse and then to leave actors sitting doing nothing for the whole day. Some directors will draw up an entire week's rehearsal plan, whilst others, myself included, find it more practical to plan a day or so in advance. Since it's never really possible to envisage how long a scene, song or dance will take to block, stage or choreograph, I prefer to have more flexibility than a weekly schedule will allow. Nevertheless, I always try to keep this rough rehearsal schedule at the back of my mind so as not to lose sight of the overall picture.

In reality, of course, there never seems to be ample time to rehearse a show, and whilst it would be perfectly easy to spend weeks rehearsing the first couple of scenes, it's important to be practical about what's achievable in the time available. The rough schedule shown above, whilst only a guide-line, helps to prevent the director from being over-indulgent with some sections of the show, whilst neglecting others. This skeleton schedule is geared towards providing time for three full run-throughs in the last week of rehearsals. For these final runs, the actors should be 'off-the-book' (without scripts), and the lighting and sound designers should be in attendance for as much time as possible. For the very last run some rehearsal props may be replaced with show props, and some costumes may be worn, especially those which are likely to affect the dance moves.

Advice to understudies

A quick word about understudies (or covers); if the show is being produced professionally then there'll usually be at least one set of understudies. It's important to emphasise to this group that as well as learning their ensemble tracks they will also need to get on top of the understudy material as quickly as possible. Since inevitably they won't get much attention until the principal cast is well rehearsed, it's vital that these actors take responsibility for themselves and try to absorb as much of the work going on in the rehearsal room as possible. I've experienced on several occasions, both as an actor and a director, situations where the understudy is thrown on with little or no rehearsal. This is terrifying for everyone concerned. For this reason I always try to talk to the understudies early in the process, often on the first day, to remind them of their responsibilities. This is also why I try to schedule an understudy read-through at the end of the first week; it helps the actors to engage with the characters that they're covering and to start to take ownership of these rôles.

End of the day

By the end of the first day of rehearsals everyone should be feeling excited about the task ahead. The company will now have some idea about the type of show being presented and will have seen some images suggesting how it will ultimately look on stage. They'll also begin to realise that there's plenty of work to do and that they will all need to be working at the top of their game. It's often worth reminding the actors that there are plenty of challenges ahead, that they will be expected to be alert, punctual and focussed throughout rehearsals, and that they should try to be prepared for each work session by memorising the music and script in advance.

8
REHEARSALS 1: CREATING A COMPANY

Before we go into rehearsals, I like to know why I am creating a piece, what the world is and how to start the process – but there should be lots of delicious unknowns as well.

EMMA RICE

The exciting thing about starting rehearsals is that nobody really knows how the production will finally turn out. No matter how much preparation has been done by the creative team, there's an alchemy that takes place in the rehearsal room that no one can quite anticipate. And this is down to a unique combination of talents – the director, the musical director, the choreographer, the actors and the stage management – they will all have an influence in defining what takes place in the room and how the creative atmosphere develops.

It's the director's job, I believe, to create a positive working environment, and to help generate an atmosphere in rehearsals which is stimulating, challenging and enjoyable. The actors should feel free to experiment, without sensing that their efforts are constantly being judged or criticised. And everyone should feel that they have a valuable contribution to make, no matter how large or small their part in the show. Early in rehearsals it is a good idea to get the actors working together, even if further down the line they're required to split into separate groups. The reason for this is obvious: if you can develop mutual trust early on in the process the actors will quickly start to work together in a less inhibited, more engaged manner. In other words they'll start to become a team. No two directors will work in the same way, of course, and there's no set formula which will ensure a productive rehearsal period. Throughout the following few chapters are suggestions which may help to facilitate the rehearsal process, but they are by no means the only options, and every director will, by trial and error, find out what works best for them.

Theatre games

We always play games. Mostly we play ball games as it is a great way of levelling the room and taking people away from their understandable fears.

EMMA RICE

Theatre games are often used to help actors loosen up, lose their inhibitions and work together in a playful, unpressurised atmosphere. Since most of us have a child lurking somewhere within, actors tend to respond well to these games, and will throw themselves wholeheartedly into pursuits more often identified with the playground than anywhere else. Most directors will have a different stock of games to draw from and will tailor them to suit the specific requirements of the group, whether this be a class of school children, a group of students, a company of amateur adults or a cast of professional actors. There are numerous theatre games to choose from and countless books have been written on the subject. A word of warning, though: theatre games should be used as a means to an end, not just as a way of filling time. Once the actors are warmed up and working well together it's important to turn to more focussed activity, preferably something which relates to the show. Having done some very basic warm-up exercises, for example, I will often move on to more specific improvisations which enable the actors to start working on their particular characters. These improvisations are still, if you like, theatre games, but they are subtly moving towards something more directly related to the piece itself.

It's important to come together as a team, games can be great levellers and can reveal the dynamics of the group – who's shy, competitive, a leader, a nurturer . . .

SHARON D CLARKE

Group research

In the first few days of rehearsal it's a very good idea to share ideas about the particular show being produced. The director and other members of the creative team will already have done a large amount of research (see Chapter 4) and will often want to discuss their findings with the company. This can, of course, be fascinating and extremely illuminating, but it's also a good idea to get the cast to do some of the work for themselves. Not only does this mean that lots of information can be gathered fairly swiftly, but it also helps to engage the actors in the project from the very start.

My own particular process usually involves splitting the company into smallish groups of three or four and setting them a task. This might involve gathering information about fashion, politics or music during the period in which our production is set. Or the task can be more specific, depending on the nature of the show. For a recent production of *Kiss Me, Kate*, for example, I asked each group to research one of the following topics: Shakespeare's *Taming of the Shrew*, the life and work of Cole Porter, and American theatre in the late 1940s (the period in which the story is set). The actors were told that there would be a 'show-and-tell' of all the material towards the end of the first week and that each group should aim to present their findings in presentations lasting approximately fifteen minutes. Another stipulation was that every group member should speak during these presentations. This activity has three specific objectives: to gather lots of useful information, to enable the actors to start working together towards a common goal, and to make sure that everyone has equal opportunity to take centre stage and have their voice heard. This last objective is particularly good for those members of the company who play small rôles and can sometimes feel somewhat invisible in the room. Actors generally seem to relish these research tasks, and the presentation itself can be informative, thought-provoking and great fun too. By asking the actors to do some of the research, the director is actually making them an integral part of the process and this is something to which most actors respond extremely well.

Group activities

There are, of course, other ways to help performers familiarise themselves with the subject matter of a show. During rehearsals for a production of *Jesus Christ Superstar*, we presented the cast with edited highlights from various films concerning the life of Christ: Martin Scorsese's *The Last Temptation of Christ*, Pier Paolo Pasolini's *The Gospel According to St. Matthew*, and Denys Arcand's *Jesus of Montreal*. These three films, though vastly different in the treatment of their subject matter, all gave us valuable insights into Christ's life, and provided lots of topics for discussion. In a similarly biblical vein, I once worked as an actor on a production of the Stephen Schwartz musical *Children of Eden*. Most of the cast were required to play animals at some point in the show, and for research purposes we visited London Zoo to observe at close quarters the physical behaviour of our chosen animals. Back in the rehearsal room we talked about our discoveries, and did some detailed improvisations based on our zoological observations. Again this research not only provided us with invaluable material which later became an intrinsic part of the show, but also helped to make the actors feel that their specific contribution was an important and much valued part of the whole enterprise.

Similar group projects could be devised for all sorts of other shows; for example, a company preparing a production of Cy Coleman's *Barnum* would inevitably benefit from a trip to the circus to examine at first hand the type of showmanship required for this style of theatrical extravaganza. Likewise, a company in rehearsal for *Sunday in the Park with George* might draw inspiration from a group outing to an art gallery – especially one featuring the work of the post-impressionist artist Georges Seurat – where the actors could examine at first hand the 'colour and light' so often referred to in Sondheim's poetic lyrics.

Improvisation

I have no strict rules about improvisation; I use it on some shows and not on others. Students, I find, are often very receptive to it, whilst some experienced professionals find it indulgent and time-wasting. Personally, I think that it can be an extremely effective method of allowing the actors to explore their characters in fine detail. It's often useful, I think, to take moments from a story which aren't presented on the stage. With a piece like *The Last Five Years*, for example, which focusses on the breakdown of a relationship and is told in reverse from the woman's perspective and in a conventional linear fashion from the man's, much of the story happens offstage. We see specific moments, but the rest we only hear about. Focussing on these unseen situations can be illuminating as this sort of improvisational detective-work allows the director and the actors to explore events in the story which aren't featured in the script. With a richer, fuller understanding of these offstage moments the written scenes take on an added resonance which is extremely helpful for the actors playing these two pivotal rôles.

Group improvisation

With the ensemble I often use an exercise early in the rehearsal process which helps the actors to start making initial decisions about their characters. They're asked to stand in front of an imaginary full-length mirror and told that their character is getting dressed for the day. They have to be very specific about the type of clothes that they're putting on, very clear about colour and texture, weight and design. They're then asked to add accessories – shoes, hats and jewellery, if appropriate. They can take as much time as they like to put these things on, but once this task is completed they're asked to walk around the room in character in order to get a sense of how it feels to move in these particular outfits. Then all sorts of different instructions can be added: the actors can be asked to interact with other characters in the room, they can be told that it's starting to rain, or that there's a pick-pocket on the loose. At times they may be asked to return to their imaginary mirrors and to answer questions, still in character, about the clothes that they're wearing, and how it feels to move about in them. This exercise is particularly useful when the show is set in a period before or after the present day since it forces the cast to start thinking about another era and about how they would present themselves in a society somewhat different from their own. The main objective of this exercise is quite simply to get the actors to start experimenting with their characters without feeling exposed or inhibited. Further improvisations can follow which are more challenging and can involve dialogue and specific scenarios.

Other group improvisations can be useful when exploring hierarchy and community. A musical such as *The Baker's Wife* explores both these themes. The show opens with a scene centred around a small village café in Provence, and slowly the audience is introduced to various local characters. The café is clearly an important focus for the community, somewhere they all go to laugh, drink, gossip and argue. A simple improvisation for this particular musical can be achieved by setting up a make-shift café in the rehearsal room, using tables, chairs, glasses and bottles. Some of the named characters in the show will already have obvious rôles to play in this scenario: Denise and Claude, the café owners, and Monsieur Martine, the teacher, for example. Others will be playing un-named villagers and will need to start imagining how they fit into the social structure of this specific community.

Once the improvisation is underway, the director may decide to add some more colour by suggesting to one of the actors that he starts to argue with the waiter about the quality of the food, or that one of the village gossips finds something unexpected in her soup. Pretty soon the scene will start to take on a life of its own, and the actors will begin to make some early choices about their respective characters. This sort of group improvisation can be very useful, especially for actors in the ensemble, since they can begin to work on a specific identity for their character, rather than simply trying to play a nebulous 'villager'. If an actor decides, for example, that she is the local postmistress, that she's secretly in love with a waiter in the café, and that she has a personal vendetta against the café owner's wife, then the ensemble scenes in which she's involved will inevitably start to become more detailed and nuanced.

Character detail

Actors should always be encouraged to discover as much as possible about their character. This is particularly useful for actors in the ensemble as there's often very little information provided in the script. It's a fairly obvious observation to make, but the more detail the actors have at their fingertips the easier it will be to play the scenes and to interact with the other characters on stage. They can start by creating a biography for their character. This can include information about family relationships, personal character traits, and any significant life events which may have had positive or negative influences on them. Actors generally enjoy this sort of forensic detail and will be happy to engage in this type of intricate character study.

Once the character has been scrutinised in this way it's often helpful to have group discussions about these invented histories. By exchanging information the actors may decide that their character has a particular connection with another character on stage; they may be related, engaged, best friends, or even rivals. After this sort of discussion it's often useful to get the actors back up on their feet again to attempt some more detailed improvisation based on the information that they now all possess. With a production of *Carousel* we found that this sort of work was invaluable. In the script it simply specifies that there are 'mill girls' and 'fishermen'. In order to create any sense of this tight-knit New England community we needed to make sure that the actors knew precisely who they were, and how they fitted into the social structure of the village. By making very clear decisions based on character histories and improvisation, we were able to flesh out these individuals and create a community of young people who felt realistic and credible.

Involving stage management

It seems to me that a happy company is generally one in which everyone feels that they have a valued contribution to make. This doesn't simply apply to the actors, but also to stage management. Just as I will always try early in rehearsals to find opportunities to involve the actors in research, I also try to ensure that the members of the stage management team feel fully engaged in the process too. One of the best ways of doing this, I find, is to start discussing the set changes as soon as possible since stage management will inevitably be involved in these and will be keen to know how they are going to be achieved. Whilst the actors may end up being involved in these set changes too, it's best to make sure that stage management know exactly what is happening before enlisting the help of the performers. Leaving such conversations until the tech really is asking for trouble and it's best for all concerned if a plan is made during rehearsals when things are relatively calm and there's adequate time to talk things through properly. Nothing can be set in stone until the technical rehearsals on stage, of course, but a good deal of planning can be done beforehand. With our production of *The Addams Family*, scene changes were generally done by a mixture of cast and stage management. We went through these changes in minute detail during rehearsals, aided by having some parts of the physical set in the rehearsal room, and consequently saved ourselves a great deal of time when it came to the tech.

Regular breaks

It may seem like an obvious thing to say, but regular breaks are really important during rehearsals, not just for the actors, but for the creative team too. It's a chance to re-charge the batteries, certainly, but it's also an opportunity for the director, choreographer, musical director and stage management to interact socially with the actors and get to know them better. On a production of *West Side Story*, which featured a predominantly young cast, I found out some fascinating details about the diverse ethnic backgrounds of various cast members by talking to the actors in the coffee breaks. Since ethnicity and a sense of belonging are subjects which dominate this particular musical, it was fascinating to discover just how many cast members felt intimately connected to the themes of the show. An innocent coffee break chat actually made me realise that the piece meant so much more to some of the cast than simply an opportunity to display their singing and dancing talents.

As far as professional productions are concerned, breaks are mandatory and specified by Equity for all rehearsals. Stage management will constantly monitor rehearsal breaks and ensure that the rules are appropriately applied.

Accent work

'What accent are we doing?' is a question regularly asked during the first few days of rehearsal. Actors, not surprisingly, want to get this clarified as quickly as possible, and decisions about accent should ideally be made early in the rehearsal process. Often it's pretty obvious; *Legally Blonde* is a show which centres around a group of all-American teenagers. It's hard to see how this particular story would work in a different context and with different accents. Similarly, *My Fair Lady* focusses on language, and without the contrast between Higgins's perfect received pronunciation (RP) and Eliza's cockney accent the story would start to unravel. Lines are a little more blurred with a piece like *She Loves Me*; the characters are Hungarian, but the writers conceived it with American accents in mind. Working on this particular show forced us to confront the accent question full-on. We decided that it would be risible to attempt Hungarian accents, and meaningless to try American ones, so the decision was made to use British ones. In the event this worked extremely well and Maraczek's perfumery became a melting pot of different regional accents which highlighted class differences and a subtle sense of hierarchy.

If all the characters in a show are speaking the same language, of course, it's not really a problem if the actors perform with their own accents. After all, no one expects to hear *Les Misérables* sung with a French inflection. Complications arise, though, with a show like *Cabaret,* as it's obviously important to differentiate between the British, American and German characters. Unless the latter have clearly-defined accents the story will be very difficult to follow. And here's where an **accent coach** can be invaluable. Not only can they help the actors to make sensible, informed choices about their accent, but the focussed work required often leads to the performers becoming more interactive and more playful with each other. After a session with an accent coach small groups of actors will often gather to reiterate what they've just been learning, and this, I find, can be very good for team building and company morale.

Accent coach

An accent coach will be able to give the cast helpful tips about a particular accent or dialect, will often supply written notes on pronunciation, and may also provide a voice recording with extracts read by native speakers. They will usually work with the actors in the first week or so to lay down some basic rules, returning later to check on their progress. Often watching a run and giving subsequent notes can be the best way of consolidating advice. With amateur or student productions it may not be possible to pay someone for these services, but it's worth asking around because someone in the cast or production team may know of someone with the requisite accent skills. Whilst a huge selection of accent coaches can be found online, I always think it advisable to ask around for recommendations. The best accent coaches aren't just specialists in their field, but also extremely good communicators and will make accent sessions with the cast both informative and fun.

Other specialisms

Sometimes directors will call in specialists to help with an aspect of the show which lies outside their own particular field of expertise. Since musicals deal with all sorts of different subjects it's impossible to list every specialism, but here are some of the more obvious ones.

Stage fighting

If the show requires fighting of any description (Photo 7) a specialist in this field is invaluable. With professional productions fight sequences come under the heading of health and safety and the execution of these needs to be taken extremely seriously. Not only will a good **fight director** ensure that the stage action looks convincing, they'll also show the actors the safest possible way to achieve the desired effect, whether it be a knife fight as in the final scene of *Oklahoma!*, or a choreographed bout of judo as demonstrated by a squabbling couple at the start of *Company.* Once the fight director has set the fight sequences the actors will need to stick very closely to this choreography. Whilst blocking and stage business can usually remain flexible to some extent, fight sequences, once set, really do need to remain consistent. Any changes can be dangerous and result in injury to the actors. Once a fight has been choreographed there should be a scheduled run-through before each performance.

Photo 7 Fight sequence: *West Side Story*, Kilworth House Theatre (Benjamin Yates, Justin Thomas). (Photo, Jems Photography.)

Circus skills

It would be unwise to approach a show like *Barnum* without first seeking the advice of a circus specialist. A pivotal moment in the show involves P.T. Barnum balancing precariously atop a high wire; unless you're extremely lucky it's unlikely that your leading man will have previous experience in this field. A circus specialist will be able to help in all sorts of areas, advising not just on tight-rope walking but on skills such as juggling, tumbling and fire-eating.

Puppetry

Puppetry is central to *Little Shop of Horrors*, so much so that the plant often becomes the star of the show. Without a puppet specialist this challenging musical will be very difficult to pull off. It's essential that someone experienced teaches the cast how to handle the smaller puppets in the first half of the show, and when it comes to the gigantic plant in Act 2 (Photo 8), whoever operates this will need a high level of fitness and will require some expert guidance from a specialist. Alternatively, because of the skill and stamina required, an experienced puppeteer may be engaged from the start to manipulate the physical plant in performance (the voice is usually provided by a different actor). Puppets are now used more extensively than ever before in shows such as *Avenue Q*, *The Lorax* and *The Lion King*, and experienced puppeteers have become invaluable members of the creative team.

Photo 8 Puppetry: *Little Shop of Horrors*, Duke of York's Theatre (Sheridan Smith, Paul Keating). (Photo, Marilyn Kingwill.)

Magic

Some shows, such as *The Wizard of Oz*, *Wicked* and *Into the Woods*, require illusions or magic tricks to help tell the story, and most directors will need to call in a consultant to help in these areas. It's no use leaving decisions until the last moment, and anything which involves any sort of illusion will need to be carefully planned in advance. It's true, of course, that some tricks, such as the sudden appearance or disappearance of a person or object, will rely heavily on stage lighting and can only really be achieved once the actors reach the stage, but there are many other illusions which can be practised in the rehearsal room. It may seem fairly obvious, but by identifying these specific moments as early as possible, and by practising them regularly during rehearsals, many of these particular challenges can be overcome before the actors even set foot on the stage. Any illusions which require specific lighting will need to be discussed with the lighting designer at the start and factored into the tech schedule as they may take up a disproportionate amount of time to rehearse.

Culture and religion

On a less practical level, specialists can also be useful in helping the cast get to grips with the subject matter of a particular show. During rehearsals for *Jesus Christ Superstar* a local vicar agreed to come and talk to us not only about the life of Christ, but also about political and social aspects of this particular historical period. With productions such as *Rags*, *Fiddler on the Roof* and *Falsettoland*, all shows which are centred around Jewish characters and themes, the input from an expert can be invaluable, giving the actors a better understanding of the customs and traditions which inform daily life in a Jewish community.

A more secular example of this type of specialist advice was extremely helpful during rehearsals for *She Loves Me* at the Menier Chocolate Factory in London. We decided that since none of us knew much about perfume, it would be helpful to talk to someone who did. Our designer contacted a former actor who now works for one of the big perfume companies. He subsequently arrived at rehearsals and proceeded to spray all sorts of scents around the room, telling us fascinating details about the perfume industry in the 1930s (our specific period), including all sorts of information about application and general perfume etiquette. The presentation was informative, illuminating and ultimately fragrant – the rehearsal room smelled wonderful for days after!

Actor-musicians

This is another specialist area which is becoming increasingly important, particularly in musical theatre. Traditionally plays have included the occasional actor-musician – someone who appears sporadically playing a portable instrument and provides suitably atmospheric accompaniment. With musicals the orchestra or band is typically separated from the action, often situated in an orchestra pit, and occasionally playing unseen from a separate room. Actor-musician shows break down these barriers and feature performers who both act the scenes and provide the musical accompaniment. Shows such as these, thoughtfully crafted and imaginatively staged, can be a revelation, with the musical and dramatic elements perfectly aligned. Successful actor-musician shows are complicated to achieve, though, and require detailed planning, expert casting and skilful execution.

Drama schools are now becoming much more switched on about actor-musicians and there is consequently a growing pool of highly-trained performers. Whilst many actor-musicians have keyboard skills, most will play a portable instrument too and this enables them to move about the stage holding it, acting with it, and sometimes even dancing with it. Guitars and accordions are particularly useful as they can provide a chord-based accompaniment and can therefore be used in place of a keyboard.

Casting a musical with actor-musicians is a complex procedure and has already been touched on in Chapter 5. Finding a suitable cast for a show like *Sweet Charity*, for example, will necessitate a search for performers whose skills include acting, singing, dancing and playing at least one instrument. This is no mean feat and will probably require compromises in certain areas. The written orchestration provided by the licensing company may be impossible to achieve with the given pool of performers and may therefore require some minor tweaking or a complete re-write. In both cases the licensing company will need to be informed before any changes can be made. A colleague of mine who orchestrates and musically directs actor-musician shows explained to me that casting briefs in the early stages can sometimes be based on instrumental ability rather than character suitability and that the matching up of rôles happens later in the process. This feels counter-intuitive but can actually be a more pragmatic way of starting the casting process.

There are clear advantages when it comes to working with casts of actor-musicians. Firstly, the company becomes very tight-knit from the start, since everyone will be working together to create the musical framework of the piece. The very act of playing in an ensemble of musicians means that very quickly the actors have to learn to support each other, and ideas of hierarchy immediately start to dissolve. There is therefore a sense of collective responsibility since every person in the room is a vital piece of the jigsaw. This can lead to a healthier working environment and a close communication between each of the performers. Other positives include the fact that with all the actor-musicians in the room from the start there's no need for a sitzprobe and the sound department will be able to get a sense of the overall mix much earlier in the process.

There are, of course, downsides too. Because each person in the team is unique, playing a certain instrument and acting a certain rôle (or rôles), covering these tracks can become incredibly complicated. And this is where producers can sometimes come unstuck. Whilst it may appear on the surface that an actor-musician show may be a cheaper undertaking because of the absence of a conventional band, in practice it may be more expensive to provide understudies for the performers. It's also practically impossible to ensure that each musical track will be covered, and often the consequence of illness or injury is that a certain musical layer will be lost or, at best, played on a different instrument; it's simply too costly to provide covers for all of the instrumental tracks in the show. A good dance captain or resident director will draw up a detailed grid as damage limitation to ensure that the show can continue in the event of a performer's absence.

9

REHEARSALS 2: SONGS, SCENES AND CHOREOGRAPHY

I very much rely on instinct, what feels truthful, what honours the material. Rehearsals are about the mechanics for me, blocking, marks, props. I 'feel' my characters when I've got my costume and I'm on set . . .

SHARON D CLARKE

Some of the best musicals are those which flow seamlessly from scene into song, and from song into dance. In rehearsals, however, the different disciplines are very often divided up, ensuring that the performers are kept as busy as possible, and that every available moment is used effectively.

Split calls

Musicals involve a combination of disciplines, most often acting, singing and dancing, and this means that there's always lots going on in a variety of different rehearsal spaces. Plays, on the other hand, are generally much easier to schedule as there's usually only one rehearsal taking place at any one time. Assuming that there's more than one space available, it makes absolute sense to schedule **split calls** so that the director can work with a group of actors in one room, whilst the musical director or the choreographer works with another group elsewhere. There may even be the opportunity for an assistant to run a third set of rehearsals, if there's space available. I quite often try to schedule an accent session, or an understudy call, to run alongside the other rehearsals; this can take place in a smaller room, or even a bar area. The advantages are obvious; the actors are kept busy and stimulated, the director, choreographer and musical director get more time with the performers, and rehearsal time is used much more efficiently.

Kiss Me Kate

Rehearsal Call *14*

For Tuesday 16th May

Location	Director	Musical Director	Choreographer	Company Stage Manager	Deputy Stage Manager
Dance Attic	Matthew White	Michael England	Sam Spencer Lane	Naomi Hill	Hannah Halden

TIME:	CALL FOR:	DETAILS:
9.30	Stage Management	**Arrive at Rehearsal Space**
10.00 – 12.00	All Ensemble	**Another Openin' With Sam Large Room**
11.30 – 12.00	To Join: Mr Gary Davis	**Another Openin' With Sam Large Room**
10.00 – 13.30	Miss Caroline Sheen Miss Monique Young Mr Gary Davis Mr Matthew McKenna Mr Justin Thomas	**Scene Work With Matt Small Room**
12.00 – 13.30	To Join: Mr Cory English Mr Carl Sanderson	**Scene Work With Matt Small Room**
12.00 – 12.15 Break		
12.15 – 13.30	Female Ensemble	**Various Dance Work With Sam Large Room**
13.00 – 13.30	To Join: Miss Monique Young Mr Thomas Audibert Mr Davide Fiensauri Mr Andrew Gordon-Watkins Mr Justin Thomas	**Recap Suitors With Sam Large Room**
13.30 – 14.30 Lunch		
14.30 – 16.15	Full Company	**Finales Act 1 & 2 With Matt/Sam/Michael Large Room**
16.15 – 16.30 Break		
16.30 – 18.00	Miss Molly May Gardiner Miss Tash Holway Miss Helen Turner Miss Holly Wilcock Mr Matthew McKenna	**Where Is the Life? With Matt/Sam/Michael Large Room**
16.30 – 18.00	Miss Emily Squibb Mr Andrew Gordon-Watkins	**Cover Work With Bex**

Diagram 4 Split rehearsal call: *Kiss Me, Kate*.

When drawing up a rehearsal schedule it's important to try, where possible, to be specific about which actors will be needed for each call. It isn't always possible to predict how much can be achieved in any one rehearsal, and actors who only appear towards the end of a scene may find themselves redundant if the rehearsal pace is slow. Sometimes this is unavoidable, and it's not the end of the world, but it's preferable to keep everyone busy. No one wants a room full of disgruntled actors who've been sitting around for hours doing nothing. An example of a typical split rehearsal call is shown in Diagram 4.

To complicate matters, this sort of complex scheduling also often involves wardrobe fittings, haircuts and **press calls**. This is an added reason why stage management must go through schedules with a fine-toothed comb. An experienced deputy stage manager will always take care to check the schedule before sending it out and will realise when an actor is potentially double-booked.

Whilst trying to make the most of the allocated rehearsal time it's also important to remember that from time to time members of the creative team will need to attend rehearsals other than their own; it's not healthy for the director, musical director and choreographer to work in isolation all the time and the opportunity to watch other rehearsals is important. The choreographer will almost certainly want some input from the director, the director will no doubt want to be present at some of the vocal calls, and the musical director will need to be very clear about the way in which the choreographer responds to the dance arrangements. Whilst split calls can be a very economical way of dividing up the rehearsal time, it shouldn't be forgotten that a lot of important work will be collaborative and the director, musical director and choreographer will need time and opportunity to work together in the same space.

Music rehearsals

In a musical, or indeed an opera, the music is first and foremost a vehicle for telling the story and expressing the characters' thoughts and emotions. It's not just music for music's sake. In order to be a good theatre conductor, you must understand that the composer is essentially a storyteller.

DAVID CHARLES ABELL

Vocal warm-up

Most musical directors will start each rehearsal with a short vocal warm-up. This will usually involve some basic breathing exercises, a few tongue-twisters and some work on diction. Even though the actors ought to arrive at rehearsals already vocally prepared, the warm-up can be a great way of kick-starting the session and getting everyone focussed and energised. In the US vocal warm-ups are considered to be the responsibility of the performer and the musical director isn't required to offer them.

Teaching the music

These days, a musical director has to have excellent keyboard skills.
Most of the new shows coming to Broadway and the West End require
musical directors who play and conduct simultaneously.

DAVID CHARLES ABELL

As I've indicated in the skeleton schedule (see Chapter 3), with a four-week rehearsal block it makes sense for the cast to learn the bulk of the music in the first week. The reason for this is simple; it often takes a while for an actor to assimilate the musical numbers, and if the score's a complicated one, such as *Passion* or *Pacific Overtures*, it really helps to learn the music early and to keep brushing it up as rehearsals progress. With shows in which the performers are singing and dancing at the same time, the process will also be much smoother if the music can be learnt in advance of the dance rehearsals. Naturally some of the vocals may be forgotten as the choreographer sets the dance moves, but if they've been well taught, and the cast has had time to absorb them properly, they will soon come flooding back.

Whilst every musical director will have a slightly different approach to rehearsing the music, the majority will want to start teaching the score as soon as possible. They'll often begin with the company numbers; this is a good idea, since it gets everyone singing together and working as a team. In many cases the musical director will be an accomplished pianist and will teach the company from the piano. However, there are some who prefer to conduct from the start and will require a rehearsal pianist to accompany the singers whilst they concentrate on teaching the music. It comes as a constant surprise to me that musical theatre performers are often not very good sight-readers. The musical director, therefore, will spend a lot of time in the early music calls bashing out single vocal lines so that the actors can record them. They may not be great sight-readers, but musical theatre actors often have a very good ear, and it doesn't usually take too long for them to learn their parts. Of course, the sooner they can memorise the music and dispense with the vocal score altogether the better. The director will find it much easier to stage a scene without the cast peering into their copies, and the actors will be freer to explore the physicality of their rôles without having to contend with musical scores or vocal books. It's more-or-less an unwritten rule that once it comes to the staging rehearsals, the performers will be 'off-book' as far as the music is concerned. In opera, after all, the singers are expected to arrive at the first rehearsal having already studied the music and consigned it to memory.

Allocating vocal parts

Whilst the musical director will probably have a fairly clear idea from auditions about the vocal range of each of the ensemble members, the early music calls are a good opportunity to re-assess the singers' voices and to divide them into their respective vocal groups: soprano, alto, tenor and bass. Once this is done the musical director can start teaching the harmonies; refining these vocal passages can happen at a later date.

Vocal calls for the principals

Where possible it's best to call the principals individually or in small groups when initially teaching them their solo parts. No one likes being put on the spot, and it's unfair to expect them to learn new music whilst being scrutinised by the rest of the cast. These calls are also a good opportunity to address any technical issues which the singer may have. Getting into good habits at this point will help once the staging rehearsals start in earnest. As far as the principals are concerned, the musical director will often want some early input from the director, as ideas about character will influence the way in which the music is sung. It's often a good idea for the director to attend some of these early principal music calls so that thoughts about character can be discussed before the actors make any strong decisions concerning interpretation. Where the director has a good musical sense, and the musical director a sound dramatic one, these sessions can be illuminating for everyone, and a good foundation for subsequent staging rehearsals.

Ongoing music calls

Once staging rehearsals are underway it's sensible for the musical director to have occasional brush-up calls in order to check that harmony lines are being remembered correctly, and that musical detail has been retained. It's amazing how quickly things can change as the actors become more confident with the material. In many cases this is a good thing, and lots of great musical discoveries can be made during the rehearsal process. However, it's important for the musical director to keep a close eye on these developments to ensure that the musical integrity of the piece is maintained.

Once the music has been taught, and the actors have had time to assimilate it, the musical director will usually be anxious to join the director for the staging rehearsals. At this point there needs to be some flexibility on the part of the musical director as the actor will now be starting to explore the character in new ways and may find that some of the vocal choices made in the early music calls are no longer appropriate. Astute musical directors with a focus on good story-telling will understand this instinctively and adapt accordingly.

When it comes to rehearsals you have to be ready for anything: at one moment, you might need to take full charge of the room, teaching music, inventing harmonies or arrangements on the spot, doing vocal warm-ups. Later, you might need to adopt a supporting rôle while the director or choreographer works with the cast.

DAVID CHARLES ABELL

Dance rehearsals

Ideally the choreographer and the director will have discussed in advance the choreographic style of the piece. They will also need to decide who'll take responsibility for the various different numbers in the show. With some sections it'll be perfectly obvious; the dream ballet in *Carousel* and the high school prom in *Grease* will clearly be on the choreographer's 'to do' list as they both involve prolonged sections of dance. Not all decisions are clear-cut, however, and the lines are sometimes blurred between what is danced, staged and acted. The following guide-line may help to differentiate between the various types of movement in a show: staging involves the movement of the actors around the stage, musical staging tends to incorporate heightened movement (usually to music), and choreography generally denotes choreographed dance-based steps.

There are certainly grey areas, however, and the degree to which a number is choreographed or staged depends on interpretation. A number like 'A Bushel and a Peck' from *Guys and Dolls*, for example, could be staged in a variety of ways. Depending on how talented Adelaide is deemed to be, the number could be done with complicated choreography, or with hardly any dance at all. This will depend on the vision of the director and choreographer, and also on the talents of the performers involved. If the actor playing Adelaide is a gifted comedian but not a dancer then obviously the staging will reflect this. These grey areas will be discussed later (see Chapter 10) but my focus for the moment will be on the purely choreographed sections of the show.

Preparation

I do a lot of pre-production. I almost have the whole show blocked and choreographed before rehearsal starts. However, I'm inspired by the actors, so I will always shift and change my initial thought as I work with each of them. It is almost like building a net that they can fall into.

SUSAN STROMAN

Rehearsal time is precious, and inspiration doesn't always strike when it's most needed; for these reasons it is a good idea for the choreographer to have a fairly clear idea of how to approach the dance sections before starting rehearsals. Often choreographers will work with an assistant in the planning stages, someone who can try out the dance steps, partner the choreographer and commit the routines to memory, if required. Frequently these preparatory sessions will be filmed, ensuring that there's something tangible to refer to once the choreographer starts rehearsing with the cast. As Susan Stroman indicates, it's not advisable to set everything rigidly in stone until the choreographer has a chance to work creatively with the actual performers, but doing detailed preparation beforehand and then being flexible in the rehearsal room will make the process a whole lot easier. It's worth mentioning that some choreographers also use improvisation as a basis for their work; this may be done prior to rehearsals with a group of students or hired dancers, or during the rehearsal process itself.

Justifying the dance

Many musical scores, especially the more old-fashioned ones, include extended sections of dance music. There may have been good reasons for this when the show was written – the desire to show-case the talents of a particular performer, perhaps. Or quite simply it might have been the fashion at the time; many shows in the 1940s, for example, feature a dream ballet. Nowadays these elongated dance sections can feel a bit excessive, and it's worth the choreographer and director discussing whether some judicious cuts could be made to tighten things up and keep the story moving. Dance for its own sake is very seldom effective in a narrative musical, and the director and choreographer should always try to justify the existence of these sections. Put at its simplest, dance needs to help create mood, tell the story and give the audience a deeper insight into the characters. In most cases a succession of impressive dance moves, however virtuosic, won't be particularly effective unless motivated by character or story-telling.

Before cutting a section of dance music it's important to touch base with the licensing company. With some shows, for example *West Side Story*, there are very strict rules concerning cuts. Thankfully with many other musicals there seems to be more flexibility, and the licensing company will be able to provide some clarity on this.

Dance warm-up

Dance calls will usually begin with a physical warm-up. These are often tailored to suit the type of show being performed and can range from a ballet barre to a physical work-out. The main aim of the warm-up is to make sure that the dancers are prepared for the type of movement required in the ensuing rehearsal; complicated lifts and pas de deux work are often challenging both mentally and physically and require proper preparation. Often, however, the dance warm-up also provides an opportunity for the choreographer to work through specific steps which may later be incorporated into the routines. Music for the warm-up is usually provided by the choreographer and relayed through speakers in the rehearsal room. With larger productions the choreographer will sometimes delegate the warm-up to an assistant or to the dance captain. The latter is appointed by the choreographer and is usually selected from amongst the ensemble members (see Chapter 5). In the US, dance warm-ups are the responsibility of the performer and not the choreographer.

Setting the dance numbers

Depending on the size of the budget and the availability of personnel, most productions will provide a pianist for the dance rehearsals. Whilst it's not impossible to use pre-recorded music, it just takes longer to stop and re-start, and also means that everything is done at the pre-recorded tempo. It's important for the choreographer to liaise with the stage management in advance of these dance rehearsals in case any specific equipment is required, such as chairs, hats or canes. With *Top Hat*, for example, our choreographer requested some very specific canes for 'Puttin' on the Ritz'. Various sample canes were bought and tested before he was ultimately satisfied. To start rehearsing routines without the right equipment can be extremely counter-productive and often leads to much time wasting.

Sometimes the wardrobe department will provide **practice skirts** for the performers (the type of skirt will depend on the period of the show) and these can be very beneficial, especially in shows featuring lots of dance. Ideally they will be introduced at the start of rehearsals and used throughout until the actual costumes arrive in time for the tech.

The choreographer will decide whether to rehearse the numbers in show order. Sometimes there will be a particularly complicated section which requires attention from the start. With a production of *Kiss Me, Kate*, for example, our choreographer was anxious to focus on two numbers in the musical – 'Another Openin'', which comes right at the top of the show and introduces most of the key characters, and the second act opener 'Too Darn Hot', a great opportunity for some show-stopping choreography (see Photo 9). By prioritising both of these she was able to map them out early in rehearsals, which was very good for company morale. By the end of the first week these numbers had begun to take shape beautifully and there was a palpable sense of excitement in the room.

It's important during these early choreographic sessions that the director has an opportunity to see the work in development. After all, there's no point in the choreographer working flat out on a dance routine, only to discover once the number has been set that the director doesn't like it; this is time-consuming and dispiriting for all concerned. As with the choreography, the director will need to keep an eye on all departments so that stylistic unity is maintained throughout the whole production.

Photo 9 'Too Darn Hot': *Kiss Me, Kate*, Kilworth House Theatre (Tarinn Callender and company). (Photo, Jems Photography.)

Rehearsing the scenes

Directing a group of actors is a great privilege – it's the chance to work together in a creative environment, to make interesting choices about character and motivation, and to experiment with challenging ideas. Above all, it's great fun. But the job of the director, in my opinion, is to facilitate rather than to dictate. Being a good listener and a good observer are important aspects of the job. Being a good editor is also a useful skill; I often let the actors play with a scene for a while before helping to refine characterisations, select certain bits of stage business, and modify or re-work the blocking.

As far as the staging of scenes is concerned, this will depend on the type of show being rehearsed, the number of actors in the company, and above all the director's personal working method. Some directors will arrive at rehearsals with a very clear idea of staging, having already mapped out the scenes and blocked the actors' moves in advance. Others will have no preconceived ideas and will wait until the actors are present before making any staging decisions.

My own personal approach falls somewhere between the two. If the scene involves a small group of actors, I'll certainly give it some thought beforehand, but I try not to anticipate specific blocking as this inevitably limits the actors' choices. However, if the scene involves the whole ensemble I'll usually have a rough plan suggesting where and when movement might take place (see Chapter 10). This is mainly because it's more of a challenge dealing with larger

Photo 10 Blocking a scene: *The Addams Family*, UK tour (Grant McIntyre, Dale Rapley, Cameron Blakely, Samantha Womack, Dickon Gough, Matthew White). (Photo, Craig Sugden.)

numbers, and it's just not practical to give everyone carte blanche as far as blocking is concerned. With a smaller group it's much easier to remain flexible and to incorporate the ideas of the individual actors (see Photo 10). After all, there's no point casting a talented group of performers and then forcing them to adhere to a rigid, preconceived plan. Actors aren't chess pieces to be moved around the stage at the director's whim; they are collaborators and their creative input is often invaluable.

Scene work

I usually begin with a read-through of the scene that we're about to rehearse. Before putting it on its feet we'll then discuss any questions that have come up and talk more generally about themes and character motivation. We also try to see how the scene relates to the rest of the show – it's often useful to talk about what happened directly before the section being rehearsed. This will in turn help to identify what state of mind the characters are in when they appear and how they're affected by what's gone before. If there's time I'll sometimes ask the performers to improvise the scene that's just taken place offstage, so that they have a tangible sense of how their character feels going into the scripted scene. This generally helps the actors to find the right emotional tone for the scene being rehearsed. This approach is most suitable for musicals with well-written, naturalistic dialogue, such as *Kiss of the Spiderwoman* or *Billy Elliot*, but not always appropriate for the more caricatured, stylised type of show. *A Funny Thing Happened on the Way to the Forum* or *Seussical* are shows which make no pretence at naturalism, and with musicals such as these it may be better to focus on the heightened characters, and explore physical ways of expressing them, rather than spending valuable rehearsal time talking about context and character history.

Having read through the scene, discussed it in some detail, and perhaps improvised around it, it's now time to put it on its feet. Some actors will try to be off-book for the very first staging rehearsals, others will steadfastly cling to their scripts claiming that they cannot learn the lines until they've had a chance to block the scene, a fairly dubious claim, in my opinion. I'm usually happy to let the actors use the script for the first rehearsal of a particular scene, but I try to encourage them to get the lines under their belts for subsequent rehearsals. It's very difficult for actors to be totally in character if they're still having to refer to the written text, and holding a script is clearly limiting as far as physical movement is concerned. It seems to me that a scene only really starts to take off once the lines have been memorised and all copies have been set aside.

Stage terminology

Most directors will use some stage terminology when starting to rehearse the scenes.

Blocking

This refers to the mapping out of the actors' moves. Once the cast has had a chance to rehearse a scene in detail the physical moves of each actor will begin to fall into a regular pattern. This pattern is known as blocking. Once the scene has started to settle the deputy stage manager will make detailed notes so that there's something to reference should the actors forget the blocking in subsequent rehearsals. Some directors are very precise about the actors' moves and once set prefer that they remain fixed. Others have a less rigid approach and allow a certain amount of flexibility. My own personal feeling is that the actors should be allowed some leeway; they shouldn't feel that they're re-producing their performance like a robot. However, too much freedom and there's a danger that the scene unravels and that the work of the other actors is compromised. It's evident that clear guidelines need to be set down from the start so that the actors are fully aware of how much freedom they have in this respect. Once this is established the deputy stage manager should keep an eye on the blocking, gently reminding the actors whenever they stray beyond the agreed parameters.

Upstage/downstage

If asked to go upstage the actors should move towards the back of the stage area, and if requested to go **downstage**, they should move towards the front. Historically stage floors were often wedge-shaped (angled up towards the back and lower in the front). This **rake** effect was, of course, to enable the audience to view the actors more clearly.

Stage right/stage left

This is a somewhat confusing term since, from the director's point of view, it's the opposite of what's expected. Assuming that the actors are facing out towards the audience, they should move to their right if requested to move **stage right**, and to their left if asked to move **stage left**.

Wings

The wings are quite simply the areas to the right and left of the performance space from which the actors enter and exit. This term tends to be used with reference to a conventional proscenium arch configuration.

Flies

The area above the actors' heads from which various stage elements are flown in is called the **flies**. These can include all sorts of things: pieces of set, chandeliers, overhead lamps and even actors on wires.

Privacy in rehearsals

First staging rehearsals can be a nerve-wracking experience for the actors and the creative team alike, and it's important to try to make everyone feel as comfortable as possible. So for the first few rehearsals I try to keep any extraneous people out of the room, so that the actors feel able to experiment, make fools of themselves, and generally engage with the piece in an uninhibited manner. Later on, of course, various other members of the team will need to start watching rehearsals, including the lighting designer, sound designer, wardrobe department and producer. Hopefully by this time, though, the actors will have got to grips with their characters and will be feeling much less self-conscious. Where understudies are concerned it is often best to follow a similar plan and allow the principal actors some breathing space before letting the covers in to watch; it's important not to make the principal cast feel scrutinised or judged during the first few rehearsals.

Creating the right environment

I like to work in a relaxed, collaborative and joyful way and I love the thrill of surprise; the moment when the work becomes more than the sum of its parts, more than any one person could imagine.

EMMA RICE

The rehearsal room should, I believe, be a playground in which the actors are free to experiment – a place where they can laugh and cry and never feel judged. It should be a safe environment which enables them to interact with each other in an unselfconscious fashion. The director and the stage management team need to ensure that nothing jeopardises this creative space. It may seem a bit pedestrian, but all sorts of things can affect the atmosphere in the room, including bad sound-proofing, poor ventilation and inadequate heating. I was recently rehearsing a dance show in a rehearsal space which was absolutely fine when the sun was shining, but when it rained was nothing short of a disaster. We were forced to place large buckets in strategic positions in the room to catch the raindrops which threatened to sabotage the entire rehearsal. This may seem like a comic anecdote, but problems of this sort can very quickly undermine the good work that's taking place in the room, and subsequently create an unhappy, disgruntled group of performers.

Not only does the physical space need to be fit for purpose, but equally important is the attitude of those in the rehearsal room, and this includes not just the actors, but everyone else too. Members of stage management who chat or gossip whilst the director is trying to motivate the company, or rehearsal pianists who sit glued to their mobile phones, can be extremely disruptive. Anyone present in the room needs to contribute something positive to the rehearsal, and this really stems from an interest in the process and a willingness to engage fully in the whole experience.

10
REHEARSALS 3: MUSICAL STAGING

Musical staging is essentially the process of bringing to life a section of the show which is sung or musically underscored. It can be deceptively difficult and requires conscientious preparation and detailed work in the rehearsal room. It can cover anything from the simple blocking of a solo song, such as Hodel's 'Far from the Home I Love' from *Fiddler on the Roof*, to the organisation of a huge ensemble number involving the whole cast; the opening number, 'Tradition', from the same musical, is a good example.

There are no firm rules dictating who'll take responsibility for the musical staging. In some cases it'll be the choreographer, in others it will be the director, and often it's a collaborative process involving both of them. In effect, any section of a show which is neither a full-out dance routine, nor a passage of spoken dialogue, could be described as being suitable for musical staging. If there's movement and music involved, whether this be vocal or purely instrumental, then some degree of musical staging is usually required. A good example of this is the 'Ascot Gavotte' from *My Fair Lady* where a group of haughty aristocrats introduces the Ascot racing scene. It's intended to be satirical and highly stylised, but since the characters are squashed into an enclosure at Ascot there's not much room for expansive choreography. Whilst the movement opportunities may be limited, great fun can be had with synchronised head and upper body movements (not to mention facial expressions) as this snobbish crowd of onlookers scrutinises the racehorses thundering down the track.

An altogether different type of staging challenge arises with a number like 'Over the Moon' from *Rent*. It's intended to be a piece of performance art, and Maureen presents it with a passionate sense of political purpose. It doesn't require dance as such, but it will certainly need some specific movement since Maureen is using her voice and body to deliver her political message. The person staging this number would, in this instance, need to work with the actor playing Maureen to find out how she can best physicalise the story that she's trying to tell. Based on how the actor uses her body, the director or choreographer will

Photo 11 'Two Ladies': *Cabaret*, English Theatre, Frankfurt (Kelly Ryan, Nigel Francis, Melitsa Nicola). (Photo, Bärbel Högner.)

need to build on what comes naturally to her, harnessing her creative ideas and helping to shape them. So the staging of a number such as this becomes truly collaborative, and isn't merely a set of preconceived physical moves grafted onto the performer.

Another useful example of musical staging is 'Two Ladies' from *Cabaret*. The number takes place in the Kit Kat Klub and can be suggestive or outrageous according to the sensibility of the director and choreographer. Depending on the type of performers involved, the piece can be highly choreographed with synchronised movement and intricate dance-steps, or much more 'rough-and-ready', using the acting talents of the trio more than their physical prowess. I worked on a production of this show in Germany where the two Kit Kat girls were both experienced dancers whilst the Emcee was first-and-foremost an actor. The choreographer skilfully managed to incorporate the talents of each of these performers and the result was a combination of daring, inventive dance moves, and quirky, Vaudevillian-style posturing (see Photo 11).

Director/choreographer collaboration

As a director, I find that collaboration with a choreographer can result in some extraordinary discoveries. Before rehearsals began for our production of *Candide*, the choreographer and I decided that we would work together on some of the more stylised sections of the show, including a battle scene, a scene onboard an eighteenth-century galleon, and one set in the mythical land of Eldorado. We decided to workshop our ideas with some willing students at a London drama school, and duly arrived at their studio staggering under the weight of suitable props and assorted paraphernalia. By using ropes, shields, swords, masks and cotton sheets the students were able to improvise these various scenarios and helped us to come up with some ingenious staging solutions. This was a win-win situation since we were able to successfully workshop our ideas, and the students were able to take part in a stimulating session with professional theatre practitioners. Having explored these ideas in a workshop situation we were then able to go into rehearsals with our professional actors with a much clearer idea of how to approach these particular scenes. The students were later invited to a preview of the show to witness the fruits of their labour.

Sharing staging responsibilities with another member of the creative team can, of course, throw up some challenges. It's important that the work of one supports the work of the other; open disagreement can contribute to confusion amongst the cast members. I generally prefer to present a united front to the actors and keep arguments and disputes out of the rehearsal room. Not all directors and choreographers work this way, but I feel that it leads to a healthier atmosphere in the room. Establishing some basic ground rules before rehearsals begin is always helpful. These may include agreeing a certain style of presentation (naturalistic or stylized, for example) and being clear about who has responsibility for each of the staged numbers.

Staging

Staging the ensemble

The ensemble is a common feature of the musical. Certainly, most classic musicals written during the 1930s and 1940s include a large ensemble, and the '**mega-musicals**' originating in the 1980s and 1990s, such as *Miss Saigon*, *Cats* and *Phantom of the Opera* are also shows featuring a sizeable chorus.

There's no one way to stage scenes involving a large ensemble since the function of this group differs from show to show. However, it does make sense to make everyone feel that they have an important contribution to make, and often the best way of doing this is to ensure that all the performers are clear about their character and their motivation. With ensemble work it's all too easy to fall into the trap of generalised reaction. This may be acceptable in some operas (although I'm sceptical about this), but with musical theatre it very seldom works. My strong feeling is that, however small the ensemble rôle, it's still important for the actor to understand how their character fits into the whole picture.

There are various exercises mentioned in Chapter 8 which will help the actors to start creating their characters, and also get a sense of how they fit into the social structure of the piece. The more information the actors have about their characters the more textured the scenes will be. The performers will find this sort of work empowering and it'll make subsequent rehearsals much easier and more satisfying. Once they've got a handle on their characters they'll be able to make interesting and individual choices, even if the directive is simply to cross the stage from one side to the other.

Large ensemble scenes

As previously mentioned, it often makes sense with large numbers of performers to do a certain amount of planning beforehand. Logistically it may not be possible to bring in an entire ensemble from one entrance, for example, so it makes sense to have some idea about who'll appear from where before the start of the rehearsal. With larger numbers it may be wise to split the actors into smaller groups to create some variety of movement, but also to make the whole thing more manageable. With a school production of *Into the Woods*, for example, we split the ensemble into two parts – 'trees' and 'villagers'. Not only did this enable more students to get involved in the project, but it also allowed us to create some dynamic pieces of staging which really helped to tell the story. A favourite moment for me was the sudden formation of a huge human tree which towered above Cinderella's Mother's grave and magically dropped a ball gown and two golden slippers at Cinderella's feet.

Small ensemble scenes

Smaller ensemble scenes are generally easier to manage, partly because there's more time to focus on each character, but also because it's possible to allow the actors themselves to have more input. For example, with *West Side Story* we discovered that Maria's 'I Feel Pretty' worked much better when it felt utterly spontaneous, and so we started by doing a series of improvisations before finally piecing the number together. Our choreographer came in towards the end of the rehearsal to help give the number some shape but was very careful not to interfere with the spontaneity that she saw developing between the characters. In performance the scene sprang to life and never failed to feel joyful and spur-of-the-moment (see Photo 12). The femininity and playfulness of this number provide an interesting contrast with the all-male 'Gee, Officer Krupke' that the Jets sing later in the show in order to distract themselves from the tragic events that are unfolding around them. Once again we discovered that by improvising the song before setting it, many exciting discoveries were made by the actors themselves which felt somehow more appropriate than specific choreographed moves. The choreographer was able to build on these character-driven impulses

Photo 12 'I Feel Pretty': *West Side Story*, Kilworth House Theatre (Annie Guy, Charlie Johnson, Leila Zaidi, Michelle Andrews, Naoimh Morgan). (Photo, Jems Photography.)

and create a number which was funny, troubling and show-stopping, all at the same time.

Focus

It's important to decide what the focal point of any staging moment should be. Many things will draw the eye of the audience, such as bright colours, sudden movement or the specific position of an actor on stage. The lighting will also help to guide the eye, of course, and follow spots can be very useful tools in making sure that the audience witnesses what it needs to see. It's unwise, though, to rely too heavily on lighting and the director and choreographer will need to make focus a priority in the rehearsal room. A fairly obvious example of this would be a song such as 'Oom-Pah-Pah' from *Oliver!* During this number Nancy and the ensemble sing a bawdy drinking song which is usually staged with riotous energy. It's not a number which necessarily requires complex choreography, but it needs to be carefully plotted, with lots of stage business to accompany Nancy's saucy lyrics. If there's too much activity going on around her, however, the audience will inevitably become distracted and Nancy will cease to become the main focus. It's the job of the stager to make sure that the audience keeps Nancy in its sights throughout the entire song and that any background activity supports her and contributes to a clearer telling of the story.

Having established in Chapter 8 the importance of empowering the ensemble actors by helping them to build their characters, it's also worth reminding them that focus is one of the key elements of good staging, and that the audience needs to know where to look at any given moment. For this reason they will require very clear instructions, and these may sometimes conflict with ideas about their own, developing characters. For example, there's a wonderful moment in *Top Hat* when Dale, our heroine, arrives at an elegant soirée dressed in one of the most eye-catching outfits in the entire show – a white feather dress. The whole point is that she's the belle of the ball, and it's vital that when she arrives, everyone notices her. It doesn't matter, in this case, if an ensemble member feels that their character would consciously look away – 'But my character hates her!' Any distractions will weaken the moment, and so for story-telling purposes it's vital that Dale is the focus here.

Actors will inevitably pull focus if they're in a commanding position on the stage. Height will often give an advantage, and an actor standing on a chair, a ladder or a platform will generally be in an authoritative position. The centre of the stage is also a good place to command attention, not least because it's usually visible from every seat in the house. Focus is often difficult to achieve in theatres where the audience is seated at some distance from the actors. This may be due to the size of the auditorium, or simply because there's an orchestra pit separating the audience from the stage. On occasions it can be hard to make out who is actually singing, especially if the voices are amplified and the sound is coming from speakers at the side of the stage. In such cases, the stager needs to help the audience by shifting the focus clearly and deliberately. There are various ways of achieving this, but one of the most obvious is to have the actor move just before singing the solo line. The eye of the audience is drawn by the movement, the actor subsequently becomes the focus, and attention will be given to the vocal line. When there are lots of actors involved, and the lyrics are being thrown from one to the next, as in 'There is Nothin' Like a Dame' from *South Pacific*, it's particularly important to make sure that the focus shifts from performer to performer, otherwise the result is simply chaotic and confusing.

Visual variety

It may seem like a fairly obvious observation, but it's important to maintain visual interest during a show and creating different stage pictures and using every area of the stage is a good way of achieving this. If there are different levels on the set it makes sense to make use of them. I like to think of the stage as a big adventure playground; allowing the actors to explore this playground can result in some great discoveries. If the set includes lamp-posts, staircases, pillars, poles or ladders these can easily be incorporated into the staging, and it's worth encouraging the actors to experiment with them. Of course, health and safety should never be ignored, and stage management will need to keep a watchful eye out for any staging that might be potentially dangerous. Making the most of the stage environment, though, will help to energise the performances, and keep the audience visually stimulated.

Whether staging songs or scenes, it's important to remember that there should always be a reason for any specific piece of blocking. It should never feel as though a character moves for no purpose. An actor who wanders stage left with no motivation will generally look unconvincing, but if there's a reason, such as a new person to talk to, the move is more likely to feel natural and unforced. Depending on the type of piece being presented it's generally not a good idea to keep the actors static for too long. An unchanging stage picture, however striking, is likely to lose its appeal if there's little or no variation. There are, of course, exceptions to every rule, and if the acting is compelling, or the situation suitably riveting, unnecessary movement can sometimes get in the way and become distracting. The director and choreographer will need to use their judgement here, making sure that clear story-telling is at the heart of their decision-making.

Upstaging

Actors will often start to worry if they sense that they're being 'upstaged' by other actors and that the focus isn't on them when it needs to be. **Upstaging** is often the result of stage business occurring at an inappropriate moment and pulling the eye of the audience away from the actor who's speaking or singing. It can also occur when there's an imbalance in the lighting and the key character is in shadow. Actors generally feel that they're being upstaged if they have to turn to deliver a line to someone standing upstage of them. They will often resist this by delivering the line downstage and therefore ignoring the actor they're supposed to be communicating with. This can be avoided to some extent by positioning the listening actor downstage of the actor in question, but if they're having a conversation then it's not really going to solve the problem. Obviously placing the actors side-by-side will help, but it may result in the stage picture looking undynamic and a bit flat.

Upstaging becomes slightly less of an issue with musical theatre mainly because most musicals are mic'd and the voice is therefore heard whether the actor is facing the front or the back. Since directing several productions 'in the round' (see Diagram 2, Chapter 4) I've actually become quite a fan of watching the actors from all angles, and it really doesn't bother me if, from time to time, I'm seeing the back of an actor's head. Audiences seem to be getting more accustomed to this too, and a recent Young Vic production had the audience surrounding a central, slowly-revolving circular stage. This meant that there were moments when a particular actor disappeared completely behind a piece of the set, but this didn't seem to worry the audience; as long as the actors could all be heard clearly, the occasional disappearance of one of them wasn't only perfectly acceptable, but actually added to the dramatic tension of the scene.

Staging the songs

Hearing the lyrics

Song lyrics, especially in the hands of a master lyricist such as Oscar Hammerstein II, can be complex, subtle and illuminating. They often carry emotional weight and can be vital in terms of story-telling. Since they are, in most cases, accompanied by some form of instrumentation it's important to make sure that nothing gets in the way of clarity. For this reason, when working on musicals, I aim to ensure that the audience can hear every single word. Rehearsals are therefore quite often punctuated by frustrated outbursts from either myself or the musical director – 'I can't hear the lyrics!'

With acoustic productions where there's no vocal amplification it makes sense to try to keep the actors facing the front when they're singing solo lines. Not only will this help with audibility but seeing the actors' faces will also enable the audience to understand what's being expressed. Radio mics obviously give the greatest degree of freedom and will allow an actor to face away from the audience without any loss of vocal power. As previously mentioned, this liberates the actor and allows for greater flexibility of movement. Sometimes, though, an inability to hear the lyrics is nothing to do with microphones and everything to do with lack of diction. The musical director will usually be able to help here with vocal exercises focussing on clarity and clear enunciation of consonants.

Solos

People sing because they can no longer express in words what they are feeling; the song takes them to the next stage of emotional storytelling.
JAMES ORANGE

The first question to ask is, what is the purpose of the song? This is something which is often overlooked but which always needs to be addressed. Why was the song written? Is it there to further the story, to explore a character's emotional state, or simply to entertain? Is there an arc to the song, is there any character development, and how has the protagonist changed by the end of the number? Good musical theatre songs will always exist for a reason. It's up to the actor, with help from the director, the musical director and the choreographer, to find answers to these questions.

Solos come in all shapes and sizes; some are like dense, complex **soliloquies** packed full of detail and character development; these can be a huge challenge even for the most experienced performers and will take time to master in the rehearsal room. Other types of solo include the more romantic, lyrical songs written to express emotion, to display the vocal talents of the soloist, and to tug at the heart-strings, such as Amalia's 'Will He Like Me?' from *She Loves Me*. At the other end of the spectrum come the comedy songs, intended to highlight certain character traits, showcase the comedic talents of the performer, and above all, make the audience laugh. Ado Annie's 'I Cain't Say No' from *Oklahoma!* fits neatly into this category.

It seems to me that the best way of approaching solo numbers isn't to do too much blocking beforehand, but to work with the actor, making joint decisions about the staging and allowing the actor's instincts to have at least some influence. There's nothing worse for a performer than being shoe-horned into a preconceived sequence of moves which feel unconnected to the character they're attempting to portray. The director may, of course, have some staging ideas in mind when approaching the song, but it's a good idea to remain flexible and to workshop these ideas with the actor before setting them in stone. With a recent production of *Kiss Me, Kate*, the choreographer and I worked together on Kate's solo 'I Hate Men'. Traditionally this number is presented with Kate on stage alone singing straight out to the audience. We decided that a more interesting approach would be for our heroine to interact with various townsfolk who would appear and disappear throughout the song. This led to many great suggestions from the actor playing Kate, lots of unexpected humour, and some enthusiastic audience reaction. What on paper comes across as a rather repetitive number, in performance blossomed into something funny, quirky and vibrant.

Solos featured in shows from the 1930s, 1940s and 1950s often begin with a musical introduction, a short section of music which pre-empts the singer. In the wrong hands this can create an awkward hiatus between the spoken dialogue of the previous scene and the main content of the song. It's important that the drama doesn't grind to a halt during these musical introductions, and the performer needs to take great care to act through them and use them as a springboard into the number. Such moments can actually be extremely effective, and sometimes very touching, as the actor sets the emotional tone for the ensuing song. In *Top Hat*, for example, as the musical introduction begins for her solo 'Better Luck Next Time', Dale slowly takes out a flower that in the previous scene she's been given by Jerry, the man she's fallen in love with. It's a simple piece of business, but this action, combined with the haunting Irving Berlin music, makes perfect theatrical sense and reminds the audience of the highly-charged romantic scene which played out only moments before. At the end of the solo Dale realises that this is a doomed love affair and regretfully tosses the flower away, thus book-ending this bitter-sweet song perfectly.

Soliloquies

As someone who loves to sing, musical theatre enables me to directly address an audience in a way you don't often get a chance to in straight plays. I love breaking the 4th wall and having a direct connection with the audience.

SHARON D CLARKE

Many musicals feature soliloquies, which are essentially monologues intended to express the private thoughts of the featured character and often concern their romantic aspirations, their hopes and fears, or the various challenges facing them. They are usually performed with just a single actor on the stage. Good examples of this type of song include 'Soliloquy' from *Carousel* and 'Meadowlark' from *The Baker's Wife*. In the former the carousel barker, Billy Bigelow, having just heard that his wife is pregnant, sings about the joys of fatherhood, first envisaging a young son, and then realising that the baby might be a little girl. He finally decides that in order to give his child a chance in life he'll need to make money, and he resolves, by the end of the song, to do anything to achieve this end, therefore setting the scene for the disastrous robbery in Act 2 and his subsequent shocking death. There's a lot of information in this particular song, and Billy's emotional journey is skilfully revealed in a dramatic, but also poetic manner. It is a master-class in story-telling and seems to me to be one of the finest examples of a sung monologue to be found anywhere in musical theatre.

In 'Meadowlark' Stephen Schwartz presents a similar moment of personal revelation in the form of a fable. The baker's young wife, Geneviève, sings about a mythical lark which falls in love with a beautiful young god but has to abandon her protector, the King, in order to follow her romantic dream. This parallels Geneviève's own personal dilemma, and by the end of the song she resolves to leave her new husband and run off with a dashing young suitor. An extraordinarily touching piece of writing, this monologue allows the audience a unique insight into the thoughts and feelings of this struggling, vulnerable woman and provides the actor playing Geneviève with a powerful, and potentially show-stopping number.

There's a huge amount of detail in both these narrative songs, and in staging them various decisions will need to be made. Most importantly, who is the protagonist singing to? It may be theatrical convention for a character alone on stage to voice their inner thoughts in the form of a song, but it's not always clear where the focus of the song actually lies. It seems to me that there are several choices. The character can address the audience as though the inner debate has become externalised; this results in a very direct relaying of ideas and an acknowledgement that the audience is sharing this particular communication. On the other hand, a different directorial choice would be to allow the audience members to remain as observers, with the singer expressing inner emotions but without specifically focussing out to the audience. Both are valid and can be extremely effective; the director will need to decide which version is most appropriate and make sure that there's a consistency of approach throughout the entire show.

Lyrics as text

With most well-written musicals the lyrics will stand up on their own, and a good exercise in the early stages of rehearsals is to separate them from the music and to encourage the performers to use them as a script, without referring to the music at all. This forces the actor to concentrate on the content of the song, its themes, images and the subtleties and nuances of its lyrics. It's surprising how illuminating this can be; without the preoccupation of having to navigate the various technical challenges of the song, the actor can focus entirely on the meaning and the emotional content.

This approach also works well with duets, providing an opportunity for the actors to work off each other and to explore the lyrics as dialogue. A passage, such as the wonderful scene towards the start of *Carousel* which introduces the awkward, touching courtship of Billy and Julie, can therefore be played as a dialogue scene, relieving the actors of any vocal anxieties and allowing them to focus exclusively on the text. As it stands, the scene dips in and out of dialogue, weaving underscored spoken sections with sung passages of great lyrical beauty. With a well-crafted scene such as this one, separating the lyrics from the music can pay dividends as the actors start to explore the language and begin to move away from a more generalised presentation of the scene towards something more intimate, layered and compelling. Once this sort of initial exploration has taken place, the musical element can be restored and the scene can be rehearsed as written. By now, though, some sort of alchemical change will have occurred as the actors start to connect more instinctively with the subtleties of the language.

Billy: Well, anyway . . . you don't love me. That's what you said.

Julie: Yes.

Some blossoms drift down to their feet. Billy picks one up and smells it.

          I can smell them, can you? The blossoms? The wind brings them down.

Billy: Ain't much wind tonight. Hardly any.

          (*Sings*) *YOU CAN'T HEAR A SOUND, NOT THE TURN OF A LEAF,*
          NOR THE FALL OF A WAVE HITTIN' THE SAND.
          THE TIDE'S CREEPIN' UP ON THE BEACH LIKE A THIEF,
          AFRAID TO BE CAUGHT STEALIN' THE LAND.
          ON A NIGHT LIKE THIS I START TO WONDER
          WHAT LIFE IS ALL ABOUT.

Julie: *AND I ALWAYS SAY TWO HEADS ARE BETTER THAN ONE TO*
          FIGGER IT OUT.

Billy: I don't need you or anyone to help me. I got it figgered out for myself. We ain't important. What are we? A couple of specks of nothin'.

                                        Carousel – Act 1, scene 2

Photo 13 'Tonight': *West Side Story*, Kilworth House Theatre (Liam Doyle, Leila Zaidi). (Photo, Jems Photography.)

Love duets

Duets, especially love duets, can be problematic to stage as they often involve two people in close proximity, and this can sometimes have the effect of excluding the audience, or at least making it hard to see the actors' faces. With a love duet I will often try to keep the actors apart for as long as possible so that the moment when they come together feels as if it's been earned, and doesn't seem like a repetition. If the writing's good, of course, these problems often solve themselves. A fine example of this is the exquisite balcony scene from *West Side Story* when the two young lovers meet alone for the first time. Because Maria is on a balcony, and Tony is down below on the street, there's already an obstacle to their union, and watching how they overcome this is one of the great pleasures of the scene. Even when Tony manages to scale the wall and scramble onto the balcony, however, they only have time for a stolen kiss before the voice of Maria's protective father warns Tony away. Maria follows him down to the street, and in our production we continued to keep the lovers apart at this point by placing them either side of a wire fence as if the world was intent on separating them too (see Photo 13).

Rehearsing musical comedy

Musicals are often referred to as **musical comedies**. It's not a title which suits every show, of course, as witnessed by some of Kander and Ebb's darker works:

Kiss of the Spiderwoman and *Cabaret*, for example. In fact the history of musical theatre is peppered with works which defy that description; even as early as 1927 audiences were witnessing musicals as challenging as *Show Boat*, a story which features racial division, alcoholism and claims of historic murder. Many musicals, on the other hand, are unashamedly light and entertaining and need to be staged with a deft touch (see Photo 14). Shows like *Kiss Me, Kate*, *Anything Goes* or *Babes In Arms* are packed full of wonderful tunes. Without clever, sparkling choreography, though, and characterful, charismatic performances, the comedy in these musicals can sometimes feel dated and a little underwhelming. Until the show is presented to an audience, of course, no one really knows how funny it actually is. And therein lies one of the difficulties of rehearsing musical comedy – we can only find out if it's funny by putting it in front of a live theatre audience. Until then we just have to trust our instincts and hope for the best.

Watching each other's scenes in rehearsal the actors will often laugh and cry in all the right places, but these responses aren't always representative of an authentic theatre audience. Besides, this reaction will inevitably subside as rehearsals continue; after all, even the funniest bit of stage business isn't funny when you've seen it fifteen times. The cast reaction will sometimes diminish to the point where the actors begin to doubt whether there's a single witty line in the whole show. 'It's just not funny anymore' is a leitmotif which I often hear towards the end of the rehearsal period. It's time to remind the performers how they felt when they first sat listening to the read-through, or how they reacted when they watched the scenes come to life in the early stages of rehearsal. They

Photo 14 Musical comedy: *Kiss Me, Kate*, Kilworth House Theatre (Matthew McKenna, Caroline Sheen). (Photo, Jems Photography.)

may, however, have to wait until there's a real audience out there in the dark before their faith is fully restored. At this point the cast will almost certainly regain confidence, realising with relief that the comedy was there all along, it just needed the spontaneous reaction of a fresh audience to reignite it.

Run-throughs

The first run-through should, in my opinion, be as relaxed as possible, and it's generally better if there aren't too many onlookers. Occupants of the room should include only the actors, the stage management, the director, the choreographer, the musical director and the rehearsal pianist. Other members of the team, including the producer, should join at a later date for a **producer's run** once the cast members are more secure in their performances.

Since runs in the rehearsal room are joint enterprises involving both actors and stage management, this particular subject will be explored in more detail in the next chapter. However, it's worth mentioning here that in my experience actors feel much more comfortable once they've had a chance to run the show in its entirety. It is advisable not to leave this until too late in the process or the performers will start to feel understandably anxious. Even a shambolic run has certain benefits, and seeing the whole thing, even if it's rough and slightly chaotic, will help to focus on those aspects of the show which need more attention. By the second run many problems will have been ironed-out and the shape of the show will start to become much more clearly defined.

11

REHEARSALS 4:
STAGE MANAGEMENT
RESPONSIBILITIES

A good stage manager should be enthusiastic above all else. I love a generous spirit who will join in company games and know they are a valued and integrated part of the team.

EMMA RICE

Previously I've looked at rehearsals with particular reference to the creative team and the company of actors. In this chapter the focus will be on stage management and its contribution to the rehearsal process. Whilst it's clear that one of the most joyful aspects of staging musicals is the way in which the different departments work together, I'm choosing, for the sake of clarity, to separate the rehearsal process into two parts, one creative, the other practical. I'm not suggesting, however, that the actors, production team and stage management operate solely within their own little bubbles. The reality is quite the opposite – everyone works together. I've already given a fairly detailed account of the various tasks that fall to each member of the stage management team (see Chapter 6). Now it's time to show how they all work together to provide vital support for the actors and the creative team throughout rehearsals. As mentioned previously, there are slight differences in job description with stage management teams in the US (see 'Stage management in the US', p. 94).

Before rehearsals

It's not unusual for the stage management team to be assembled fairly late in the day, and they often have to hit the ground running when it comes to assessing the production and its specific needs. The best way of doing this is for the stage manager to talk in detail with the producer and the director to get an overall sense of how they're planning to approach the show. Advance knowledge of the rehearsal space is of primary importance, and the stage manager will want to know the following details.

1 Are there suitable transport links to the rehearsal rooms and nearby parking? If anyone in the company has any specific needs the subject of access may also be relevant. This information, alongside address and contact details for the venue, should be conveyed to the company before rehearsals begin.

2 How many rehearsal rooms are available, and what are their dimensions? It makes sense for the main rehearsal space to be at least as large as the stage area on which the show is to be performed, and ideally it'll be quite a lot larger than that so that there's space for the creative team to watch rehearsals from a reasonable vantage point.

3 Is there a company office? This is often a small room close to the main rehearsal space. The stage management will usually take over this area and share it with the company manager.

4 How many changing rooms are there on site? The performers will clearly need somewhere to change, and ideally this will include shower facilities, especially if the show involves a lot of dance.

5 Is there a piano or keyboard in the rehearsal room? Rehearsal room pianos are subject to lots of wear-and-tear and they're often not in the best condition and seldom in tune, so it's best to check with the musical director to make sure that the instruments provided are suitable. If not then keyboards will need to be brought in, and this will obviously have a financial implication. The producer will need to be involved in this discussion.

6 Is there adequate space for a drum kit in the rehearsal room? Often a drummer will be introduced at some point during rehearsals for a musical, and it's wise to factor this in from the start.

7 Are there enough chairs in the rehearsal room for the whole company for the first day of rehearsals? This may be the only time when this number of seats is required, but it's important to check in advance as you don't want to have members of the company sitting on the floor during the initial read-through.

8 Are there enough copies of the script? If there's to be a read-through on the first day the stage manager will need to check that there are enough copies for the actors and for various members of the production team. Some of the principals may, of course, have already received scripts and scores before rehearsals begin.

9 What activities will take place on the first day of rehearsals? If the director has any intention of getting the actors to do anything physical on the first day, theatre games or preliminary dance rehearsals, for example,

the stage manager should pre-warn the actors so that they can bring along suitable clothing.

10 What supplies are needed for the first day of rehearsals? Some producers like to begin with an informal meet-and-greet, and this often involves tea, coffee and biscuits (or doughnuts if the producer's feeling generous). This will usually be organised by stage management.

Clearly the stage manager will need to liaise with the director before the start of rehearsals to find out what activities are intended for the first few days. A rough schedule will usually be devised which will probably need to be amended as everyone starts to get to grips with the process. The stage manager will also need to find out what the director and designer have in mind for the first day's design presentation. They may require a projection screen to show images of the set and costume designs, for example. The choreographer may also want to play sections of music to the cast or start the ball rolling with some basic movement. Suitable sound equipment will need to be available in this case. Stage management will also want to know when a mark-up is required and what rehearsal props will be needed for the first few days of rehearsal.

Starting rehearsals

The first day of rehearsals is a busy time for all involved. I've already explained in some detail what a standard first day might look like (see Chapter 7). The stage management, whilst facilitating these various activities, will also need to start preparing for the rest of the rehearsal period.

Mark-up

The mark-up (taping in the US) is quite simply a representation of the set marked out in coloured tape on the floor of the rehearsal room; the dimensions should be exactly the same as the set. Most directors won't get around to doing much specific blocking on the first day, so it's usually fine to leave the marking out of the space until rehearsals begin. This can be done whilst the actors are having their lunch, or at the end of the day. Before laying down the mark-up the stage manager will need to liaise with the director and choreographer to find out how they intend to use the rehearsal space. There's no point doing a complicated mark-up only to discover that the director wants to use the room in a different way. This may be to do with the position of the door, the light from the windows, the general shape of the rehearsal space, or simply down to personal preference. Also, rehearsal rooms often have mirrors running the length of one wall. These can be very useful in dance rehearsals, but very distracting when the actors are playing a scene. Ideally there will be curtains to hide these mirrors when not required, but if there's no way of concealing them, it's probably best to do the mark-up with the mirrors at the back or the side of the room.

The creative team will need some space in front of the acting area so that they can see how the show will look from an audience point-of-view. If they're nose-to-nose with the performers with their backs pinned against the rehearsal room wall it'll be very hard to judge the work objectively. Later in the rehearsal process it's useful for the stage manager to set up a **production desk** in front of the stage area so that the creative team can watch the show and take notes. There will need to be adequate space for this too.

Once these various issues have been addressed the mark-up can commence. Usually it's supervised by the stage manager who will reference the ground plan in order to work out the exact dimensions of the stage design. Using coloured tape, the stage management will then create a fantastic spider's web of markings on the floor which will represent to the actors the size and complexity of the stage design. All doorways and entrances/exits should be indicated, and if the set is designed as a series of levels, then this should also be clear from the layout. Once this has been done to the satisfaction of the director the cast members should be given a tour of the newly marked-up room so that it's clear to them what the various coloured strips represent. From this point onwards the director and choreographer will adapt their work to ensure that it fits in the space available. Occasionally the mark-up may need to be renewed as it can get quite a battering during rehearsals, especially if tap-dancing is involved.

Rehearsal schedules

During the first few days of rehearsals the director, with help from the choreographer and the musical director, will work out the first of a series of rehearsal schedules, usually planning one or two days in advance. Sometimes the stage manager will assist with this, especially if there are complications such as wardrobe or wig fittings. The director should take great care to call actors only when they're needed, since having them hanging around for hours is counter-productive and can contribute to a bad atmosphere in the room.

Schedules are rather like jigsaw puzzles and can be complicated to organise. In the case of split calls (see Diagram 4, Chapter 9) it's important to double-check that no actor is expected to be in two places at the same time. Stage management (usually the deputy stage manager) should make sure that the schedule is neatly laid out and unambiguous so that no confusions arise. After all, there is nothing more annoying for a director than a half-attended rehearsal, and nothing so frustrating for an actor as a missed one.

Once the schedule's finalised the stage manager or deputy stage manager will send it out to the company, also posting a copy in the rehearsal room so that the actors can refer to it throughout the day. The schedule will usually include the following details:

- The location of each rehearsal.
- The names of the actors required.
- The start and finish time.
- The scenes, songs or dances to be rehearsed.
- The name(s) of the creative team member(s) in charge.

Props

Even the simplest of productions will usually require some props (see Photo 15). The term refers to anything on stage which is handled by the actors and which isn't a piece of costume or a part of the set. There are various types of props, some which will need to be replaced on a regular basis, some which may be eaten during each performance, and some which will need to be repaired, re-polished or re-painted from time to time.

Items of furniture, such as chairs and tables, are often referred to as stage furniture and are usually the responsibility of the set designer. If the piece is very specific, perhaps needing to be painted in a similar way to the rest of the set, it will probably be handed over to the set builders, but if there's a props supervisor

Photo 15 The props desk: *Candide*, Menier Chocolate Factory. (Photo, Nobby Clark.)

on board then they might source or even make the required item themselves. If, however, it can be easily purchased off-the-shelf then it's more likely that the assistant stage managers will take responsibility for it. Whichever department builds, buys or sources it, the designer will need to be in close contact with them and will ultimately have the final say. The assistant stage managers will usually list these pieces as props in order to keep track of them, even if strictly speaking they are more aligned to the set.

Props list

At the start of rehearsals, a member of stage management (often an assistant stage manager) will liaise with the designer in order to begin compiling a provisional props list. This is easily done by reading through the script and noting any props which are specified in the text. Some scripts helpfully include a fairly comprehensive props list to use as a starting point. The director may, of course, end up dispensing with any or all of these suggestions, and will almost certainly want to add additional props once rehearsals are underway.

A provisional list is useful for several reasons. Firstly, an assistant stage manager can start to think of suitable items to use as rehearsal props, so that when it comes to a new scene and the director suddenly requires a briefcase, or a parasol, they'll have something to offer up. These rehearsal props will usually be up-graded once they've been confirmed by the director and a show prop will subsequently appear, often in time for the final runs in the rehearsal room, but always in time for the tech. Secondly, the list is useful since it flags up any unusual items which may need to be hired or specially built, and the sooner the director, designer and stage management are aware of this the better.

We soon discovered in rehearsals for Candide *that one of the leading characters, the pedantic tutor Pangloss, would need to be in a small boat for one specific scene. Since the style of the production was tongue-in-cheek the boat didn't need to be realistic, but was required to be very light so that the actor could move about in it. Our assistant stage managers searched high and low, but in the event were unable to find anything suitable. Consequently, with assistance from the designer and production manager, a bamboo framework was constructed for our Pangloss to 'wear', and this was used in rehearsals to represent the boat. Once we knew what was required of both actor and prop we were able to refine the design and make it look more like a suitably nautical vessel. It always had a slightly make-shift feel about it, though, which totally suited the production (see Photo 16).*

Photo 16 Pangloss in the boat: *Candide*, Menier Chocolate Factory (James Dreyfus). (Photo, Nobby Clark.)

Props budget

Most shows will have some sort of props budget and this needs to be managed wisely. There's no point investing in expensive props at the start of rehearsals as they may end up being cut by the end of the first week; it's not unusual for a director or an actor to jettison a prop having experimented with it for a couple of days. If the stage management team is over-zealous with the budget in the early stages there may be financial issues further down the line, so it's important to wait until firm decisions have been made before investing in anything costly.

Specialised props

Conversely, there are some props which will need more consideration right from the start. If they're likely to be used for any stage 'business', such as a knife, a gun or even a walking stick, it makes sense to get the right prop sooner rather than later since the actor will need to get used to it before various bits of staging can be finalised. With our production of *Top Hat* the choreographer was insistent, quite rightly, that the ensemble members were issued early in rehearsals with the correct canes for a complicated dance routine. The weight and size of these canes had a significant impact on their use, and the routine could not really be choreographed until the actual show props turned up.

Stage furniture

If the set design includes furniture of any description, or a specific piece of set which the actors might utilise, a fence or a lamp-post, for example, suitable substitutes should be found until the proper items are available so that the actors have something to work with in rehearsals. Since there's usually very little time on stage during the tech to re-block scenes or to work out complicated bits of business, it's worth trying to get as much sorted in the rehearsal room as possible. Our design for *The Addams Family* included two sets of moveable stairs which were positioned differently for each successive scene. We actually had two skeleton sets of stairs brought into rehearsals so that we had something tangible to work with. Whilst this wasn't a cheap solution, it certainly helped us to get to grips with the scene changes well before we reached the theatre and therefore saved us lots of time in the tech.

Show props

As the rehearsals progress and the director, choreographer and actors work out what is needed for each scene, the provisional props list will slowly transform into a definitive one. Usually the designer will be heavily involved in making decisions about props, especially those which need to have a period feel and which may look out of place if they're not carefully chosen. On some commercial productions with larger budgets the services of a props supervisor or **props maker** may be required to design and make soft furnishings such as curtains and cushions, and they will sometimes be tasked with making more unusual items such as bespoke wedding cakes, table decorations and half-eaten meals. A suitably gruesome delicacy was required for the banquet scene in *The Addams Family*; this was out-sourced to a props maker, and the results were delightfully ghoulish (see Photo 17).

There are many specialist prop hire companies listed on the internet, and shopping online is the easiest and most time-efficient way of handling this particular task. Alternatively, trawling round charity shops and second-hand stalls can result in some cheap, and often very suitable purchases. Local shops will sometimes help out in return for a mention in the programme, and it may also be possible to track down other companies who've done past productions of the same show; if they're no longer in need of various props they may be persuaded to lend them out on a temporary basis.

Some items, though, may be impossible to source and will have to be specially made, either by the designer, a member of stage management or a specialist props maker. On a particularly prop-heavy production of Sondheim's *Into the Woods*, one of our tasks was to find a white cow with a hinged jaw which would be able to 'eat' various articles: a red cape, an ear of corn and a golden slipper. It was also required to move about the stage accompanying

Photo 17 The banquet: *The Addams Family*, UK tour (Valda Aviks, Les Dennis, Dickon Gough). (Photo, Matt Martin.)

Jack on his journey into the forest. Not surprisingly, this prop was nowhere to be found and had to be specially made by a very frazzled member of the stage management team.

Props setting list

As rehearsals progress, a props setting list will need to be drawn up by the deputy stage manager; this will ultimately be handed to the assistant stage managers and become their responsibility. This list is a detailed account of where each prop will be located, and who's responsible for it. There is usually a 'shout check' before each performance, during which members of stage management read out every item on the list and visually check each prop.

Some props need pre-setting and will be placed onstage by an assistant stage manager either before the show begins or during a scene change. Others will be set offstage on a props table and clearly divided up so that the actors can easily pick them up before going on stage. Some, called **personal props**, will be pre-set in the actors' dressing-rooms. These tend to be items that the actors can carry themselves, such as cigarette lighters, handkerchiefs, spectacles, watches and other types of jewellery. It's wise, though, for the assistant stage managers to double-check with the actors before they go on stage that they have their personal props with them, particularly those which are integral to the action of a scene. Some show props will need replacing on a regular basis, including any food and drink which is consumed during the performance. Newspapers and letters, which often start to look tatty after several days, will also need to be replaced regularly too.

By the end of rehearsals there should be a definitive props list (created by the assistant stage managers) and a provisional props setting list (created by the deputy stage manager). Obviously, some details concerning the latter can only be finalised once the company has moved into the theatre and stage management has had a chance to work out the best way of utilising the backstage areas. Final decisions about the placement of props tables and more specific information about the use of backstage areas will have to wait until the technical rehearsals begin.

Deputy stage manager in rehearsals

A good deputy stage manager is a key member of the team (see Chapter 6). Not only will they run the rehearsal room, taking blocking notes, liaising with the assistant stage managers about props and scene changes, and generally keeping an eye on the cast, but crucially they will also cue the show in performance. During rehearsals they will spend most of their time in the main rehearsal space taking detailed notes and setting them out clearly in the prompt copy (or prompt book).

Prompt copy

The prompt copy is essentially the production bible; it contains information which is slowly gathered throughout rehearsals so that by the time the actors move into the theatre it's usually overflowing with lighting cues, sound cues and detailed information about scene changes and blocking. It also includes any script alterations that have taken place during rehearsals. The prompt copy is usually constructed by taking the script and the score, dividing them into separate pages, and inserting them into a large folder or ring-binder. On one side will be displayed the script or score, and on the other specific numbered cue points and concise instructions about blocking, usually colour-coded so that the deputy stage manager can tell at a glance where to find certain bits of information. Since blocking inevitably develops as rehearsals progress, much of the detail in the prompt copy will change from one rehearsal to the next. And this process doesn't stop once the production moves into the theatre. Nothing is set in stone until the show officially opens, and in some cases this isn't until the end of a lengthy preview period. Consequently, the deputy stage manager is forever writing things in pencil and then rubbing them out again.

Once the production reaches the theatre, the prompt copy becomes the nerve-centre for the whole show. For this reason it's vital that the deputy stage manager makes all notation legible, so that if ever someone else is called in to cue the show at the last minute, the information in the prompt book can be easily deciphered. The golden rule concerning this vital resource is that once it reaches the theatre, it doesn't leave until the show closes. After all, if this book were to go missing, the entire show would grind to a halt. A sensible deputy stage manager, of course, will make a digital version or **e-prompt copy** as a back-up.

Prompting in rehearsals

During rehearsals, in addition to note-taking the deputy stage manager will keep a watchful eye on the script and prompt the actors whenever necessary. Any cuts or script changes implemented by the director will also be noted. As far as prompting is concerned, certain rules will need to be set out at the start of rehearsals. It's customary for an actor to say 'line' or just 'yes' when they forget a scripted line. It's important to stick to the agreed rules and an actor who starts shouting 'prompt! prompt!' indiscriminately is likely to be frowned on by the other performers. Conversely it can be very distracting for the actors if they pause for breath (or for dramatic effect) and the deputy stage manager bowls in with an immediate prompt. Prompting is a delicate task and needs to be approached sensitively; it takes a certain amount of experience to know when to prompt a performer and the deputy stage manager will have to remain focussed and flexible, particularly during early rehearsals. Some actors will approximate their lines for a while until they've got the scene firmly under their belts and prompting them may be distracting or cause them to stray even further from the script.

If a prompt is required the deputy stage manager should deliver it clearly and unapologetically. Attempting to be discreet about this is usually counter-productive and it can be very unsettling for the actor if the prompt is inaudible and they're forced to ask for it a second time. In the case of a confident actor who never asks for help, but constantly paraphrases the lines, the deputy stage manager should make a note during the rehearsal of these approximated lines and find a convenient moment to talk to the actor later and correct any mistakes. It is best not to interrupt the flow of the rehearsal for minor script inaccuracies but finding the actor in a coffee break to chat things through is perfectly acceptable. Letting the actor get away with script errors will lead to general sloppiness and an inaccurate rendition of the piece, so it really is worth correcting these mistakes as early as possible.

In my experience prompting in performance happens extremely rarely. By the time the production arrives on stage the deputy stage manager will have far too much to do cueing the show and keeping an eye on things backstage; prompting won't usually be a priority. Actors tend to rely on each other during performance, and if a line gets dropped one of the other cast members will usually come to the rescue. Actors are pretty instinctive in these situations and usually find a way of helping their fellow performers out of a hole.

Sound effects

As rehearsals progress it'll become increasingly clear which sound effects are going to be used in the show. The deputy stage manager will make a list of these and note specific cue points in the prompt copy. A member of the sound department, usually the sound designer, will then source these effects and check with the director to see if they're appropriate. It's always good to have a choice at this stage as sound effects vary enormously; the sound of a clock, for example, can range from the sonorous pealing of Big Ben to the faint chimes of a carriage clock. It helps if the sound designer is given precise instructions from the start, and early discussions with the director will obviously make this task a lot easier.

Some sounds are very difficult to reproduce, and in certain circumstances a live effect will be more suitable. For example, trying to replicate the sound of gunshot is surprisingly difficult and it's much better to use a prop gun firing blanks than a pre-recorded version. There are obvious health and safety issues when using guns and this will, of course, need to be taken into consideration. Other sounds which are hard to replicate include the sound of smashing glass and also that of rainfall. For some reason both these sounds often come across as unconvincing once they're pre-recorded and amplified through a sound system.

Depending on the show, it's sometimes a good idea to introduce sound effects during rehearsals, rather than waiting until the technical rehearsals on stage. This will enable the actors to get used to them and will also give the deputy stage manager a chance to start cueing them. With shows which are very cue heavy this can be extremely productive and can make the tech a lot less stressful for everyone. It's fairly easy to set this up assuming that stage management has access to a laptop and a spare set of speakers. In the second half of *Into the Woods* there's a scene in which the Giant's pre-recorded voice is heard, whilst the Giant herself remains invisible. Each one of her scripted lines will need to be cued independently, and this may take some time for the deputy stage manager and the actors to get used to. Hearing the sound cues in the rehearsal room will definitely speed things up in preparation for the tech and dress rehearsal.

Safety

Stage management will need to keep a close eye on all aspects of safety in the rehearsal room. Since the deputy stage manager is usually present in rehearsals, any concerns can be flagged up immediately if it looks as though a piece of staging may be potentially dangerous. In the giddy whirl of the rehearsal room it's not unheard of for a director or choreographer to turn a blind eye to health and safety and to allow the actors to experiment with physical work which is actually beyond their capabilities, or which may simply be impossible to repeat night after night. A subtle word in the director's ear may just save an actor from being rushed into hospital with a broken limb. In my experience, anything which isn't flagged up by stage management is usually identified by the production manager, who will often have a clearer idea of the potential hazards once the actors reach the stage. With our production of *West Side Story*, for example, our production manager was particularly concerned about a scene which required the actor playing Tony to scale some scaffolding leading up to Maria's balcony. This action had to be repeatedly rehearsed slowly and calmly until everyone was satisfied that there was minimal risk involved.

It's important for stage management to monitor the number of hours that the actors are working since the latter will need to be alert at all times, and tiredness in the theatre can be hazardous. In professional theatre, of course, over-running in rehearsals has very clear financial implications, but it's just as important to regulate the hours of a group of unpaid actors, and stage management should try to ensure that they're given regular breaks and that they're not expected to work ridiculously long hours, especially as the performance dates loom ever closer.

Communication

A crucial part of the deputy stage manager's job is to make sure that any decisions reached during rehearsals are immediately disseminated to the appropriate departments. If an actor is expected to climb a tree, or jump onto a fence, this information needs to be conveyed to the set builders so that specific parts of the set can be reinforced. There's no point reaching the technical rehearsals only to find that various bits of staging are impossible because no one has passed on vital information. Similarly, with reference to lighting, if a special effect is required – a stroboscope, mirror ball or a specific gobo, for example – the lighting designer will need to know this in advance so that the correct equipment can be hired and installed. The deputy stage manager acts as a sort of go-between and will liaise with all other members of the production team to facilitate good communication. They will usually send out a rehearsal report via e-mail on a daily basis to all relevant departments (see p. 163).

As far as communication with the theatre or performance venue is concerned, the production manager will usually liaise with the theatre management concerning a running time for the show, the number of intervals required, and whether there are likely to be any of the following: loud noises, gun-shots, stroboscopic effects, nudity or strong language.

Production meetings

Production meetings are organised regularly during rehearsals and should involve the heads of each department. The production manager or stage manager will usually chair the meeting and will ask each representative in turn briefly to outline how things are going in their separate departments. It's also an opportunity for the director to give some feed-back concerning rehearsals and for members of the production team to voice any particular concerns. For those people whose work takes place mainly outside the rehearsal room, such as the set, costume, lighting and sound designers, these production meetings provide an excellent opportunity to ensure that their departments are working in tandem with the ongoing work in the rehearsal room. The producer should always try to be available for these production meetings as decisions taken at this stage will often have financial implications. The producer will also be anxious to find out how rehearsals are progressing, especially if there has been no opportunity to observe them at first hand.

These meetings also provide a good opportunity for the heads of department to discuss a provisional technical schedule. The production manager, with help from the designer, should be able to estimate the time it'll take to construct the set in the theatre, the lighting designer will do the same for the rigging and focussing of the lights, and the sound designer will calculate the time it'll take to install suitable sound equipment. With this information at their fingertips the producer, production manager and director should be able to come up with a realistic technical schedule. Where possible, someone from stage management should take the minutes at these meetings, so that any members of the production team who aren't present can catch up later and access any relevant information.

Wardrobe fittings

Costume design, unlike set design, will often remain flexible throughout much of the rehearsal process. This makes the costume designer's job more last-minute, and therefore more stressful. For this reason it's vital that costume fittings are factored into the schedule so that the designer and wardrobe staff get a chance to fit the actors with their costumes and make subsequent alterations or changes in good time.

The job of scheduling is often delegated to the deputy stage manager who will try to organise the costume fittings without wasting precious rehearsal time. Stage management will usually supervise these fittings and make sure that the actors arrive at the designated time and return to rehearsals promptly afterwards. This is important as a late arrival will create a knock-on effect meaning that actors are subsequently missing from a staging call. Some performers will also require wig fittings and these should also be organised to dove-tail with the directors' rehearsals.

Pre-empting the tech

Since there never seems to be enough time to tech a show properly it makes sense to try and solve some problems whilst still in the rehearsal room. Assuming that the wardrobe department has been able to organise the correct costumes, quick changes can be looked at in rehearsals and subsequent adjustments can be made swiftly and efficiently. Quick changes aren't usually dependent on the set or the lighting, so they can just as easily be rehearsed before the tech. In our production of *The Producers*, the actress playing Ulla had several jaw-droppingly quick costume changes in the course of her first number, 'When You've Got It, Flaunt It'. Because the costumes were ready in advance we had time to work them into the number before she ever reached the stage, therefore saving us lots of tech time.

In the same musical we decided to try pre-empting some stage business by bringing a selection of scenic elements into the rehearsal room. The set designer had created a series of desks for Leo Bloom's 'I Wanna Be A Producer' which each contained a hidden showgirl. During the number the girls were to emerge spectacularly as if from a magician's cabinet. Having these desks in rehearsal in their basic form (without paint or decoration) made it possible for the choreographer to work out the precise staging for this number, without having to leave anything to chance. This meant that once we arrived on stage the routine was very quickly blocked during the **spacing call**, and precious time was saved.

Rehearsal photos

As far as rehearsal photographs are concerned the company manager, or stage manager, will liaise with the production office; these photos will generally feature the entire cast and sometimes the creative team too. They're intended to represent a rough 'work-in-progress' rather than a glossy final result and will often be featured in the theatre programme. As a courtesy to the cast it's important that the actors are warned in advance about forthcoming photo sessions; whilst the pictures may be intended to look like informal rehearsal shots, the performers may wish to make the odd adjustment to their make-up or outfit so that they don't end up looking as though they've just tumbled out of bed.

Obtaining licences

Depending upon the specific requirements of the piece, the production manager, the production office or the stage manager may need to consider obtaining a licence for one or more of the following:

Children

There are strict rules concerning the appearance of children in professional theatrical productions and a licence will need to be obtained from the relevant local authority before a child actor can appear on stage. If in doubt the production office should contact Equity (UK), Actor's Equity (US) or the relevant local authority, preferably prior to the start of rehearsals.

Firearms

It's necessary to obtain a firearms licence before using a firing gun on stage. There are also specific regulations which apply to the handling of guns in the theatre. A gun must never be left unattended in the wings, for example, and when not in use must be locked away in a safe. Actors will be handed the firearm by stage management just before going on stage and it will be taken from them as soon as they exit. For more information about obtaining a firearms licence the production office should contact Equity (UK), Actor's Equity (US) or the relevant local authority. Whilst the rules aren't as strict when it comes to prop knives (or replica knives), great care must be taken when handling or storing anything that looks like an offensive weapon.

Fire

Professional theatres have designated fire officers to make sure that safety procedures are observed at all times. If the production includes smoking or naked flame (candles, flame-throwers or pyros) the relevant fire officer will need to be informed. In the case of school, college or community projects the local authority should be notified. Where fire is concerned stage management will need to take certain precautions to ensure that safety remains an absolute priority. For example, if lit cigarettes are required, there must be fire extinguishers in each wing, and ash-trays should contain sand or water so that the cigarettes can be extinguished immediately. The entire set and all set dressings will also require fire proofing; this will include paper props and any costumes which come into close contact with naked flame.

Electronic cigarettes (**E cigarettes**) are now designed for theatrical use and are beginning to eclipse the real thing since they are safer to use, don't give out obnoxious fumes, and are generally more consistent. Unfortunately they are also heavier and less convincing to look at since they don't realistically burn down and therefore don't decrease in size or create any ash. Technology is, of course, moving at a dizzying pace, and no doubt there will soon be an affordable alternative which is every bit as believable as the real thing.

Animals

In my opinion animals should only appear on stage if it's absolutely necessary. I would rather see a well-manipulated puppet than a real animal, but there are occasions when a more naturalistic approach is suitable. Musicals such as *Oliver!*, *Annie* and *The Wizard of Oz* are shows which arguably would suffer without the appearance of a live canine companion. To use an animal on stage a certificate will need to be obtained from the relevant local authority and a handler will be required to look after the animal when it's not on stage. None of this comes cheap, and if a director decides to feature a live animal in their production the producer will need to be consulted at an early stage to check that suitable finances are in place.

Rehearsal reports

After each rehearsal day the deputy stage manager will send out an e-mail to the production team giving an account of the rehearsal room activities and any matters arising which may have an impact on any of the separate departments. These rehearsal reports are vitally important for anyone who isn't a regular in the rehearsal room: a new sound cue may have been added, a costume may require pockets to hold a specific prop, or the set may need adapting to accommodate a new piece of blocking. Any of these additions will need to be actioned quickly, and the rehearsal report will ensure that the relevant department knows all about it. Diagram 5 is a rehearsal report sent out during our production of *The Addams Family*. It clearly states that during one single rehearsal day several new props have been added, that there are various new accessories which the costume department will need to source, and that low-lying fog will be required for the final exit of the ensemble. The producer will always require a copy of the daily rehearsal report so that all new developments in the rehearsal room can be closely monitored and budgeted for, if necessary.

REHEARSAL NOTES	
Show: Addams Family **Venue**: Dance Attic, North End Road, Fulham, London, SW6 1LY	
DATE: 05/04/17	**REPORT #19**

GENERAL:

1. There was a production meeting held at lunchtime. Minutes to follow from Ms. Warnaby.

PROPS:
1. GRANDMA will carry basket for Act 2:10. Inside that she should carry a lunchbox and a map of the stars for FESTER, and a bunch of flowers and a ring box for FESTER to give to the Moon, a bottle of polish and a cloth so that PUGSLEY can clean FESTER's rocket. The ring inside will be revealed and should be like a jewelled spider or similar. The map will be briefly opened up and checked for directions.
2. FESTER's rocket should have a hatch in it so that the aforementioned items can be packed into it.

SET:

No notes today

COSTUME:
1. GRANDMA should have a thin scarf that she uses to 'hold' PUGSLEY round the neck in Act 2:10.
2. Please can MAL have a headband that he can put on during *Crazier Than You*. Would his dressing gown be able to have a pocket in it with the headband pre-set in?

WIGS & MAKE UP:

No notes today

LX:
1. See props note 2 re. Fester's Backpack Rocket.
2. For the Ancestor's exit at the end of Act 2:10 before the bows, the doors of the stairs will be opened and there should be low fog

SOUND:

1. The Ensemble wont be able to get off stage unseen after their exit through the staircases for their final 'Love love love....'.at the end of Act 2:10. Can we make sure they can see an MD monitor from USC ?

MUSIC:

No Notes today

Amy Wildgoose
Deputy Stage Manager

Diagram 5 Rehearsal report: *The Addams Family*.

Accident book

Stage management will need to set up an accident book during rehearsals so that any injuries sustained by either the cast or stage management are officially recorded. This book will stay in operation throughout the run of the show. This is particularly important with a production which features lots of dance as the chances of cast injury are likely to be higher.

Keeping the rehearsal room tidy

This is a fairly obvious point to make, but stage management will need to ensure that the rehearsal room remains a productive place to work, and this means that it must be kept clear of rubbish and unnecessary clutter. The cast will need to be reminded on a regular basis that they, too, have a responsibility to make sure that the room stays clean, and this will involve checking at the end of the day that they take their rubbish away with them. Coffee cups will need to be washed, newspapers and magazines put in the recycling bins, and lunch boxes and bags removed from the premises. Unfortunately it often seems to be the stage management who end up doing these menial chores long after the actors have disappeared into the night. A stage manager friend of mine recently told me what the title ASM (assistant stage manager) really stands for; the acronym is apt, she says: 'Always Sweeps and Mops'.

Staging notes

Once the show has been staged it's important to keep detailed notes about the blocking and choreography; this is useful for several reasons. Firstly, it's helpful for the actors to remind them of their moves, especially if a scene hasn't been rehearsed for a while. It's also valuable for future reference during understudy calls when a new set of performers will need to get to grips with the staging and choreography.

The deputy stage manager will take detailed notes concerning the blocking and will ensure that the prompt copy is kept up to date with any changes that are made in rehearsals. The assistant director will usually keep blocking notes too. The assistant choreographer and dance captain will similarly keep track of the choreography and make sure that all the dance moves are recorded and easily accessible. Some will film the choreographed sections of the show so that they have a complete record of all relevant material. Others prefer to use specific choreographic notation such as Benesh Movement Notation (BMN), which is a complex, detailed system used to record ballet steps.

Final run-throughs

As the rehearsals progress, the prompt copy will gradually start to fill up with sound and lighting cues, staging notes and script changes. By the final rehearsal week the production should be starting to settle into some sort of shape, and what seemed like an untameable beast in the first few days should now begin to feel much more manageable. There are still, of course, many challenges to face before the show is ready for an audience, but by now the actors and stage management should all be pretty clear about their contribution to the piece, and how their work affects the others around them.

In my rough rehearsal schedule (see Chapter 7) I suggested that for a musical with four weeks of rehearsal, the aim should be to have three full run-throughs during the final week. This may not, of course, always be achievable, and sometimes due to a variety of factors the first full run doesn't happen until the dress rehearsal on stage. This situation should, if possible, be avoided, since it throws everyone into a panic – cast, production team and stage management alike. Running the show several times in the rehearsal space gives everyone a chance to get to grips with the piece, it helps to build stamina, and also gives some much-needed confidence to the cast and production team before having to face the challenges of teching and dressing the show in the theatre (see Chapter 12).

The stage manager will usually be in charge of the rehearsal room for these final runs, taking responsibility for starting and stopping the rehearsal, and for ensuring that the run is tightly coordinated. The cast members will usually adjust pretty quickly to the stage management activity around them, and a 'backstage ballet' will begin to take shape. This is a term which I think best describes what's going on behind the scenes; it refers to the complex manoeuvres which occur offstage of which the audience is blissfully unaware. This backstage choreography will, of course, become even more complicated once the show reaches the theatre.

During these final runs it's best to try not to stop unless there's a very good reason to. Sometimes a complicated scene change will mean that the entire stage management team, and often some of the actors, are racing around trying to set chairs, desks, tables and other assorted bits of furniture. Once on stage these changes may be fairly simple to achieve, taking place behind a front-cloth, or the result of a simple moving truck, but in the rehearsal room, with no crew and only a small stage management team, they may take longer and therefore interrupt the flow of the piece. This is sometimes unavoidable and will need to be taken into account when timings for the show are noted at the end of the rehearsal. In short, these final runs should really be viewed as performances, so that both the actors and stage management can start to get an idea of how much energy will be required to get them through the show. A continuous run-through will also enable the actors, and wardrobe and wig staff to assess how much time to allow for costume and wig changes.

By the second or third run there will probably be some sort of audience, usually comprising members of the extended production team. In addition to those normally present in the room there may now be the set, costume, lighting and sound designers, and various members of the wardrobe staff. If the show is to be mic'd it's vital for the sound operator who will be mixing the sound (Sound no. 1) to attend several of these runs too. This crucial and highly skilled member of the team mixes the sound at the **sound desk**, and adjusts the levels of each singer throughout the performance, whilst also mixing the band. Other members of the production staff, including PR and marketing, may also be in attendance.

For these final runs, the stage management will need to make sure that the rehearsal room remains as uncluttered as possible; the only items allowed anywhere near the stage area should be props and set dressing. If the actual show props are available it makes sense to incorporate them at this stage; if not the rehearsal props will suffice until the real ones appear for the tech. Similarly, if any of the show costumes are ready it'll certainly benefit the actors to start wearing them at this point. However, unless previously rehearsed, costumes should only be used in these rehearsal room runs if they're unlikely to cause problems; this isn't the time to be battling with costumes, especially ones which still need adjustment.

If the real costumes aren't available the cast members should be sensible about what they wear for these run-throughs. If an actor has some business taking off a jacket, for example, it makes sense to bring something suitable so that the stage action can at least be approximated. Anything that's a nod towards the period and the type of costume to be worn in the actual show is probably going to be beneficial. As previously mentioned in Chapter 9 ('Setting the dance numbers') the wardrobe department will often provide practice skirts for rehearsals; these can be particularly helpful when it comes to running the choreographed routines.

If the piece is dance heavy then it's likely that show shoes will have been ordered well in advance so that they're available for rehearsals. This makes complete sense as the shoes will need to be 'broken in', and it's important to make sure that they're not going to inhibit the dancing or movement in any significant way. Show shoes will inevitably have a bearing on the way an actor moves, and should therefore be worn as early as possible, and certainly for the final runs in the rehearsal room.

Stage management will need to make sure that timings are taken for each act, as the box office usually likes to inform the audience members about estimated timings for the interval and for the end of the show. This is information which may also appear in the programme, and since printing will need to happen in advance of the first performance the sooner this is supplied the better.

Sometimes one of the final runs will be filmed by stage management and this will often be used for reference once the performers have left the rehearsal room. In some cases the deputy stage manager will view it when practising cueing the show, but it can also be invaluable for the dance captain and the swings, who'll be able to check blocking and original dance moves once the company move into the theatre. From a health and safety perspective it also makes sense to have any fight sequences on film so that the choreographed moves can be checked once the fight director has left. With professional productions the **book**

cover (or standby deputy stage manager) will also benefit from a filmed copy of a rehearsal run.

Notes

After each run it's customary for the director, choreographer and musical director to give notes to the cast. My own preference is to have a small note session with the actors sitting on chairs in the rehearsal room, and then to do a larger session of **working notes** with the cast up on their feet. During these note sessions it's important to have a member of stage management present since any changes for the cast are likely to impact on their department too. For example, a change in blocking will need to be noted in the prompt copy, as will any alterations to the script or to the cue points.

Positive encouragement can be most important at this stage in the process, and it's worth tempering any critical notes with one or two words of praise. Unless things are going disastrously badly this shouldn't be too difficult to achieve as there are usually lots of delightful things which become apparent as the show starts to come together in the course of a run. Whilst the principal actors often receive a fair amount of attention in these note sessions, the ensemble tend to get slightly ignored, or at best receive very general notes about their group performance. I try, if possible, to offer more personalised feed-back, either during the general note session, later on in a coffee break or at the end of rehearsals. Ensemble members are often surprised to find that their particular contribution has been noticed, but as soon as they start to feel singled out they will visibly blossom. It's also important to encourage the individual members of the stage management team; nobody likes to think of themselves as an insignificant cog in a vast machine and giving everyone a sense that their contribution is appreciated can have a positive effect on the mood of the whole company. Ideally there should be time for each member of the creative team to give notes, and often the stage manager will also want to talk through various technical issues or practical details.

Lighting design in rehearsals

Light for light's sake isn't something I do well. . . I tend to light musicals as if they were all Chekhov plays which move quickly!

PAULE CONSTABLE

Throughout rehearsals the director will begin to envisage certain lighting effects which may help to enhance the look and atmosphere of each scene. Communicating these thoughts to the lighting designer is an important part of the process, particularly if the director has special effects in mind such as stroboscopes, gobos, pyrotechnical flashes or smoke effects. The lighting designer may choose to adopt some of these ideas, modify them or jettison them completely, but it's important for this dialogue to take place so that creative ideas can be exchanged and developed. As a director I enjoy working alongside a lighting designer but try not to be too prescriptive. When I first began directing I gave my designers very specific requests regarding lighting cues, colours, textures and effects. My policy nowadays is to give them a more general brief but to leave the specifics to them. Good lighting designers are instinctive story-tellers and will understand how to enhance each scene without constant input from the director.

Following a number of meetings with the director and set designer early in the process the lighting designer will have devised a provisional lighting plot for the show. Unlike the job of the other production designers, much of the work of the lighting designer has to happen later in the process. Lots of preparation will take place in the early stages, of course, but until they can see how the show is developing in rehearsals it's all a bit theoretical. They will always want to be kept up-to-speed with rehearsal developments and will do so by scrutinising the daily rehearsal reports, attending sporadic rehearsals, and ultimately watching as many run-throughs as possible. This will enable them to get a sense of the blocking, to see how the actors interpret the material, and to assess the mood of each scene. After watching these final runs, usually sat alongside the director, a more detailed lighting plot can be devised which will now become the basis for lighting the show in the tech.

Sound design in rehearsals

Whilst much of the sound designer's work will be done in the theatre, it's obviously important for them to watch the run-throughs to start assessing the quality of each actor's voice (both singing and speaking) and to begin to make some preliminary decisions about the positioning of mics. They will also want to see if and when hats are worn and whether there are occasions when two people are likely to be singing directly into one another's mic. Both these scenarios may lead to sound issues and a suitable solution will need to be found. The person operating the sound in performance (Sound no. 1) will also need to attend these final runs and may want to watch earlier rehearsals too. Their job is a complicated one and will involve constant monitoring of each actor's mic and continual adjustment of the sound balance during the show.

Producer's run

This usually takes place on the last day of rehearsals and will be the final opportunity for any of the production team to see a run of the show before the start of the tech. Most producers will have seen at least one run already, but even so the performance will need to be taken seriously by the cast and stage management as it'll be the last opportunity to consolidate their working notes before other complications arise at the theatre involving set, lighting, costumes and sound.

Whilst I do take general notes at this point I tend not to do a big note session after the producer's run as I'm aware that many of these will be redundant once the actors get on stage. I do, however, like to give the cast a quick talk about the way in which things are about to change. If things have gone well the rehearsal venue, however shabby, will often feel like a place of safety and comfort. Even with the most experienced casts I like to remind them that this forthcoming change of location is likely to feel disconcerting to begin with. Furthermore, the show, which felt so tight in the final stages of rehearsal, is about to fall apart as soon as the other production elements are added: the costumes will be unflattering, the band inaudible, the scenery won't fit on stage, and the dressing rooms will be freezing. But, I remind my company, that's what always happens when you leave the warmth of the rehearsal room for the unknown vicissitudes of the theatre. And it's only a temporary glitch. Once the show's been painfully pulled apart during the tech, it will inevitably rebuild itself and become something greater than the sum of its parts. Another type of alchemy is about to take place.

12
TAKING TO THE STAGE

During the last few days of rehearsals it's likely that the band will have been getting to grips with the score, often in a different venue. This can cause problems with productions where the musical director has no assistant as it's clearly impossible to be in two places at the same time and someone will need to stay in the rehearsal room to represent the music department. It helps, of course, to have an assistant musical director or at least a very proficient rehearsal pianist. Depending on the complexity of the score, band calls (see Photo 18) can take up a fair amount of time and it's always important to factor them into the overall production schedule (see Chapter 3). Ideally they shouldn't conflict with the final full runs in the rehearsal room since the musical director will need to be available to conduct these.

Photo 18 The band call: *The Producers*, UK tour (Andrew Hilton and band members). (Photo, Russell Wilcox.)

Sitzprobe

It can be a great morale-raiser for the cast after spending weeks in a rehearsal room with just a piano for company.

DAVID CHARLES ABELL

The sitzprobe is the point at which the actors and musicians come together for the first time and the whole score is worked through, usually in chronological order. It's often one of the most exciting moments in the entire process and it can be a joyous, bonding experience for all involved. There is something about hearing the score played for the first time by a group of accomplished musicians which never fails to excite, energise and delight a company of actors. For me, as director, it feels like a gift. Coming at a point when the rigorous work in the rehearsal room has been completed, but prior to the challenging technical period, it seems like a well-earned treat. For the musicians, though, this is another very important rehearsal as they will still be getting to grips with the music having only had a relatively short amount of time to rehearse it. During the sitzprobe the actors will usually stand in front of microphones and sing through the entire show, omitting any unaccompanied sections of dialogue. However, any spoken passages which are underscored with music will also need to be rehearsed. This sometimes comes as a shock to the actors who can find it oddly disconcerting to recite the spoken text without doing the usual blocking.

The sitzprobe will generally last for one session of three to four hours; for financial reasons it's not usually extended beyond this. Whilst undeniably enjoyable, it's a pivotal part of the whole process and needs to be carefully organised and efficiently run. Whilst the musical director will be in charge during this rehearsal, the sound department and stage management will usually look after the technical aspects. There are several things to take into account to ensure that everything runs smoothly:

1   The rehearsal space for the sitzprobe needs to be large enough to seat the entire band, the cast and most of the production team.

2   Music stands will be needed for the musicians, and a well-tuned piano is essential, unless the keyboard is electric.

3   Amplification will usually be provided for the singers (unless the band is very small and uses only acoustic instruments). Mics are required, not only so that the solo voices can be heard, but also to stop the actors trying to compete with the musicians and straining their voices. There should be enough mics for each of the soloists, and several additional ones for the ensemble to share.

4   If possible the sitzprobe should take place in a sound-proofed room so that the rehearsal isn't compromised by external noise. Rooms

which are particularly resonant and have a noticeable echo are also not ideal.

Sometimes the sitzprobe will take place in a convenient room in the theatre, but away from the main acting space. This is an efficient way of organising things because it means that everyone's in the same building and the production team are all within easy reach of one another. Occasionally, and this is fairly rare in my experience, the stage is actually available, and the sitzprobe can turn into the exotically named **wandelprobe**. This is when the actors are in radio mics and rehearse on stage with the musicians in their designated area. This is more like the 'stage and orchestra' rehearsals common in the world of opera. Whilst it's great for the actors to start rehearsing on the stage, there are disadvantages too. The actors and musicians are separated and therefore don't really start to get to know each other, the detail in the music is often hard for the actors to hear when the musicians are some distance away and amplified through directional speakers, and with the actors free to move about the set the musical director can sometimes feel side-lined, the focus shifting away from the music and onto more physical aspects of the production. There's no denying, though, that the wandelprobe is generally a hit with the sound department because the sound operator (Sound no.1) is able to start mixing the show much earlier than usual and consequently there's more time to develop the overall sound design.

My personal preference is for the good old-fashioned sitzprobe as it is the only time that the actors are likely to hear the band acoustically. From this point onwards the musicians will probably end up tucked away in an orchestra pit, squashed into a corner of the stage or, in extreme cases, hidden away in a separate room. The whole cast should be encouraged to attend the sitzprobe even if there are some performers who don't actually sing in the show. It's probably the last opportunity for everyone to concentrate solely on the music, and from now on the technicalities of the piece will take precedence. Once on stage the performers will be inundated with problems of a fairly uncreative nature, such as ill-fitting costumes, wobbly sets and irritable directors. The sitzprobe is often the calm before the storm, and the actors should be encouraged to savour the experience accordingly.

Organising the get-in and fit-up

The get-in (or load-in) refers to the process of bringing all the technical elements of the production (the set, the lighting equipment and the sound system) into the theatre and the fit-up indicates the period during which they are installed. Many theatres, of course, will already have a fair amount of lighting and sound equipment, but inevitably some extra kit will be required for each new production. Touring shows tend to rely less on the theatre's existing stock of equipment and the team will usually bring in most of their own kit. Follow spots are an exception, though, and whilst being variable in terms of quality, are often inherited by the incoming company. Whilst these various technical elements are being sorted, wigs, costumes and props will be sent to the theatre and organised by their respective departments. The production manager will usually oversee the get-in, with assistance from the stage manager and the rest of the stage management team. This period of preparation requires skilful planning and the time-frame is usually decided following detailed discussions with each department head during the regular production meetings held during rehearsals (see Chapter 11).

Estimating the amount of time each department will require in order to set up in time for the tech is a skilful operation, and the production manager will need to take all sorts of things into consideration. One of the most important decisions at this point is to calculate how many crew members are required for the get-in. With professional productions this will have a financial implication and the producer will therefore need to be consulted. Once crew numbers have been decided the production manager will have to work out in what order various pieces of equipment need to arrive, how many people will be required to install each of them, and where they should be positioned in the theatre.

Seating the band

Seating the band will happen just prior to the start of the tech. It can actually be quite a complicated process because the band is often squeezed into a fairly tight space. Decisions will need to be made about where each instrument is positioned; this will mainly be dictated by the musical director, but the sound designer may have a hand in this too. The sound department will usually have to mic each instrument, and this can be a time-consuming process. Individual music stands will also need to be provided and stand lights will be required so that the musicians can read their music under show lighting. These will often require dimming during the performance to enhance lighting effects or to help achieve a **blackout** on stage. Television monitors and cameras may also be set up at this point; these are often used to help the actors see the conductor and, in some cases (depending on the positioning of the band) to enable the conductor to have a clear view of the stage.

It's also important, whilst positioning the band, to make sure that the musical director has a direct eye-line both to the other musicians and, ideally, to the actors on stage. Because of the need to communicate quickly with the deputy stage manager, a telephone handset and cue light is usually provided for the musical director. This will enable the former to cue the start of the show or in extremis to stop it in mid-performance. If the band are on stage then there are other things to take into consideration too. Clearly the chairs and music stands will need to be in keeping with the set, and ideally the musicians will be costumed accordingly. If the show is a period piece, then any electric keyboards, synthesisers, speakers and cables will have to be hidden from view. The stand lights will need to be subtle and adjustable to prevent them pulling focus from the actors, and the musical director will have to be positioned carefully so as to be seen by the musicians and performers without becoming a distraction to the audience. Often television monitors will be provided up at dress circle level so that the actors can keep an eye on the musical director at all times. This is particularly useful if the band is situated on stage or somewhere other than the orchestra pit.

Lights: focussing and plotting

Once the get-in and the fit-up have been completed and the lights have been rigged, the lighting team will begin focussing. Ideally the set will be ready by the time the focussing takes place so that the lighting designer can clearly see how the stage looks in each scenic configuration. They can now begin to look at suitable lighting states for each scene and start working through the previously devised lighting plot. The lighting designer, like a painter, will now be able to choose from a varied palette of colours, to isolate the lights, mix them and change their intensities. This is the point at which theatrical magic can start to take place. We should never underestimate the importance of stage lighting; with an experienced lighting designer at the helm the lights can make all the difference: a character suddenly vanishes in front of our eyes, a bare stage becomes an enchanted forest, the sun starts to rise and the entire stage is flooded with light. Even the drabbest of sets can suddenly spring to life when lit with sensitivity and imagination.

In some ways lighting designers have the hardest job of all, since most of their creative work takes place during the tech, a time which is usually compromised by unforeseen challenges and a tight schedule. They consequently have little time for experimentation but are always expected to deliver great results no matter how short a time-frame they have to achieve this in. For these reasons, it's important for the lighting designer to work calmly and efficiently, even in the most frenetic of circumstances.

I prep really, really well. I run. I eat well. I don't drink when I'm in tech and previews. I tell terrible jokes and try to keep the atmosphere of the room light.

PAULE CONSTABLE

Another challenge for the lighting designer is to plot lighting states before the arrival of the actors on stage. This preliminary plotting therefore has an element of guess-work attached; until the start of the tech various members of stage management will usually stand in for the actors to approximate their positions so that the lighting designer can start to light them against the backdrop of the set. However, there's often another complication; the set won't always be completed by the time the lighting designer wants to start building the lighting states and some creative guesswork may have to take place until the set is ready and the tech can begin. Most lighting designers are pretty sanguine about this, having presumably had their expectations lowered after numerous similar experiences. They will, however, usually have agreed certain cue points with the deputy stage manager in advance; these can be called during the tech even though the fleshing out of these cues may have to happen later.

Often it is easier for a director to react to something rather than to have to generate it from scratch. So I make something – they can then respond to it. If in doubt I go to black and start again. Darkness is our best friend.

PAULE CONSTABLE

Smoke and haze effects are usually supplied by the lighting department, and ideally should be tested before the actors arrive on stage. If there's a dance element to the show, testing these effects will be a health and safety priority as they can make the stage floor slippery and dangerous to work on. It's not really worth trying them out in the rehearsal room, since smoke, haze and dry-ice are pretty temperamental and will behave differently in each venue. Whilst pyrotechnics are usually supplied by the lighting department, it's the responsibility of the stage management to ensure that these effects are tested on stage without anyone standing nearby. The set will need to be fire-proofed in advance, of course, regardless of whether or not pyros are being used.

Early sound checks

Just as the lights need focussing before any plotting can be done, the sound designer will require some time before the tech to adjust sound levels and check the positions of loudspeakers and fold-back monitors. For shows involving a sophisticated sound system, especially musicals which require each actor to have a personal body mic, early sound checks are advisable, giving the sound department the chance to set basic levels for each performer, which can then be tweaked during the various technical and dress rehearsals on stage (see Photo 19). For shows involving a band or orchestra, it's sensible to have a pre-tech balancing session just for the musicians, to allow the sound designer time to adjust sound levels according to the acoustic of the building. Often the musicians won't be called for the tech and will only appear for the first dress rehearsal; if there's no time for a band sound check before the tech begins then time will have

Photo 19 The sound desk: *The Producers*, UK tour. (Photo, Russell Wilcox.)

to be allocated at some point before this dress rehearsal. Without the opportunity to prepare properly the sound will inevitably suffer and the dress rehearsal is likely to be seriously compromised. For all sound sessions silence will be required in the building as it's impossible for the sound department to do their job properly if hammering, drilling or even talking is happening nearby.

Actors in the theatre

Before the cast arrive in the theatre the company manager or stage manager will have allocated specific dressing rooms to the actors. It's normal practice to separate the leading actors from the ensemble. The former will usually be given single or joint rooms, whilst the latter will be divided into male and female and will be expected to share larger communal dressing rooms. Allocation of rooms is often influenced by costume and wig requirements; an actor may, for example, require more space for multiple costumes or wigs. In my experience it's often better for company morale when dressing rooms are larger and the actors are expected to share. This seems to take ego out of the equation and helps to remind the performers that they're part of a company working together collaboratively. It's also much easier for the director or dance captain to give notes if the cast are all together in one place. This is a slightly Utopian dream, however, since most theatres, especially the older ones, are built with a theatrical hierarchy in mind.

Backstage

Before the tech begins the actors should be taken on a tour of the theatre by stage management; this is called **familiarisation**. They will need to know how to get from the dressing rooms to the stage, of course, but they should also be shown the backstage areas with particular reference to props tables and quick-change areas. Most importantly they will be taken for a tour of the stage, and the stage manager will point out any relevant health and safety issues. The stage can be a hazardous place, especially under stage lighting when the wings are often in darkness, so it's really important that the cast are shown any potential safety risks such as low-hanging lights, trap-doors or steep staircases. Fire-exits should also be pointed out. Most importantly the actors will need to be reminded that they're not allowed to enter the stage area without permission from stage management; during this period of intense activity there are potential hazards everywhere and it's important to stress this to the company. A member of the theatre staff should also be on hand to go through venue rules and evacuation procedures.

If there's a raked stage (where the floor of the stage slopes down towards the audience) the stage manager will need to allow the performers time to try walking on it, and dancing too, if appropriate. In some older theatres the rake can be quite steep, and the performers will need to adjust their movement accordingly. The choreographer will be on hand to help out, especially during the spacing call when there will be more time to address this particular challenge. In the US, Equity requires a qualified physical therapist to work with the company to ensure that they understand the difficulties of standing, moving and dancing on a raked stage.

Production desk

The **production desk** will usually be positioned in the middle of the auditorium towards the back of the stalls. In most cases this is where the director and the deputy stage manager will sit during the tech. Often the lighting designer will occupy a similar position in the auditorium so that there's easy communication between all three. In larger theatres the sound department will often supply a **god mic** so that the director's voice can be amplified during the tech, thus making communication with other departments (including the actors) much easier. Most theatres or theatrical venues will also have some sort of backstage intercom system which the deputy stage manager can access from the production desk. There's usually a **show relay** which enables the actors in their dressing rooms to hear what's happening on stage during the tech, the dress and subsequent performances.

Tech

I love techs! I love watching my team take on the work like the baton in a relay race. They amplify and reveal it with their own story-telling brilliance, understanding, and magic.

EMMA RICE

This is the period when everything comes together, the set, the lighting, the video projection, the sound, the music, the costumes, the choreography and, of course, the staging. It's a period of intense activity, sometimes fairly stressful, when every technical element of the show is introduced chronologically, then rehearsed and refined. In my experience the tech never feels long enough and there's always the underlying worry that things won't come together in time for the first performance. Will the rehearsal grind to a halt because of unforeseen technical issues? Will the radio mics start playing up? How will stage management cope with the scene changes? There are many challenges at this stage and the clock is always ticking quietly in the background reminding everyone that there's a public performance just around the corner.

The way to deal with all of this, certainly from the point of view of the director, is to delegate. It's really important to have confidence in all the heads of department and to make sure that each of them is fully in charge of their specific team. Most often in tech there will be one main activity taking place, such as the lighting of a certain sequence or the spacing of a dance routine, but in every pocket of the theatre people will be hard at work: sewing on buttons, mending a prop, re-writing the scene-change music, adjusting the sound levels, or re-setting a wig. There is constant activity in the building which makes it an exciting, if slightly frenzied, place to be.

The length of the tech will have been determined in advance, the result of various production meetings held during rehearsals. Everyone will have to work together to make sure that the tech time is well spent and that everything is ready for the dress rehearsal and subsequent first performance. It's important to give adequate stage time to stage management to ensure that there's ample opportunity to solve ongoing problems. There is no point having the actors on stage throughout the tech and trying to push through without solving the various technical issues that arise. For this reason I'm in favour of limiting the tech sessions with the actors to the afternoons and evenings and keeping the mornings free for stage management to do technical work on stage. This doesn't suit all directors, but personally I find that it's the most efficient way of working.

It's a good idea to approach the tech by dividing the show into segments and aiming to reach a certain point by the end of each session. If, for example, there are six three-hour onstage sessions, then five of these might be used to tech the show with the final session as a dress rehearsal. If two dress rehearsals are required then four sessions will have to suffice to achieve all the technical work. In reality, the tech normally starts off fairly slowly and the pace picks up as everyone becomes more familiar with the set-up, the surroundings and the equipment.

Spacing calls

A spacing call at the beginning of the tech can be a very good way to kick-start the rehearsal. This is an opportunity for the choreographer to space the larger dance numbers with the correct scenery in position. It doesn't require lighting, or sound, and the performers won't usually need to be in costume either. There should be time during this spacing call for the choreographer to adjust the choreography to ensure that it fits into the confines of this new space, and also to check that the dancers have adequate room to execute their moves. This isn't an opportunity to hone the dance steps or invent new choreography – there's no time for that – it's a practical rehearsal which aims at solving staging issues as quickly and efficiently as possible.

Running the tech

The tech is usually run by the director and stage manager in tandem. The former will stay out in the auditorium and the latter will remain on stage or in the wings. (The process is slightly different in the US where the production stage manager will usually run things from the auditorium.) Whilst the stage manager monitors all things technical, the director will try to bring together both the technical and the creative elements of the show. The stage manager will, of course, be on hand to stop the rehearsal if there are any problems, especially those involving the safety of the actors, stage management or crew. It's often the director, though, who will interrupt a scene in order to give the lighting designer more time to plot a cue, the choreographer the opportunity to alter some staging, or the wardrobe department time to rehearse a costume change. This isn't, though, the right time for the director to start adding new business or doing character work with the actors. A technical rehearsal is just what it says on the tin; it's all about the technical aspects of the show and shouldn't be high-jacked for any other purpose.

As far as music is concerned, if the musical director is playing keyboards in the band then it's likely that they will also play the piano for the tech. If not, then they will almost certainly be conducting and someone familiar with the show will be drafted in to play keyboards, ideally the rehearsal pianist. Because of the slow-moving, laborious nature of the tech, the musical director will need to be very patient, but also alert and able to spring into action at a moment's notice. As previously mentioned, the band isn't normally called during the tech.

Actors and the tech

There are various things that the actors will need to take into account at the start of the tech.

- Ideally a separate physical and vocal warm-up will be organised by the choreographer (or dance captain) and musical director and scheduled accordingly. If the stage is busy (which it usually is at this point), stage management will try to find an alternative location for the various warm-ups. If there's no time then the actors will need to be warned in advance so that they can organise their own warm-ups. In the US, warm-ups are the responsibility of the individual performer, of course.

- They will need to be in costumes, show shoes, wigs and mics for the entire tech, unless told otherwise.

- They will need to stay focussed, even when offstage, and be ready to get straight back onstage as soon as they are asked to by the director or stage management.

- They shouldn't change costumes until requested to do so by stage management. Often the director will need to go back over a scene, and if some actors have already changed for the next scene much time will be wasted waiting for them to get back into their previous costumes.

- They will inevitably be asked to repeat sections of the show several times and should take care not to strain their voices. Whilst the sound department will need to hear them singing full out on occasions, they should be allowed to 'mark' their performance when repeating the same section over and over.

- When not on stage they should be encouraged to run lines with the other actors, experiment with a particular personal prop (having checked first with stage management), practise some of the dance steps, or rehearse understudy material. As long as they are ready at a moment's notice to rejoin the tech, they should be able to use this spare time productively.

Creatives and the tech

There are also a number of things that the director and choreographer should bear in mind during the tech.

- Before starting, it's often a good idea for the director to address the whole company to explain how the tech rehearsals will be structured;

this is particularly valuable if there are any younger, inexperienced actors in the cast. Information such as that just listed will be useful for the cast to hear and will set some basic ground rules. It's also worth reminding the actors that the focus during these rehearsals will be on the technical aspects of the show and not on their personal performance. They shouldn't expect to get acting notes at this stage.

- In my opinion, it generally works best if the director stays in the auditorium during the tech; if the actors need re-blocking or some piece of stage business needs refining it's often better for the choreographer to deal with it whilst the director continues to liaise with the rest of the team out front. In large theatres it can actually take quite a long time to reach the stage from the auditorium, making it fairly impractical for the director to keep jumping up and interacting with the cast.

- The choreographer will need to work swiftly and efficiently during the tech. If there's a spacing call at the start of these onstage rehearsals then many staging and choreographic issues can be addressed straight away. Subsequently the choreographer will often act as a sort of go-between between the director and the actors on stage. This can be particularly helpful when time is tight and there are lots of staging challenges.

- It can help to save time if the director and choreographer liaise with stage management about scene changes before the actors arrive on stage. It's often possible to **dry tech** a scene change in advance without the actors being anywhere near the set. This, of course, presupposes that the actors aren't required to help with that specific scene change.

- Since time is always tight during the tech it's important for the director to use it efficiently. This means keeping in close communication with all departments and ensuring that something productive is happening at all times. If, for example, things suddenly grind to a halt as the lighting designer and the lighting programmer wrestle with a particularly complicated cueing sequence, there are plenty of other things that can be achieved during the hiatus; this might be the perfect opportunity for the choreographer to leap on stage and clarify the positioning for one of the dance numbers or for the sound team to sort out someone's faulty mic. As soon as the stage manager gives the go-ahead to continue with the tech, though, everyone needs to be ready to resume the rehearsal immediately.

- It makes sense for the director to rehearse some things before the actors arrive on set, or whilst they're on a break, especially if there are health and safety issues associated with them. In *Candide* there is a scene in which Pangloss is ritualistically hung during an 'auto-da-fé'. In order to make sure that there was no danger attached to this piece of stage business we rehearsed the section calmly whilst the actors were on a break and only attempted to include the actor playing Pangloss when stage management understood exactly how the trick worked. On a production of *Jesus Christ Superstar* we rehearsed the section with Jesus on the cross before our actors got anywhere near the stage. Knowing stage management had already worked on this scene helped the actor playing Jesus to feel much more confident. Similarly, pyros, explosions and gun-shots should be rehearsed with stage management before the actors are allowed to participate in the scene.

- The director should be very conscious of quick changes and should make sure that sections are always run in their entirety so that the change in question can be attempted at the proper speed and assessed accordingly. Costume changes often take place offstage and so the director needs to be fully aware of what's taking place in the wings; there's nothing more annoying than a director stopping a scene half-way through a quick change before the actors and **dressers** have had a chance to finish the sequence.

- The director and choreographer should try to remain calm during the tech. Alongside the stage manager, these are the people who will set the tone for the rehearsals on stage and shouting and swearing will only be perceived as a loss of control and will encourage others to behave in a similar way. A calm tech is generally a happy tech, and this is a much more productive environment for everyone to work in.

- If time is very tight it's a good idea for the director to think in advance about how the show might be 'topped and tailed'. If there are no lighting or sound cues during a scene, and no complicated stage business or quick changes, it might be possible to jump sections of dialogue. This won't always be a popular decision with the cast members, who will often want to run their scenes in full, but in extremis this is a valid approach and may just enable the director to get to the end of the tech in time for the dress rehearsal.

- The director should try to maintain a sense of humour throughout the tech, and a sense of perspective too. It's important work that we do, of course, but it isn't the end of the world if a costume comes unzipped, a prop malfunctions or an actor's mic fails.

Stage management and the tech

Stage management will usually be working flat out during the tech. Unlike the actors, who often get quite a lot of downtime during this period, stage management will be constantly occupied in a variety of different ways.

- Whilst sharing joint responsibility with the director for running the tech, the stage manager will take full responsibility for everything that happens onstage. Since the theatre can be a dangerous environment, the stage manager will always be in direct communication with other members of the stage management team and will be able to stop the rehearsals (or subsequent performances) at a moment's notice should anything go seriously wrong. The stage manager is also the official time-keeper and will try to ensure that rehearsals begin and end on time. Scheduling regular tea breaks and dinner breaks is also an important part of the job since everyone needs time to re-charge and a tired, over-worked company is never going to be conducive to a successful tech. These breaks will take into account the time needed for the actors to get in and out of costumes, mics and wigs.

- The deputy stage manager will usually stay at the production desk in the auditorium throughout the course of the tech and will generally be in charge of cueing sound, lighting and scene changes.

- The assistant stage managers will supervise the backstage areas, setting and re-setting props, helping the actors, assisting with scene changes, and generally doing everything possible to keep things behind the scenes as efficient and well-organised as possible. They will also sweep the stage floor before the actors arrive on set. The stage manager, though, will take full responsibility for the surface of the stage as this is a health and safety issue and will be part of the risk assessment. In the US the crew have greater responsibilities and will take over some of the assistant stage managers' duties once the show reaches the theatre (see 'Stage management in the US', p.94).

- The crew are there to help the assistant stage managers and will often do the majority of the heavy lifting and flying (this refers to any pieces of set which need to be lowered from above). Crew members will spring into action for the scene changes, especially complicated ones which involve a significant transformation. They will also help with the pre-set, making sure that everything's ready for the actors when they arrive on stage. Different rules apply in the US where the crew tend to handle more of the assistant stage managers' responsibilities (see Chapter 6).

The prospect of the tech can be daunting for stage management, especially on complicated shows with a large amount to achieve and little time to achieve it. On balance the tech for a musical tends to be more complicated than that for a straight play, partly because there are often more scenic variations to navigate, but mainly because there are a greater number of disciplines to pull together. However, if there's good communication between departments, thoughtful preparation and a calm and productive atmosphere, a huge amount can be achieved technically and creatively in a relatively short amount of time.

Bows and curtain calls

Whilst there's an old theatrical tradition which dictates that curtain calls should never be rehearsed until the day of the first performance, this is a superstition which I'm happy to ignore. The truth is that bows often get left to the last minute because there's so much else to worry about. A better approach, I think, is to map them out roughly in rehearsals, and refine them at the end of the tech. This makes sense for the following reasons:

1   Sometimes there will be music accompanying the bows and the musical director will need to ensure in advance that something appropriate is available and suitably orchestrated.

2   If the curtain call ends up being quite elaborate, the choreographer will need to spend time devising and rehearsing it beforehand, and since there probably won't be time to do this at the theatre it's sensible to address this issue during rehearsals.

3   With commercial productions it's important to consider the order of the bows since celebrities will usually expect to appear towards the end of the curtain call. In some cases this will be contractual and will therefore need to be discussed with the producer in advance. No matter what scale of production I'm working on I always make a point of liaising with the producer when it comes to the delicate subject of the order of the bows; this can be a divisive moment in the whole process and needs to be approached sensitively.

Every director and choreographer will have a slightly different attitude towards curtain calls, and this very much depends on personal preference. I tend to avoid long, drawn-out bows, which can often seem self-indulgent and unnecessary. I also like to acknowledge the company of actors, rather than focussing too much on the principals; after all, the ensemble often work just as hard as the soloists (see Photo 20). It's always important to acknowledge the band and the musical director, even if they're not visible to the audience. The same goes for stage management, and if there is a suitable opportunity it's important to reference these hard-working members of the team.

Photo 20 The curtain call: *Candide*, Menier Chocolate Factory (Scarlett Strallen, James Dreyfus, Fra Fee, Jackie Clune and company). (Photo, Nobby Clark.)

Dress rehearsal

Since the earliest design meetings the show will have been gathering momentum with new elements being added as the production slowly starts to take shape. The dress rehearsal is the first time that all these component parts come together; it's the culmination of a truly collaborative process. Despite careful planning in every department, nobody quite knows how the production will turn out once all the elements come together. And this is what makes the dress rehearsal an exciting, unpredictable and often nerve-wracking event.

Beforehand there's usually chaos, with people from all departments rushing around the building trying to sort out last-minute problems: costumes that won't stay up, props that have been mislaid, and a designer who's still onstage painting the set. There may also be a nervousness on the part of the actors, as this will probably be the first time they've run the piece without stopping since the last run-through in the rehearsal room. They may be starting to feel that they've lost touch with the show, that something which seemed so familiar in the rehearsal room has now mutated into something less tangible. These feelings are absolutely normal and will usually evaporate as soon as the dress rehearsal begins.

Cast pep talk

It is a good idea for the director to have a quick pep talk with the actors before the dress rehearsal, reminding them that they'll need to be extra vigilant during this run-through. There's usually time to catch them en masse just after the pre-show vocal and physical warm-ups. In the US the performers will manage their own warm-ups, so the director's pep talk will need to take place just before the dress rehearsal begins. It's worth reminding the cast that they will need to be alert to everything that's going on around them since there'll be lots of new elements to contend with. The aim, of course, is to run the show without stopping, but it is important to remind the actors that if anything dangerous occurs they should immediately alert the stage manager who will quickly assess the situation and stop the run, if necessary. It is also worth reminding the performers that the only real difference between a performance and a dress rehearsal is that one has an audience and the other doesn't. Every department should approach this run with the same degree of integrity as they would a public performance. Only in exceptional circumstances should the actors be encouraged to **mark** rather than perform full out and this will usually be in situations where an actor has vocal problems or a dancer is nursing a minor injury. After the disjointed and often repetitive nature of the tech it's important that the performers now start to raise their game and once again return to working at performance level.

Show calls

Ideally the production desk should now be removed from the auditorium, and the deputy stage manager should be relocated, usually into one of the wings. Whilst the actors will no doubt have been sneaking into the auditorium during the tech, they should now be reminded to stay backstage at all times when not actually performing. All show calls should now be given by the deputy stage manager just as they would be in performance. Thirty-five minutes before the dress run the half-hour call will be given over the intercom. The actors are expected to be in the building at this time, and there's an understanding that from this point on they won't leave the theatre. Some actors will elect to arrive earlier than that, especially those with elaborate hair and make-up to sort out. The fifteen-minute call will be given twenty minutes before curtain-up, the five-minute call will be given ten minutes before the show begins, and at beginners (five minutes before curtain-up) the actors will start to make their way to the stage.

Make-up and hair

Whilst the actors during the tech are usually without full stage make-up and sometimes without wigs too, for the dress rehearsal it's imperative that both these elements are added. The whole purpose of the dress rehearsal is to make sure that everything works cohesively; leaving out any one element prevents the production team from seeing the show in its entirety. Quite apart from anything else, production photographs are often taken during this run and these will need to present the show in the best possible light. In most cases make-up is supplied by the actors themselves, but if there's specific character make-up or specialist make-up required this will be provided by the production company. Examples of this would include a suitable verdigris for Elphaba in *Wicked* and for the loveable monster in *Shrek the Musical*.

Putting it together

And now at long last the show can be performed with every element in place. This will probably be the first time the cast has sung with the band since the sitzprobe, and this alone will add a whole new dimension to the piece. The deputy stage manager will instruct the musical director as soon as various **clearances** have been given; these will include confirmation from the front-of house manager that the audience has been seated, clearance from the sound department, acknowledgement that beginners are ready on stage, and confirmation that the crew are standing by in the wings. Once all clearances have been indicated then the deputy stage manager can stand all departments by, including the musical director. The musicians will now be tuned up, the cast will be anxiously waiting on stage or in the wings, and the production team will be sitting in the auditorium nervously clutching their note-pads. The deputy stage manager can now cue the house lights to fade and the dress rehearsal can begin.

Photo calls

A **production photographer** is usually called in to take photographs during the dress rehearsal. These images will then be used to publicise the show in various different ways. They may appear as front-of-house photos either outside the theatre or in the foyer, they may become part of a press pack for journalists intending to review the show, and they may be sent to local or national newspapers, often accompanied by some newsworthy information about the piece. These images will also appear on the website (assuming that one exists) and will probably be sent digitally to all sorts of different organisations (schools, local newspapers or local television stations) to help drum up interest in the show.

The production office will usually liaise with the production photographer, but it is often the stage manager who'll deal with logistics on the day. The actors should, of course, be warned in advance, because the production photographer will often dart around the auditorium taking shots from all sorts of different angles, and this can be distracting. It can also disturb the production team, who will be trying to focus on the dress rehearsal. Sometimes it helps to put the photographer up in the dress circle with the production team down below in the stalls, but this, of course, will depend on the layout of the theatre.

Some producers prefer to use **set-up shots**, rather than photos taken during a run. This way there's more control, shots can be re-taken when necessary, the lighting can be adjusted so that the image is brighter and clearer, and radio mics can be removed so there are no unsightly lumps and bumps on the actors' faces. The disadvantage here is that the photos can end up looking stagy and a bit artificial; there's nothing like the energy that comes from an actual run under show conditions, and photos taken during the dress rehearsal are often more dynamic than those which have been carefully organised and manipulated. In reality there's seldom time to do set-up shots before the first performance, and this type of photo session will often take place during previews.

Notes from the dress rehearsal

There is usually very little time between the dress rehearsal and the first performance. In most cases the final dress run (assuming there's more than one) will take place on the afternoon of the first public performance, leaving no real time for cast notes. Ideally, production notes with the heads of each department should take place straight after the dress rehearsal, but in my experience there's seldom time to do this. It's often a case of racing around the building and grabbing people when they have a spare moment.

I generally try not to give the actors notes after the half-hour call, as they will usually be preoccupied with costumes, make-up and hair and won't be particularly receptive. It's a good idea to touch base with the stage manager and deputy stage manager, though, as there are usually notes concerning scene changes and cueing which can be actioned before the first official performance.

Be your harshest critic. A piece of work is never finished. You give yourself the best notes.

                                                        PAULE CONSTABLE

13
PREVIEWS, OPENING NIGHT AND BEYOND

Previews

Previews offer another process altogether – you will be performing at night and rehearsing during the day. It can be exhausting.

DAVID CHARLES ABELL

Performances which precede the opening night are referred to as previews. The ticket prices are often lower, and there's some expectation amongst the audience members that aspects of the show are still in flux and that it hasn't yet 'settled'. Sometimes, of course, there won't be any previews and the first performance in front of the public is also deemed to be the opening night. But where runs are longer it often makes sense to have a few previews to iron out any problems left over from the tech and dress rehearsals.

There's no doubt that with the introduction of an audience a show changes profoundly, and, despite careful planning and a lengthy rehearsal period, it's never easy to second-guess the audience response. A side-splitting gag which in rehearsals had everyone in stitches provokes a polite ripple of laughter; a piece of stage business which you had long forgotten was funny makes the audience howl and practically brings the show to a stand-still. This is, of course, the beauty of live performance, and this exchange between the cast and the audience is what makes it such a unique event. The actors need to be very attuned to this new set of reactions and will alter their performances accordingly, allowing space for the audience response. Comedy, which often features in musical theatre, is notoriously difficult to gauge, and the cast may suddenly find that the balance of the show has subtly, or not so subtly, shifted. They may need a few performances to get used to this, and the director will also need to be vigilant, checking that actors aren't suddenly becoming over-indulgent and that the pace of the show isn't suffering. With a run of previews the actors will have the opportunity to experiment with pace and timing, and this is often invaluable when it comes to fine-tuning their performances.

Meanwhile, with a handful of previews, the production team will have the opportunity to refine their work. The director can start to give detailed notes to the actors, and also re-rehearse troublesome scene changes with the help of stage management; the choreographer can re-work sections of dance which aren't quite hitting the spot; the lighting designer can adjust lighting states without feeling the need to race against the clock; and the musical director can at long last start to give some detailed vocal notes.

Preview audiences are, of course, expecting to see the show in a reasonable state of readiness. However, in my experience they are often delighted if things go slightly awry. After all, there's something exciting about a show in the early stages of a run: everything is fresh, nothing's taken for granted, and the actors are constantly discovering something new. If a bit of set starts to malfunction, or a costume change doesn't quite happen as it should, the audience tends to be extremely indulgent, and in fact quite relishes these small mishaps.

It's a very good idea for the director to give some detailed acting notes to the company once the show has opened to the public. As previously mentioned, the tech rehearsal, which with some shows can go on for a number of days, focusses on the technical elements of the show and not expressly on the actors' performances. Consequently, any concerns about characterisation or character development get pushed to one side in favour of set, costumes, lighting and sound. Once the show is up and running and the previews are underway, however, there should be ample time to give acting notes to the company, and the cast will generally welcome this.

Press calls

With professional productions the producer will often have a press call in advance of the opening night and invite some select photographers to take photos of the show. This enables various publications and online companies to have suitable images to accompany reviews or articles related to the production. The director and choreographer, often with some input from the producer, will select a series of key moments of visual interest which will usually be repeated several times for the photographers.

It's important to be well prepared for these photo shoots; professional photographers don't like to hang about and are often available for a limited amount of time. Costume changes and scene changes will need to be carefully thought through so that the photographers aren't kept waiting around. It may not, therefore, make sense to photograph everything in chronological order. When organising these press calls it's worth bearing the following things in mind:

1   A running order should be devised in advance. This should be given to the actors and the wardrobe department so that everyone's clear about which costume will be required for each shot.

2 Quick changes need to be pre-empted to save time during the press call and dressers may be required to help out.

3 Stage management need to ensure that scene changes are clarified in advance so that no time is wasted during the session.

4 It's important to be realistic about what can be achieved during the press call; there's no point trying to capture every significant moment in the show. The producer may insist that a particular scene, or a particular character is featured, though, especially if there are well-known actors in the cast.

Opening night

I find press nights stressful. I always watch, but I live every breath, beat, step and song with the actors.

EMMA RICE

The opening night of any show, whether a glamorous high-profile affair, or a small amateur production in a make-shift theatre, is always a memorable event. The excitement is palpable with people racing around the dressing rooms dropping off cards and flowers and first night gifts. There will inevitably be some anxiety and tension, but there's also humour and high spirits too. The show, the result of months of detailed planning and meticulous rehearsal, is about to be officially unveiled (see Photo 21). Everything feels heightened in some way, with everyone

Photo 21 The opening night: *Top Hat*, Aldwych Theatre (Tom Chambers and company). (Photo, Nigel Norrington.)

focussed on the impending performance. At best this focus can help to give the show an extra-special something – a brilliance or luminosity which makes the opening night audience feel as though they're witnessing something unique. At worst, the actors start to push too hard and the performances become heightened and self-conscious. For this reason it's well worth assembling the cast and stage management before the opening night show for a short pep talk. I generally like to thank them all for their hard work, and remind them that this particular performance and the subsequent run is the result of a joyful collaboration to which many people have contributed, and that the opening night should be approached as they would any other performance. 'Perform to the best of your ability, and just tell the story.'

After this brief talk the actors can now head back to the dressing rooms to start preparing for the show: mics are strapped into place, wigs are fitted and make-up is applied. I try to avoid going round the dressing rooms during this time; the actors need to start thinking about the performance ahead and they really don't need the director making small talk, or worse still, giving last-minute notes.

Members of the production team will often sit together on the opening night, more for mutual support than anything else. I try to avoid taking notes (this is agony for me as I'm an inveterate note-taker) and I attempt to watch the show through the eyes of the audience – not easy for someone who's been associated with the production from the very start. Often I find myself feeling slightly detached at this point; this no doubt springs from the knowledge that there's nothing much I can do to influence the performance now. Actually, this shift in responsibility can come as a bit of a relief. Handing the show over to the actors, the musicians, the stage management and the crew feels like a necessary rite of passage, and whilst my job isn't entirely over, the emphasis has certainly started to shift.

I have never sat at an opening – I pace in the back. When opening night arrives it is out of my hands – it now belongs to the actors. I sometimes feel a sense of loss.

SUSAN STROMAN

After-show parties

Traditionally there's usually some sort of celebration after the opening night. Depending on the scale of the production this can range from a simple drink in the theatre bar to a lavish themed party with catering and entertainment. Whatever shape it takes, the opening night celebration is a great opportunity for everyone to relax after the intense activity of the previous few days and weeks. Everyone involved with the show should be invited, of course, and it's not unusual for the producer or the director to say a few words of thanks to the assembled team before the celebrations really kick off. With shows which are limited to a short run, the producer may decide to delay the party until the last night. This has one distinct advantage – no one has to work the following day!

Opening night is when the show is usually claimed by everyone else and you walk away.

PAULE CONSTABLE

Reviews

The result of a successful opening night can be a slew of great reviews. The reverse is also possible, and an unfavourable review, especially one which picks out particular performances, can be extremely damaging as far as cast morale is concerned. I try to encourage the company to avoid reading reviews, positive or negative. The former can lead to inflated egos and an unappealing arrogance in performance, and the latter can result in real anxiety and distress. If actors feel compelled to read reviews they should, I advise, keep them and read them once the show has finished. That way there's no danger that performances will be undermined or actors' insecurities heightened whilst the production's still running.

Maintaining the show

It's amazing how quickly a show can deteriorate if there's no one looking after it. Just as a beautiful, well-ordered garden requires regular maintenance, the same can be said of a musical or any theatre piece, for that matter. On a day-to-day basis stage management will take responsibility for the smooth-running of the show, however the production team will need to keep an eye on things too, and regular visits to the theatre will help to ensure that the show looks fresh and well maintained.

Music

The musical director will usually conduct the show and will consequently be well aware of any musical issues which arise, either vocally or in connection with the band. The odd vocal call after the daily warm-up will often be enough to sort out any problems with the singers. With longer runs there will usually be a dep system in place so that the regular band members don't have to play every single performance. These deps (or subs in the US) will usually be chosen by the player and approved by the musical director. If there's an assistant it's a good idea if the musical director does the occasional **show watch** to check things from out front, leaving the assistant to conduct. This will enable them to hear the performance as the audience hears it, rather than from within the confines of the orchestra pit. These show watches can be very beneficial as they enable the musical director not simply to check on the actors' performances, but also to monitor the sound from various different parts of the auditorium.

Choreography

If the choreographer has appointed a dance captain from within the company (see Chapter 5) it will be their job to keep an eye on the choreography and musical staging and they may also take the occasional clean-up call too. They will collaborate with other members of the team, usually stage management and the assistant director, if understudies and swings are suddenly required to go on. Depending on other work, the choreographer will usually visit from time to time to check that the dance routines and staging are being well executed and that the cast are performing to the best of their ability. Any notes can usually be given via the dance captain.

Sound

This will be constantly monitored by the sound operator mixing the show from the desk. On occasions, especially during long runs, the sound designer should return to check sound levels and the mix in general. It's important to watch the show from different parts of the auditorium as the sound quality can vary significantly from one area to the next. There may be some adjustment needed if a dep is playing in the band, or if an understudy is taking over a leading rôle, since the sound levels are likely to be different. It makes sense for Sound no.2 to mix the show on occasions so that Sound no.1 can check the balance from various parts of the auditorium.

Costume

The wardrobe department will take care of the ongoing maintenance of the costumes, including hats and shoes. They will also ensure that costumes are washed and ironed on a regular basis. Some, of course, will require dry-cleaning. Looking after the costumes is a massive job, and in my experience the wardrobe staff are often under-appreciated. On larger productions there may be a dedicated member of the team whose sole responsibility is the washing and ironing of the costumes.

Wigs

Wigs can be temperamental and need to be carefully maintained by a skilled team. A period wig, for example, will usually need re-setting after each performance, and this takes time and expertise. For this reason matinée days can be particularly challenging, especially with period shows where most of the characters are likely to be wearing wigs. The wig designer will usually try to visit the show from time to time to check that the setting of the wigs is consistent with the original designs and that the wigs and hairpieces remain in good condition.

Lighting

Lighting will also need to be checked on a daily basis as lamps can get knocked, they can malfunction (especially moving lights) and they can blow. The **chief electrician** will keep an eye out for any problems, as will the board operator, but stage management should also be aware of any issues too. The lighting designer should try to see the show once in a while, especially if the run is a long one.

Set and props

It's the responsibility of stage management to check the set and props regularly and to action any repairs, if required. In the US the crew will take more responsibility for this (see 'Stage management in the US', Chapter 6). Even on a short run there's bound to be a certain amount of wear-and-tear, and the set will probably require maintenance at some point. Stage floors are particularly susceptible to damage, especially if there's heavy scenery or vigorous dancing in the show. Tap dancing in particular can be detrimental to the floor and can create an uneven surface which may cause problems for the performers. If there are paint effects on the stage floor these may become scuffed and worn, especially during a long run; they will therefore require regular attention. As previously mentioned, some props will need replacing on a daily basis, and this job will usually fall to one of the assistant stage managers (see Chapter 11).

Cast performances

The director should try to visit the show regularly, especially if there's no assistant or resident director involved. Whilst keeping an eye on all aspects of the production, a particular emphasis should be placed on the actors' performances. Actors aren't automatons and can't be expected to slavishly repeat the same performance night after night, especially during long runs. Even if they could, this would result in a stolid, uninspiring piece of theatre. It's important, therefore, to allow the actors some degree of flexibility. I believe that they should be encouraged to continue to develop their characters and make new discoveries, but this has to be done with a sensitivity to those around them. Too much freedom can lead to unruly, ill-judged performances and a general lack of focus. It can also lead to serious confrontations with other members of the cast. This is why it's important that someone monitors the show on a regular basis. Ideally this should be the director, but if this isn't possible then there should be someone else, usually an assistant, who has the authority to give acting notes, where necessary. Regular note sessions will help to keep things on track and will also reassure the actors that the show is being well looked after. The director or assistant director may also decide to call the occasional rehearsal in order to tighten things up, change a bit of tired staging or re-motivate the actors.

With musical comedy the audience response will always have a rôle to play, and the cast can be affected quite significantly by a perceived lack of enthusiasm on the part of the punters. 'It was a terrible audience tonight' is actor-speak for 'they didn't laugh very loudly and didn't give us a standing ovation at the end'. This doesn't mean, of course, that they were having a miserable time. Different audiences respond in different ways, and it's often misleading to judge them by the noise that they make during a performance. 'You can't hear an audience smile' is an old adage which I find quite useful when the actors start complaining. I know from sitting out front that a quiet audience isn't necessarily an indifferent one. It's important to remind the actors of this, and to caution them against making an enemy of their audience.

From time to time the director should try to watch the show from different parts of the auditorium to check sight-lines and blocking and should be particularly aware of any sound or lighting issues. Regular notes to each department will help to keep everything in good shape and will also give the correct impression that the show's being closely monitored and scrupulously maintained.

Understudies

Many shows, of course, don't have understudies, and the prospect of rehearsing them won't be an issue. For those that do, however, it's a good idea to get them ready as soon as possible (see Chapters 5 and 7). Ideally some work will already have taken place during rehearsals; at the very least the understudies will have been closely observing the principal performers and taking notes on characterisation and blocking. Once the show has officially opened there should be time for understudy rehearsals to commence (or recommence) and the aim should be to do a run of the show as soon as possible, ideally on stage with props and costumes. If the run is a long one there should be regular, scheduled understudy rehearsals to make sure that the covers are ready to go on at a moment's notice. These understudy runs will usually be organised by the assistant director or the deputy stage manager, but this will depend to some extent on the size of the production and the allocation of responsibilities within the team. In the US, the cover rehearsals will usually be taken by the production stage manager.

Warm-ups

As previously mentioned vocal and physical warm-ups are an important part of any musical theatre production (see Chapter 9). Not only do they achieve the obvious, which is to make sure that the actors are physically and vocally prepared for the performance, but they also provide an ideal opportunity for everyone to meet up before the show to focus on something together. This isn't only good for company morale, but it also gives the assistant director, the stage manager or the dance captain the opportunity to give notes, and to address any other matters concerning the company. In the US, warm-ups are generally the responsibility of the individual performer.

Show reports

After each show, whether this is a preview or a regular performance, the deputy stage manager should provide a show report (see Diagram 6). This will usually include timings for each act, general audience reaction, and a short account of any problems experienced during the performance, including any technical issues, wardrobe malfunctions or cast injuries. It will also indicate any changes in show personnel, such as understudies or deps. The show report is usually written up as soon as the show finishes and sent out to all relevant departments, including the producer.

Final performance

The final performance tends to be a fairly emotional affair, not just for the cast, but for stage management, front-of-house, the musicians and all the backstage departments too. Theatre productions are the result of teamwork and consequently everyone should feel that they've played their part, whether on stage or off. As a director I think it's important to get the company together before the last show to acknowledge the contributions that everyone has made. The stage is usually a good place to do this, and I find that a few well-chosen words before the half-hour call can help to give the last show a sense of occasion, and also remind the actors that nothing extra is required; like any other performance they just need to 'tell the story'. From the point of view of the performers, of course, the show will inevitably have an extra resonance since they'll be singing the songs, speaking the lines, and dancing the routines for the very last time. It's not surprising, therefore, that the final curtain call tends to elicit a few more tears than usual.

No matter how emotional the last performance, what follows never fails to feel abrupt and untimely. As soon as the show finishes the building becomes a hive of activity: costumes are folded up and packed away; dressing rooms are stripped of make-up boxes, first night cards and wilting flowers; and the set is taken down and removed from the building. Even the front of house displays are quickly dismantled and within hours it seems as if the show never existed at all. And this, I suppose, is what makes the whole enterprise such a bitter-sweet

CANDIDE
PERFORMANCE 87

Performance: 87	Date: Wednesday 19th February 2014		Evening
	LIGHTS UP	**LIGHTS DOWN**	**PLAYING TIME**	**INTERVAL TIME**
ACT ONE	20:06	21:23	1 hour, 17 minutes	
INTERVAL				18 minutes
ACT TWO	21:41	22:40	59 minutes	
			TOTAL PLAYING TIME	2 hours, 16 minutes
			TOTAL RUNNING TIME	2 hours, 34 minutes

MD / Conductor	Leon Charles
SM / Lighting Operator	Ciara Fanning
ASM's	James Enser Katherine Tippins
Wardrobe	Corrie Darling Justin Allin
Wigs / Hair	Camila Del Monte
Sound Operator	Mike Thacker
Sound No.2	Sarah Dickinson

Notes

- Mr Abell and Mr Alderking in the house this evening.
- Ms Spurrell was back on in her full track this evening.
- Ms Anderson was on a slightly reduced track due to injury. She was cut from Paris Waltz and the Entr'acte, and was covered by Ms Jenna and Mr Wilman in 'Easily Assimilated'.
- An insole from Mr Fee's shoe came out and fell onto the stage during the final section of 'Oh Happy We' as he undressed. It remained onstage until the flogging scene when it was cleared by Mr Lewis.
- Cunegonde's (Ms Strallen) diamond necklace flew off during 'Glitter and be gay' this evening and into the front row of audience on the South bank. It was retrieved by Stage Management at the interval.
- As the wicker boat entered during 'Bon voyage' the flag caught on the curtain, pulling it down slightly. This was temporarily fixed during the galley scene and a more permanent fix will be looked at before the next performance.
- The lights up on Cunegonde on the walkway in the final section (LXQ352) were slightly late. Operator error.
- The Paris and Cadiz sections popular as ever this evening. The Eldorado red sheep received a titter. One woman in particular enjoyed the *'Even kind hearted Cacambo grew restless and distracted'* line during the narration at the end of Venice section: she let out quite a squeal!
- Some audience members left during the curtain call, causing minor traffic issues with the company.
- A warm and responsive house this evening. A good response at the curtain call with much whooping and cheering and some on their feet.

Ciara Fanning  (SM)	

Diagram 6 Show report: *Candide*.

experience; it exists in the present and once the production ends, it's over. We can film it, photograph it or record it, but the power of a stage production lies in the connection between the live audience and the performers on stage and any attempt to capture that experience, or preserve it, somehow feels unconvincing and half-hearted. Nothing beats a live performance, and the best way to overcome the onset of last night blues is to start planning the next one.

14
MUSICALS: PAST, PRESENT AND FUTURE

Whilst musicals are often thought to have emanated from America in the first quarter of the twentieth century, there's evidence to suggest that this combination of music, drama and dance has been around much longer, and hails from a variety of different cultures. During the latter half of the nineteenth century vaudeville and music hall entertainments were packed full of entertaining skits, and amusing, satirical songs. The operettas of Gilbert and Sullivan in Great Britain and Jacques Offenbach in France also contained many of the elements of the modern musical – songs, scenes and choreographed movement – and were bursting with catchy tunes and witty, often irreverent dialogue. There was spectacle too, with imaginative sets and lively, colourful costumes. Reaching further back, John Gay's ballad opera, *The Beggar's Opera*, written in 1728, again contained various recognisable features of the musical. Scenes and songs were interspersed, and the music was eclectic: a mixture of well-known opera arias, popular ballads and folk tunes. And still further back some historians would suggest that elements of the musical were evident in the plays of ancient Greece and Rome; not only were there songs and dances interwoven with spoken text, but there was even a prototype of the modern tap shoe!

Whatever we believe its origins to be, the musical certainly came of age in the twentieth century and with the help of some extraordinary practitioners evolved into an art form which remains, at its best, challenging, thought-provoking, and relevant. Something which started out as pure entertainment, has, by turns, embraced the farcical, the political, the romantic and the tragic. Looking back over the last century, tens of thousands of musicals have been written and many have been staged and re-staged, some with spectacular success. Only a few, however, have been 'game-changers' – shows which make their mark in unexpected ways and which help to change our perception of what constitutes a musical.

Show Boat

In the late 1920s, following decades of vaudeville and frivolous revue-style entertainment, Jerome Kern and Oscar Hammerstein II wrote the ground-breaking musical, *Show Boat*. This piece, which explores the lives of those living and working aboard the 'Cotton Blossom', a Mississippi show boat, was a far cry from the light-hearted escapism of most theatrical productions of the time. Racial segregation and discrimination, alcoholism and gambling were unlikely subjects for a new musical, and the show was a major departure from the type of production prevalent on the Broadway stage. Ironically, it was Florenz Ziegfeld, the same impresario who famously presented lavish revues featuring gorgeously-costumed beauties, who saw the potential in this dark, uncompromising story. His instincts were well founded and the show became a huge success, helping to steer the musical into new and unchartered territory.

Game-changers

Musicals like *Show Boat* are few and far between; finding genuinely new ways to tell stories with the aid of music, drama and dance is a slippery and elusive pursuit. The following list presents a selection of shows which I believe really have helped to redefine the genre. Choosing one from each successive decade since *Show Boat*, I've attempted to select musicals which are original, ambitious and which don't exclusively rely on a tried-and-tested format.

1930s   *Porgy and Bess*
George Gershwin (music), Ira Gershwin (lyrics) and DuBose Heyward (book), created this 'folk opera' for a cast which exclusively featured black performers. This ambitious work introduced serious themes (drugs, violence and sexual obsession) and the story boldly gave centre stage to a group of impoverished working-class characters. Whilst the original Broadway production ran for a relatively modest 124 performances, the show has continually been revived and remains popular in both theatres and opera houses throughout the world.

1940s   *Oklahoma!*
This was the first collaboration between Richard Rodgers (music) and Oscar Hammerstein II (lyrics/book), paving the way for an extraordinary string of hits including *Carousel*, *South Pacific*, *The King and I* and *The Sound of Music*. Whilst the show's score had a freshness and spontaneity which set it apart from anything that had come before, there were darker undertones too, especially in the scenes involving the sinister Jud Fry. An early example of the 'book musical', *Oklahoma!* had songs which were skilfully woven into the fabric of the story and which helped to delineate character and motivation. The show was an unprecedented success and ran for over five years on Broadway.

1950s   *West Side Story*
This show was the thrilling result of a collaboration between
Leonard Bernstein (music), Jerome Robbins (direction/
choreography), Arthur Laurents (book) and a young Stephen
Sondheim (lyrics). The vibrant jazz-infused score set the perfect
tone for this turbulent tale of two young lovers torn apart by
hatred and bigotry in a run-down New York ghetto. Hal Prince
joined the team to helm what was to become the most
successful Shakespearian adaptation ever to grace the
Broadway stage. Everything about this show felt daring and
original, with music and choreography which perfectly captured
the seething tensions between two rival gangs, the Jets and
the Sharks.

1960s   *Hair*
From its bold, monosyllabic title, to its psychedelic rock-infused
score (courtesy of Galt MacDermot), nothing about this musical
seemed conventional. The central characters embraced drug-
taking, free love and activism, and the mood of the piece was
iconoclastic and intoxicating. This controversial new show included
nudity, sexual fluidity, racial integration and a fervent endorsement
of the anti-Vietnam War peace movement. Several of the songs
became top ten hits, and the show ran on Broadway for nearly
five years.

1970s   *A Chorus Line*
This show was a daring departure from the conventional story-
driven musical and focussed on a group of disparate chorus
dancers auditioning for a Broadway show. The script, written by
James Kirkwood Jr. and Nicholas Dante, emerged from recordings
taken from several workshop sessions with professional dancers,
and Marvin Hamlisch provided the exceptional score. With a cast
of hoofers not stars, all dressed in contemporary dance gear and
performing on a bare stage, this musical was, in some ways, the
antithesis of a lavish Broadway show. Breaking all previous box
office records and winning the Pulitzer Prize for drama, *A Chorus
Line* became an instant classic and has been revived many
times since.

1980s   *Sunday in the Park with George*
With previous work including *Company* and *Sweeney Todd*, this
ground-breaking musical continued Sondheim's quest for unusual,
challenging material. Here was an original story inspired by a
Georges Seurat painting. The musical has philosophical
aspirations, and explores the nature of creativity, the complicated

relationship between art and commerce, and the legacy left by 'children and art'. It's a fascinating, ambitious piece, with music which deftly mirrors the pointillist painting technique used by Seurat to give his works a shimmering quality. The show won the Pulitzer Prize for Drama in 1985.

1990s   *Rent*
Based on Puccini's *La Bohême*, Jonathan Larson's *Rent* was a contemporary rock opera featuring a group of misfits – artists, drop-outs, drug addicts and drag queens – all struggling to survive in New York's run-down Alphabet City. This anarchic, vibrant new musical premiered off-Broadway in 1996, but the young author/composer was never to witness the show's success; he unexpectedly and tragically died the night before the opening. This innovative show became an instant cult hit, attracting a youthful audience which enthusiastically embraced its dynamic score and cast of unlikely heroes. The show ran on Broadway for twelve years, winning a clutch of prestigious theatre awards including the Pulitzer Prize for Drama.

2000s   *The Producers*
Based on his 1967 film of the same name, Mel Brooks's *The Producers* was fast-paced, irreverent, tasteless and side-splittingly funny. Whilst the show borrows shamelessly from the conventional Broadway musical, everything is deliciously subverted; a second act show-stopper features a sequinned Hitler set against a backdrop of sparkling swastikas and assorted Nazi paraphernalia. As far as satirical entertainment was concerned, nothing in Mel Brooks's world was off-limits. The show was a phenomenal success winning a record-breaking twelve Tony Awards and running for over six years on Broadway.

2010s   *Hamilton*
No one could have predicted that a historical account of one of America's Founding Fathers would have provided the source material for a musical which would go on to take Broadway by storm. *Hamilton*, with music, lyrics and book by Lin-Manuel Miranda, is a melting pot of different musical styles; rap, hip-hop, soul, and rhythm and blues all contribute to this rich, nuanced piece. By casting an ethnically diverse group of actors to tell this particular story, Miranda successfully manages to create a musical biography which feels contemporary, cool and relevant. Hailed as a masterpiece by audiences and critics alike, *Hamilton* won eleven Tony Awards, the Pulitzer Prize for Drama, a Grammy Award and seven Olivier Awards.

There are, of course, other notable musicals which haven't quite made it onto this list by dint of the fact that they happen to share a decade with another ground-breaking show. *Cabaret* is a masterful example of a 1960s musical which can shock and entertain in equal measure and which never shies away from tackling challenging, painful subject matter. *Les Misérables*, first produced in the 1980s and based on Victor Hugo's epic novel, is a fine example of the through-sung musical and has had unprecedented success in the West End, on Broadway and around the world. And there are shows which bravely tackle mental health issues (*Next to Normal*), musicals which offer us LGBT protagonists (*March of the Falsettos*, *La Cage aux Folles* and *Fun Home*), and works which focus on tragic real-life events, treating them with integrity and ingenuity (*Floyd Collins* and *London Road*).

Where next?

Who knows what the next game-changer will be? How will it redefine the musical and what new elements will it introduce? One thing we can predict with some certainty; it won't be predictable. Most of these previously-mentioned shows came from left field; they were the extraordinary result of a new collaboration (*Oklahoma!*), a passion project, worked and reworked over a number of years by one, driven individual (*Rent* and *Hamilton*), or the product of a unique combination of talents, individuals whose artistic vision came together to produce something truly ground-breaking and enduring (*West Side Story*).

Whilst it's not always easy to find a common link between each of these game-changing musicals (apart from the very obvious combination of music and drama), what's very clear is that all the shows on this list took their audiences by surprise, forcing them to re-evaluate their preconceived ideas about the genre. And it's pretty safe to say that each of these works had a direct influence on other contemporary writers, allowing them to see how innovation really could lead to exciting new developments. *Hair*, in the late 1960s, for example, broke various taboos and demonstrated spectacularly that a musical could both entertain and be a viable means of political protest.

New ideas

We should totally be championing new musicals. I try to do as many new musical workshops as I can, to champion both the work and the writers and see what's brewing out there . . . We must nurture and take a risk on our homegrown talent and our own stories.

SHARON D CLARKE

As previously discussed, musicals have often been derivative, taking their inspiration from a diverse range of sources: novels, films, plays, biographies, operas, paintings and even comic books (see Chapter 4). Most of the best musical theatre writers have, to a large extent, relied on other art forms to inspire their creativity. Rodgers and Hammerstein famously had their first flop with *Allegro* in 1947 when they attempted to create a musical from scratch. It's interesting to note that their subsequent work was almost entirely based on pre-existing source material, and this format proved immensely successful for them.

The derivative nature of much musical-theatre writing is largely economically driven. Most theatrical producers will find it easier to sell a show if there's immediate product recognition from potential ticket-buyers. For this reason film titles are particularly appealing. The result of this, however, is that many new musicals end up being pale imitations of previous cinematic triumphs. Stories which work well on film don't automatically translate to the stage. An enchanting movie such as *Amelie*, for example, without the charismatic presence of an Audrey Tautou, or the quirky sensibility of Jean-Pierre Jeunet's sensitive direction, doesn't necessarily translate into a satisfying theatrical experience. It seems to me that we need an artistic climate to exist in which it's possible to be brave and experimental, where writers can afford to veer away from previous sources and allow their creativity to take flight. This takes courage both from writers and from producers; it also requires audiences to be open to new experiences, and not just to rely on work which feels recognisable and safe.

I'm not, of course, suggesting that writers should stop being inspired by other works of art; there will always be room for musicals which are based on pre-existing source material. But in addition to these it should be possible for musical theatre writers to create innovative stories which spring from their imaginations rather than from anything which already exists in a different format. This will require support, funding and the opportunity to workshop new ideas.

The secret of any successful original musical is nearly always 'the book'. However tuneful a musical score is, it must come out of interesting characters and propel dramatic situations. Creating a new musical that isn't based on existing material has always been very hard and even the most experienced and successful writers are dependent on finding that elusive great story to adapt. When it happens, it is magic and often from an unexpected source. The pantheon of great musicals is mostly led by great stories that people in the industry at the time thought would never work – until they opened!

SIR CAMERON MACKINTOSH

Contemporary issues

Politics

Dating back as far as Ancient Greece the theatre has always been a place where contemporary ideas can be examined, debated and, of course, satirised. With modern theatre it seems to me that plays are generally better at reflecting current political scenarios than musicals. The reasons for this aren't entirely clear, but my suspicion is that it's partly to do with a perception that musicals exist primarily to entertain. It's also the case that most musicals take longer to develop and produce; there's always the danger that by opening night the show has already begun to lose its edge in terms of contemporary relevance. Some shows, of course, have successfully captured the spirit of the age; *Hair* and *Rent* are good examples of this as they both managed to incorporate musical styles of the period and tackle subjects which felt, and still feel, topical and challenging. Sondheim's *Assassins*, first produced in 1990, feels increasingly relevant, as gun control continues to be a hugely contentious issue, both in the US and throughout the wider world.

There may also be an underlying fear that musicals might trivialise contemporary issues and that a 'heightened' dramatic environment may not be the best platform for political debate. If somebody bursts into song, for example, does this give weight to an argument, or does it merely make it feel unrealistic or overblown? There's no one answer here, of course; it all depends on the sensitivities of the writers and their skill in engaging with the subject matter and conveying it in a suitable theatrical context.

Sexuality

Commercial musical theatre writers haven't always felt comfortable putting sexuality at the forefront of their work, but there are, of course, some notable exceptions. *Cabaret* certainly wasn't a 'gay musical', but it did introduce a central character, Cliff, who is revealed to be bisexual. Other shows certainly flirted with non-heterosexual themes; *The Rocky Horror Show* and *Hair* both featured characters with ambiguous sexualities, and *A Chorus Line* included several gay characters. Shows with gay protagonists have until recently been less common. Again, there are exceptions; William Finn's ambitious and provocative musical *March of the Falsettos* premiered in the early 1980s and featured a bisexual man, Marvin, who finally leaves his family for his male lover, Whizzer. This was a bold and controversial show which not only focussed on the sexual dilemmas of its leading character, but also tackled the sensitive issue of AIDS. Subsequent shows featuring gay protagonists include, *La Cage Aux Folles*, *Kiss of the Spiderwoman*, *A New Brain*, *Taboo*, *The Color Purple*, *Fun Home*, and most recently *Everybody's Talking About Jamie*.

Multicultural casting

Early in my career I was lucky enough to gain experience as an assistant director working on Nicholas Hytner's National Theatre production of *Carousel*. The creative team made the then controversial decision to cast a black actor, Clive Rowe, as Mr Snow, the provincial fisherman who woos and weds the vivacious millworker, Carrie Pipperidge. Whilst there were other black actors in the ensemble, the decision to cast one of the leading characters in a way which challenged perceptions was a bold and exciting one. The show subsequently moved to New York and this 'colour-blind' casting was continued when a young Audra McDonald took the rôle of Carrie, and the opera singer Shirley Verrett played Nettie. These casting decisions worked because the actors were all exceptionally good in their rôles, not because their ethnicity shone a particular light on any of the issues in the show. Since the production was presented at two highly influential institutions, the National Theatre in London and the Lincoln Center in New York, it might be assumed that this casting ideology would have subsequently been adopted throughout the industry on both sides of the Atlantic. This wasn't, however, the case. It's still comparatively rare to see casting in musicals which ignores the ethnicity of the actors, and it's partly for this reason that I've chosen *Hamilton* as one of my game-changers. Lin-Manuel Miranda has taken a group of historical characters and essentially posed the question, 'if they were around today, what might they look like?' And the answer is clear: multicultural. This is a profoundly important message and will hopefully encourage many other theatre practitioners to adopt a much more inclusive attitude towards casting, both in musicals and in plays.

God bless **Hamilton***!!! Apart from it being phenomenally fantastic and fresh and funky with wonderful writing, performances, voices, storytelling and choreography, it's diverse on every level.*

SHARON D CLARKE

Gender-fluid casting

Most people are aware that the plays of Shakespeare were originally performed by men; female rôles were taken by boys, and women were excluded from participating. After the Restoration, when theatres were re-opened, women were for the first time allowed to act on the stage, although this wasn't considered a respectable female occupation and many actresses were thought of as little better than common prostitutes. Whilst there is still, clearly, an imbalance when it comes to opportunities for women in theatre (mainly because of a preponderance of male rôles), there are some striking examples of women in history who have bucked the trend and taken on parts originally intended for men. In the nineteenth century both Sarah Siddons and Sarah Bernhardt played Hamlet, and most recently Glenda Jackson, Harriet Walter, Maxine Peake, Diane Venora and Kathryn

Hunter have taken on some of Shakespeare's most demanding male rôles, including Prospero, King Lear, Hamlet and Richard III.

Where musical theatre is concerned, gender fluidity is arguably a little more complicated, for the simple reason that the rôles will have been written with a specific vocal type in mind. Changing the sex of the actor playing the part will almost certainly mean that keys will have to be changed, in some cases quite radically; this will involve re-orchestrating the numbers which can be time-consuming and costly. This isn't to say that switching genders is an impossibility. A West End production of *Company* boldly re-imagined the central character, Bobby, as a woman. This in turn lead to other necessary gender changes throughout the show. This unconventional approach certainly shed new light on the piece and with a female character at the centre of the story the sexual dynamics inevitably shifted, Bobby's emotional indecision resonating in an entirely different way. In a similar vein it might be interesting to imagine a production of *Cabaret* with the Emcee played by a woman; my suspicion is that this switch would work rather well, as this is a show where nothing is quite what it seems, and sexuality and theatricality are inextricably linked. The number 'Two Ladies', involving the Emcee and a pair of girls from the Kit Kat Klub, would in this context take on an extra layer of meaning.

A variety of Shakespeare's plays have been presented by single-gender casts and were successful both in London and New York; *Twelfth Night* at the Globe Theatre/Belasco Theatre (all-male) and *The Tempest* and *Julius Caesar* at the Donmar Warehouse/St. Ann's Warehouse (all-female) are several examples which helped to shed new light on these familiar stories. It's interesting to envisage whether similar experiments might be made with well-constructed pieces of musical theatre. For example, a director might opt to create an all-female version of *Chicago*, with the inmates of the Chicago women's prison telling this particular tale. Similarly, *Kiss of the Spiderwoman* could be performed by the male inmates of the South American jail in which Molina and Valentine are incarcerated. Both these scenarios would therefore present the prisoners as story-tellers, a device which has been used to great effect in the musical *Man of La Mancha,* a show which also takes a prison as its central location.

Whilst I don't expect that the sort of experimentation mentioned here will lead to a flood of all-male *Carousels*, or all-female *Sweeney Todds*, there should always be the opportunity to breathe new life into established musicals by envisaging them in bold and imaginative ways. It should be noted, however, that any significant changes, such as the gender of a character, will always need to be cleared with the licensing company first.

Looking ahead

As far as theatrical productions are concerned, musicals remain extremely popular. Despite many other more easily-accessible forms of entertainment, people still venture out in great numbers to participate in this unique shared experience. Successful musicals can, of course, be very lucrative, and shows such as *Les Misérables* and *Phantom of the Opera* have smashed all previous records as far as commercial long-running musicals are concerned. Erroneously seen by some as the poor relation of the play, the best musicals can be thought-provoking, challenging, moving and entertaining, all at the same time.

It seems to me that audiences will always be drawn towards stories which are told through a combination of music and drama; this has been demonstrated throughout history from the very earliest examples of staged entertainment. The musical has, as we've seen, re-invented itself on numerous occasions, and will no doubt continue to do so. Looking forward we can envisage great developments in theatre technology, with exciting advances in video projection and in set, lighting and sound design. Musically we can only guess at how styles will develop, but we can be pretty sure that popular, contemporary music will always find its way into new works of musical theatre. And what about theatres themselves? It strikes me that there is currently a renewed appetite for unconventional theatre spaces. Peter Brook taught us that all we need is an empty space and an audience for an act of theatre to take place. Contemporary theatre audiences are embracing this idea that theatre can happen anywhere, and some of the most exciting recent productions have taken place, not in the conventional formality of a Victorian playhouse, but in warehouses, railway arches, old chocolate factories, watermills, tents, and train stations.

Epilogue

Whilst there is no sure-fire way to guarantee the success of a musical theatre production, there are certain things which will help to facilitate the process, including creativity, communication and collaboration. In my guide to putting on a musical I've focussed on three groups in particular, the creative team, the actors, and stage management; they represent the fundamental elements of any theatrical project, the artistic and the practical. It's the combination of these that underpins any successful production, so there is something both reassuring and exciting about the start of rehearsals when the whole company comes together for the first time, everyone sitting in a circle waiting for the inevitable first day speeches to begin. Even though the production team will have been preparing the show for months in advance, no one in the room knows exactly how this particular project will play out. There are many challenges ahead, many artistic decisions to be made, much laughter and probably a few tears. As George says as he gazes at a blank white canvas in the final scene of Sondheim's luminous *Sunday in the Park with George*: 'So many possibilities ...'

Appendix
REFERENCED MUSICALS

A Chorus Line
Music: Marvin Hamlisch
Lyrics: Edward Kleban
Book: Nicholas Dante/James Kirkwood Jr.

A Funny Thing Happened on the Way to the Forum
Music/Lyrics: Stephen Sondheim
Book: Burt Shevelove/Larry Gelbart

A Little Night Music
Music/Lyrics: Stephen Sondheim
Book: Hugh Wheeler

Allegro
Music: Richard Rodgers
Lyrics/Book: Oscar Hammerstein II

Amelie
Music: Daniel Messé
Lyrics: Daniel Messé/Nathan Tysen
Book: Craig Lucas

A New Brain
Music/Lyrics: William Finn
Book: William Finn/James Lapine

Annie
Music: Charles Strouse
Lyrics: Martin Charnin
Book: Thomas Meehan

Annie Get Your Gun
Music/Lyrics: Irving Berlin
Book: Dorothy Fields/Herbert Fields

Anything Goes
Music/Lyrics: Cole Porter
Book: P.G. Wodehouse/Guy Bolton/Russel Crouse/Howard Lindsay

Avenue Q
Music/Lyrics: Robert Lopez/Jeff Marx
Book: Jeff Whitty

Babes in Arms
Music: Richard Rodgers
Lyrics: Lorenz Hart
Book: Richard Rodgers/Lorenz Hart

Barnum
Music: Cy Coleman
Lyrics: Michael Stewart
Book: Mark Bramble

Beautiful
Music/Lyrics: Carole King/Cynthia Weil/Gerry Goffin/Barry Mann
Book: Douglas McGrath

Billy Elliot
Music: Elton John
Lyrics/Book: Lee Hall

Bugsy Malone
Music/Lyrics: Paul Williams
Book: Alan Parker

Cabaret
Music: John Kander
Lyrics: Fred Ebb
Book: Joe Masteroff

Candide
Music: Leonard Bernstein
Lyrics: Richard Wilbur
Book: Hugh Wheeler (original script: Lillian Hellman)

Caroline, or Change
Music: Jeanine Tesori
Lyrics/Book: Tony Kushner

Carousel
Music: Richard Rodgers
Lyrics/Book: Oscar Hammerstein II

Cats
Music: Andrew Lloyd Webber
Lyrics: T. S. Eliot/Trevor Nunn

Charlie and the Chocolate Factory
Music: Marc Shaiman
Lyrics: Marc Shaiman/Scott Wittman
Book: David Greig

Chicago
Music: John Kander
Lyrics: Fred Ebb
Book: Fred Ebb/Bob Fosse

Children of Eden
Music/Lyrics: Stephen Schwartz
Book: John Caird

City of Angels
Music: Cy Coleman
Lyrics: David Zippel
Book: Larry Gelbart

Closer Than Ever
Music: David Shire
Lyrics: Richard Maltby, Jr.

Company
Music/Lyrics: Stephen Sondheim
Book: George Furth

Crazy for You
Music: George Gershwin
Lyrics: Ira Gershwin
Book: Ken Ludwig

Dear Evan Hansen
Music/Lyrics: Benj Pasek/Justin Paul
Book: Steven Levenson

Everybody's Talking About Jamie
Music: Dan Gillespie Sells
Lyrics/Book: Tom MacRae

Falsettoland
Music/Lyrics: William Finn
Book: James Lapine

Fiddler on the Roof
Music: Jerry Bock
Lyrics: Sheldon Harnick
Book: Joseph Stein

Fiorello!
Music: Jerry Bock
Lyrics: Sheldon Harnick
Book: Jerome Weidman/George Abbott

Floyd Collins
Music/Lyrics: Adam Guettel
Book: Tina Landau

Follies
Music/Lyrics: Stephen Sondheim
Book: James Goldman

42nd Street
Music: Harry Warren
Lyrics: Al Dubin/Johnny Mercer
Book: Mark Bramble/Michael Stewart

Fun Home
Music: Jeanine Tesori
Lyrics/Book: Lisa Kron

Gigi
Music: Frederick Loewe
Lyrics/Book: Alan Jay Lerner

Grease
Music/Lyrics/Book: Jim Jacobs/Warren Casey

Guys and Dolls
Music/Lyrics: Frank Loesser
Book: Jo Swerling/Abe Burrows

Gypsy
Music: Jule Styne
Lyrics: Stephen Sondheim
Book: Arthur Laurents

Hair
Music: Galt MacDermot
Lyrics/Book: James Rado/Gerome Ragni

Hamilton
Music/Lyrics/Book: Lin-Manuel Miranda

Hot Mikado
Music: Rob Bowman (after Arthur Sullivan)
Lyrics/Book: David H. Bell (after W.S. Gilbert)

Into the Woods
Music/Lyrics: Stephen Sondheim
Book: James Lapine

Jersey Boys
Music: Bob Gaudio
Lyrics: Bob Crewe
Book: Marshall Brickman/Rick Elice

Jesus Christ Superstar
Music: Andrew Lloyd Webber
Lyrics: Tim Rice

Joseph and the Amazing Technicolor Dreamcoat
Music: Andrew Lloyd Webber
Lyrics/Book: Tim Rice

Kiss Me, Kate
Music/Lyrics: Cole Porter
Book: Sam Spewack/Bella Spewack

Kiss of the Spiderwoman
Music: John Kander
Lyrics: Fred Ebb
Book: Terrence McNally

La Cage aux Folles
Music/Lyrics: Jerry Herman
Book: Harvey Fierstein

Legally Blonde
Music: Laurence O'Keefe/Nell Benjamin
Lyrics: Laurence O'Keefe/Nell Benjamin
Book: Heather Hach

Les Misérables
Music: Claude-Michel Schönberg
Lyrics: Alain Boublil/Herbert Kretzmer/Jean-Marc Natel

Little Shop of Horrors
Music: Alan Menken
Lyrics/Book: Howard Ashman

London Road
Music: Adam Cork
Lyrics: Adam Cork/Alecky Blythe
Book: Alecky Blythe

Mamma Mia
Music/Lyrics: Benny Andersson/Björn Ulvaeus
Book: Catherine Johnson

Man of La Mancha
Music: Mitch Leigh
Lyrics: Joe Darion
Book: Dale Wasserman

March of the Falsettos
Music/Lyrics/Book: William Finn

Matilda
Music/Lyrics: Tim Minchin
Book: Dennis Kelly

Me and My Girl
Music: Noel Gay
Lyrics/Book: Douglas Furber/L. Arthur Rose
Revised book: Stephen Fry

Miss Saigon
Music: Claude-Michel Schönberg
Lyrics: Alain Boublil/Richard Maltby, Jr.
Book: Alain Boublil/Claude-Michel Schönberg

Mr Stink
Music: Matt Brind
Lyrics: Matthew White
Book: David Walliams/Matthew White

My Fair Lady
Music: Frederick Loewe
Lyrics/Book: Alan Jay Lerner

Next to Normal
Music: Tom Kitt
Lyrics/Book: Brian Yorkey

Oklahoma!
Music: Richard Rodgers
Lyrics/Book: Oscar Hammerstein II

Oliver!
Music/Lyrics/Book: Lionel Bart

Pacific Overtures
Music/Lyrics: Stephen Sondheim
Book: John Weidman

Passion
Music/Lyrics: Stephen Sondheim
Book: James Lapine

Phantom of the Opera
Music: Andrew Lloyd Webber
Lyrics: Charles Hart
Book: Richard Stilgoe/Andrew Lloyd Webber

Pippin
Music/Lyrics: Stephen Schwartz
Book: Roger O. Hirson/Bob Fosse

Porgy and Bess
Music: George Gershwin
Lyrics: Ira Gershwin
Book: DuBose Heyward

Promises, Promises
Music: Burt Bacharach
Lyrics: Hal David
Book: Neil Simon

Rags
Music: Charles Strouse
Lyrics: Stephen Schwartz
Book: Joseph Stein

Ragtime
Music: Stephen Flaherty
Lyrics: Lynn Ahrens
Book: Terrence McNally

Rent
Music/Lyrics/Book: Jonathan Larson

Seussical
Music: Stephen Flaherty
Lyrics: Lynn Ayrens
Book: Stephen Flaherty/Lynn Ayrens

She Loves Me
Music: Jerry Bock
Lyrics: Sheldon Harnick
Book: Joe Masteroff

Show Boat
Music: Jerome Kern
Lyrics: Oscar Hammerstein II/P.G. Wodehouse
Book: Oscar Hammerstein II

Shrek the Musical
Music: Jeanine Tesori
Lyrics/Book: David Lindsay-Abaire

South Pacific
Music: Richard Rodgers
Lyrics: Oscar Hammerstein II
Book: Oscar Hammerstein II/Joshua Logan

Sunday in the Park with George
Music/Lyrics: Stephen Sondheim
Book: James Lapine

Sweeney Todd
Music/Lyrics: Stephen Sondheim
Book: Hugh Wheeler

Sweet Charity
Music: Cy Coleman
Lyrics: Dorothy Fields
Book: Neil Simon

Taboo
Music: Boy George/John Themis/Kevan Frost/Richie Stevens
Lyrics: Boy George
Book: Mark Davies Markham/Charles Busch

The Addams Family
Music/Lyrics: Andrew Lippa
Book: Marshall Brickman/Rick Elice

The Baker's Wife
Music/Lyrics: Stephen Schwartz
Book: Joseph Stein

The Color Purple
Music/Lyrics: Stephen Bray/Brenda Russell/Allee Willis
Book: Marsha Norman

The King and I
Music: Richard Rodgers
Lyrics/Book: Oscar Hammerstein II

The Last Five Years
Music/Lyrics/Book: Jason Robert Brown

The Lion King
Music: Elton John
Lyrics: Tim Rice
Book: Roger Allers/Irene Mecchi

The Lorax
Music/Lyrics: Charlie Fink
Book: David Greig/Dr Seuss

The Pajama Game
Music/Lyrics: Richard Adler/Jerry Ross
Book: George Abbott/Richard Bissell

The Pirates of Penzance
Music: Arthur Sullivan
Lyrics/Book: W.S. Gilbert

The Producers
Music/Lyrics: Mel Brooks
Book: Mel Brooks/Thomas Meehan

The Rocky Horror Show
Music/Lyrics/Book: Richard O'Brien

The Sound of Music
Music: Richard Rodgers
Lyrics: Oscar Hammerstein II
Book: Russel Crouse/Howard Lindsay

The Wizard of Oz
Music: Harold Arlen
Lyrics: E.Y. Harburg
Book: John Kane

Thoroughly Modern Millie
Music: Jeanine Tesori
Lyrics: Dick Scanlan
Book: Richard Morris/Dick Scanlan

Tick, Tick . . . Boom!
Music/Lyrics/Book: Jonathan Larson

Top Hat
Music/Lyrics: Irving Berlin
Book: Howard Jacques/Matthew White

Two Gentlemen of Verona
Music: Galt MacDermot
Lyrics: John Guare
Book: John Guare/Mel Shapiro

West Side Story
Music: Leonard Bernstein
Lyrics: Stephen Sondheim
Book: Arthur Laurents

Wicked
Music/Lyrics: Stephen Schwartz
Book: Winnie Holzman

INDEX